The Ethics of Creativity

The Ethics of Creativity

Beauty, Morality, and Nature

in a Processive Cosmos

Brian G. Henning

UNIVERSITY OF PITTSBURGH PRESS

Published by the University of Pittsburgh Press, Pittsburgh, Pa., 15260

Copyright © 2005, University of Pittsburgh Press

Manufactured in the United States of America

Printed on acid-free paper

10 9 8 7 6 5 4 3 2 1

Library of Congress Cataloging-in-Publication Data

Henning, Brian G.

  The ethics of creativity : beauty, morality, and nature in a processive cosmos /
Brian G. Henning.

     p. cm.

  Includes bibliographical references and index.

  ISBN 0-8229-4271-2 (hardcover : alk. paper)

  1. Ethics. 2. Environmental ethics. 3. Environmental responsibility.
4. Process philosophy. 5. Whitehead, Alfred North, 1861-1947. I. Title.

BJ1031.H46 2005

179'.1—dc22

                                                2005014856

To my beloved spouse, without whose unfaltering love, friendship, support, and patience this work would not have been possible. In beauty may we walk.

Contents

Foreword

For quite some time it has been widely acknowledged that more work needs to be done on the axiological implications of the process metaphysics of Alfred North Whitehead. In a completely different quarter it has also been widely acknowledged that there is a tension in environmental ethics between the rights claimed on behalf of sentient individuals (whether human or nonhuman) and the attention that must be paid to what is, to the naked eye, nonsentient nature.

The great merit of Henning's book is that by responding insightfully to the first problem mentioned above, he does so as well to the second. His book is thus essential reading for both process thinkers/ American pragmatists as well as environmental ethicists. The key to the book consists in Henning's rejection of axiological dualism, wherein the more familiar ontological dualism of early modern thinkers like Descartes dictates the aesthetic and ethical terms found in Kant and other late-modern thinkers.

Henning is very much in the tradition of Peirce, James, and Dewey in his rejection of the hegemony dualism and materialism have had on contemporary philosophic debates. The rapprochement he forges between the pragmatists and Whitehead (specifically, an "ecstatic" interpretation of Whitehead) enables him to defend a view of reality in general as organic. On this view there is a continuum of value in nature, contra axiological dualism.

The practical implications of this continuum of value in nature for contemporary debates in environmental ethics become readily apparent toward the end of the book, where Henning lays out, in Jamesian fashion, his view of a genuinely ethical universe. This view both borrows from virtue ethics, utilitarianism, and deontology and also improves on them. No small accomplishment!

Daniel A. Dombrowski
Seattle University

Acknowledgments

In that this work advances the view that our relationships with others are an essential part of who we are, it is particularly fitting to begin by acknowledging some of the individuals who have helped to shape this project (though I accept complete responsibility for all of the claims made herein). I extend a special note of thanks to Daniel A. Dombrowski, whose exceptional skill as an editor and generous willingness to read the many drafts which this work has undergone has benefited this project greatly. More important, in helping me to see the beauty and value of the extrahuman world, he has, by both scholarship and example, profoundly affected the way I live my life. A great debt of gratitude is owed to Jude Jones, who has contributed enormously to my work. Not only has my work greatly profited from her perspicuity and incisive appreciation of metaphysical nuance, without her own ground-breaking work in process thought, the present project would be untenable. For her invaluable counsel, continual encouragement, and persistent pluralism, I express my gratitude to Judith Green. I am most grateful to W. Norris Clark, SJ, and Frederick Ferré, whose generous, yet tenacious, challenges have significantly improved this manuscript. I extend my sincere thanks to Trudy Conway, whose generous support facilitated the final revision of this manuscript. Finally, I thank Kendra Boileau and Jane Flanders at the University of Pittsburgh Press for helping me bring this project to completion.

Without the constant support of friends and family, this project would not have been possible. In particular, I wish to thank my mother, Margo Henning, and my father, Dick Henning, whose unconditional encouragement and moral integrity have been a source of inspiration throughout my life. My greatest debt is to my wife, Suzie Henning. Without her constant encouragement, unwavering patience, and selfless support, I would not have had the courage to lead a life dedicated to the pursuit of wisdom, much less to complete the present project.

Early versions of several parts of this work first appeared in scholarly journals and are reprinted in revised form here with the permission of their editors. The articles in question are "Saving Whitehead's Universe of Value: An 'Ecstatic' Challenge to the Classical Interpretation," *International Philosophical Quarterly* 45 (2005); "Getting Substance to Go All the Way: Norris Clarke's Neo-Thomism and the Process Turn," *Modern Schoolman* 81 (2004): 215–25; "On the Possibility of a Whiteheadian Aesthetics of Morals," *Process Studies* 31 (2002): 97–114; and "On the Way to an Ethics of Creativity," *International Journal for Field-Being* 2 (2002). Charles Hartshorne's aesthetic circle in chapter 4 is reprinted by permission of Open Court Publishing Company, a division of Carus Publishing Company, Peru, Ill., from *Creative Synthesis and Philosophic Method* by Charles Hartshorne, copyright © 1970 by Open Court Publishing Company.

The Ethics of Creativity

Introduction

> There is no one behavior system belonging to the essential character of the universe, as the universal moral ideal. What is universal is the spirit which should permit any behaviour system in the circumstances of its adoption. Thus morality does not indicate what you are to do in mythological abstractions. It does concern the general ideal which should be the justification for any particular objective. The destruction of a man, or of an insect, or of a tree, or of the Parthenon, may be moral or immoral. . . . Whether we destroy or whether we preserve, our action is moral if we have thereby safeguarded the importance of experience so far as it depends on that concrete instance in the world's history.
>
> Alfred North Whitehead, *Modes of Thought*

THERE IS CURRENTLY a battle being waged in the marketplace of ideas over which relations "count," morally speaking. Traditionally, ethical theories have held that the only morally significant relations are interhuman relations or those obtaining between human beings.[1] Accordingly, human beings' relations with organisms such as insects and trees or inanimate objects like the Parthenon are not moral relations at all; they do not count in this sphere. In contradistinction to this long-held conception of ethics, Alfred North Whitehead affirms a fundamentally different model of morality: whether one's actions affect a human being, an insect, a tree, or even an inanimate object, such as the Parthenon, that action is moral if, by one's relation to such entities, one has thereby safeguarded both the value experience which in that instance is possible and all subsequent repetitions of that value.

If Whitehead is right, morality as we know it must undergo a dramatic transformation. No longer can it be limited exclusively to those relations obtaining between human beings or even those between sentient beings. Rather, morality must concern how we, as humans, ought to conduct ourselves with each and every aspect of reality. This project takes on added urgency when we consider the environmental and social crises such as overpopulation, deforestation, global warming, and species extinction that threaten not only human civilization, but all forms of life on this planet. If we are to have any hope of reversing the potentially catastrophic destruction and consumption of our natural environment, we must devise an ethical theory grounded in an axiology that acknowledges that *every* individual—from the most insignificant flicker of existence at the opposite end of the universe to complex individuals such as ourselves—has value not only for itself, but for others, and for the whole of reality.

Yet how can we claim to understand the value of an individual and its community if we do not first at least attempt to give a systematic, metaphysical account of the nature of individuality? It is in part with such a question in mind that I turn to the organic metaphysics of Alfred North Whitehead and, to a lesser extent, the pragmatism of William James, John Dewey, and Charles Sanders Peirce. One of the greatest services that a Whiteheadian moral philosophy can provide to contemporary environmental and moral philosophies is to provide the metaphysical basis for understanding not only the locus and scope of intrinsic value, but also its nature. Thus one aim of this project is to reclaim the central role of metaphysics for moral theory. Yet, as my analysis will make clear, I do not mean to affirm the traditional view of metaphysics as first philosophy. Metaphysical speculation must remain as fluid as reality itself. In a way, then, I am calling for what may be called metaphysics in "real time." That is, in seeking always to be adequate to experience, metaphysics must embrace its fallibility by continually revising its conclusions in light of new discoveries. Only in this way can it serve as an adequate basis for moral philosophy.

The aim of this project, then, is to develop and defend a holistic, organic ethical theory grounded firmly in Whitehead's aesthetico-metaphysics of process. The seminal insight of this ethic, which I refer to as the ethics of creativity, is the fundamental sense of value at the base of existence; there is no vacuous, valueless existence. This idea is the foundation of Whitehead's metaphysics and the source of my title. Creativity, Whitehead's most basic category, what he calls the "category of the ultimate," describes the unceasing process by which "the many become one, and are increased by one" (PR, 21). The full meaning of this complex and enigmatic term will become clear only gradually; let me note at the outset that my motivation for adopting it as my title is not only to acknowledge its indebtedness to Whitehead but, more important, to indicate a fundamental refusal to accept a dichotomy between the interests of the one and the many. This is to be an ethics of *creativity* in the sense that, like the creative process of the universe itself, morality must always aim at achieving the most harmonious, inclusive, and complex whole possible.[2]

The book is divided into two parts. Part 1 establishes the critical and substantive ground for developing the ethics of creativity, which is the task of part 2. Chapter 1 seeks to expose the axiological implications of the dualistic and materialistic presuppositions that often uncritically underlie much of contemporary moral and environmental philosophy. Rather than merely repudiating the invidious logic of axiological dualism and materialism, we must systematically develop and defend an alternative. With this in mind, I turn to the organic metaphysics of Whitehead.

Because both Whitehead and the classical pragmatists argue that to be an individual is to be essentially related to every other individual, they reject any form of ontological dualism or bifurcation that might seek to carve reality into unrelatable pieces. Unlike Descartes and Kant, for example, they observe no absolute bifurcation or ontological gap between human beings and nature, between the animate and the inanimate, or even between the universe and God. Thus, what they reject is not only the ontological bifurcation or reduction of nature, but also its axiological bifurcation or reduction. According to such a worldview, we must repudiate any form of dualism or materialism that makes of certain entities sheer facts, devoid of value. There is no longer dead, lifeless, valueless "stuff." In a processive cosmos, everything has value to some degree. Given such a worldview, the important question is not whether others have intrinsic value, but whether the intrinsic value of others and of the whole is recognized, appreciated, and affirmed.

Yet, as I note in chapter 2, Whitehead's bold affirmation that actuality and value are coextensive presents a potential problem for his axiology in general and for the development of an ethics of creativity in particular: if actuality is coextensive with value, but actuality is itself limited to subjects of experience, then the objective world (that is, superjects or achieved occasions of experience) and future potential individuals can have no intrinsic value. In other words, Whitehead's entire metaphysical project would be in danger of collapsing into exactly what it was designed to overcome: a universe of independent subjects selfishly seeking their own ends. In this chapter I argue that the problem of subjectivism is ultimately a product of the classical interpretation of Whitehead's metaphysics, which insists on a sharp ontological distinction between the past and the present that thereby drains the past of both creativity and value. Thus, in order to avoid the very real danger of subjectivism, I appeal to a group of process scholars who affirm the actuality and value of both the past and the present. This interpretation, which I refer to as the ecstatic interpretation, makes it possible to interpret Whitehead's metaphysics so as to avoid the problem of subjectivism.

Having established this foundation, I then proceed to deepen the earlier analysis of Whitehead's theory of value. Specifically, I examine Whitehead's use of the crucial notion of intrinsic value by contrasting it with its use in established environmental ethics traditions. I conclude that Whitehead's insistence that every individual has value not only for itself, but for others and for the whole of reality, establishes a rich axiological foundation for the development of an organic moral philosophy. Thus chapters 1 and 2 not only provide an indispensable foundation for the later chapters, but also frame the heart of the project in general.

Building on the microscopic metaphysics of process developed in the preliminary chapters, chapter 3 seeks systematically to develop what is referred to as the organic model of individuality. Contrary to popular conceptions of Whitehead's system, this chapter examines how Whitehead's rich account of microscopic process can not only do justice to the unity and self-identity of macroscopic individuals, but also supports meaningful moral responsibility. A primary goal of this chapter is to demonstrate that difference may be real without the multiplication either of ontological kinds or, what is more important for my project, of the statuses that attach to them. If individuality is conceived organically, it is possible to affirm the existence of different types of entities, but these differences of type are in reality the result of differences in the complexity of social order of the actual occasions of which they are comprised. In an ethics of creativity, then, the language of *kind* and *type* has real moral footing without being ontologically basic. That is, we are able to appreciate the very real, and potentially morally significant, differences between individuals without introducing ontological gaps in the fabric of reality. Only by systematically developing this basis can we correctly assess the scope and locus of our direct moral concern and responsibilities toward others. This will become particularly important in chapter 7 when I engage the relationship between an individual's ontological status and its moral significance.

Chapter 4 introduces one of the more novel (and for some, troubling) elements of a Whiteheadian moral philosophy: namely, Whitehead's insistence that the telos of the universe, and therefore of every actual occasion, is aimed at the achievement of beauty. Creativity, the dynamic process of the universe, is not aimless. Rather, the process of becoming is the achievement of beauty; every pulsing element of our processive cosmos is beautiful to some degree in itself and for itself. Given the view that process aims at the attainment of beauty, this chapter establishes an important bridge between Whitehead's metaphysics of creativity and the development of an ethics of creativity. For insofar as all forms of process aim at the achievement of beauty, the conditions of beauty are the conditions of maximally effective processes in general, and, by implication, of morality. Thus, by uncovering the complex conditions involved in the achievement of beauty, we simultaneously establish the conditions of good and evil.

In chapter 5, my aim is to establish the ideal of the ethics of creativity by examining the kalogenic or beauty-generating structure of reality as the source and foundation of moral obligation. However, before beginning the difficult work of developing such an ethic, it is first necessary to confront two related criticisms that arise due to the constitutive relation between beauty and goodness: (1) that, in founding reality on value experience, any Whiteheadian moral philosophy is ultimately a subjectivistic moral interest theory; and (2) that, in reducing ethics to aesthetics, such a theory is guilty of a vicious aestheticism. Having closely examined these two points, by enlisting the work of William James, I then proceed to develop the ideal of the ethics of creativity and the delineation of five different obligations, all of which are contained with the obligation of beauty: the obligation to always act in such a way so as to bring about the greatest possible universe of beauty, value, and importance that in each situation is possible.

Yet if a Whiteheadian moral philosophy is to be of any practical use, it must move beyond abstractions and concretely demonstrate how a general ideal of morality can help us make meaningful moral decisions. Accordingly, the primary goal of chapter 6 is to move beyond the abstract analysis of ideals and obligations and demonstrate how the ethics of creativity would help us address the all too prevalent moral conflicts that confront us. I begin by delineating a three-step process of decision making that follows from the obligations of beauty detailed in chapter 5. I then proceed to examine how, in general, the ethics of creativity suggests we ought to comport ourselves toward each of the primary types of individuals in the world. In addition to these still abstract analyses, I then set out to test both the adequacy and applicability of the ethics of creativity by examining how it would handle a particular instance of moral conflict. Specifically, I address how we are to decide between our own intrinsic value as human beings and the intrinsic value of the organisms we destroy in order to sustain ourselves. That is, I examine the ethics of food.

Although, throughout, I bring the ethics of creativity into dialogue with established moral and environmental theories, in chapter 7 my aim is to explicitly indicate how the ethics of creativity relates to some of the most prominent moral theories. I ask, "What is the proper classification of the ethics of creativity?" Initially, several different answers suggest themselves. For instance, in that it places a high emphasis on education and the character of the moral agent, is perhaps the ethics of creativity a form of virtue ethics? However, in calling for the maximization of beauty, value, and importance overall, is it perhaps closer to a form of utilitarianism? Or, since it affirms the irreplaceable uniqueness of every individual, maybe it is closer to a form of deontology? Then again, in that it affirms the intrinsic value of everything in the universe, maybe it should be classified with Schweitzer, Leopold, or deep ecology?

In the end, we find that although it has much to learn from established theories of moral and environmental ethics, a Whiteheadian moral philosophy is every bit as unique, speculative, fallible, and dynamic as the metaphysics on which it is based and therefore cannot be squarely aligned with any extant moral or environmental philosophy.

Anyone seeking to develop a moral philosophy based on Whitehead's work faces many challenges. One obvious reason for the relative lack of attention given to Whitehead's work by mainstream environmental and moral philosophers is the density and abstruseness of the texts themselves. Coupled with the generally unfavorable view of metaphysical speculation among most contemporary ethicists, this has led many to admire Whitehead's work from afar.[3] Given this, a secondary, though not unimportant, goal of this project is to show the value of Whitehead's complex process metaphysics for moral and environmental philosophy by presenting it in language that strives for clarity and seeks to do justice to the richness and nuances of his thought.

While the present project presents a Whiteheadian ethic, it is not Whitehead's moral philosophy. I am not primarily interested in debating what Whitehead himself may or may not have believed. Rather, in the spirit of Whitehead's own approach to philosophy, while this project is inspired by and builds upon the work of those who came before me, it ultimately stands or falls on its own merits.

1

A Processive, Kalogenic Cosmos

1

From Mechanism to Organism

When man finds he is not a little god in his active powers and accomplishments, he retains his former conceit by hugging to his bosom the notion that nevertheless in some realm, be it knowledge or esthetic contemplation, he is still outside of and detached from the ongoing sweep of interacting and changing events; and being there alone and irresponsible save to himself, is as a god. When he perceives clearly and adequately that he is within nature, a part of its interactions, he sees that the line to be drawn is not between action and thought, or action and appreciation, but between blind, slavish, meaningless action and action that is free, significant, directed and responsible.

John Dewey, *Experience and Nature*

A CENTRAL CONCERN OF moral philosophy has always been to define the scope of direct moral concern, and this is the issue that most divides the various approaches to ethics today.[1] For instance, for some the scope of direct moral concern is limited to rational agents, while for others an individual need merely be able to feel pleasure and pain or have interests to be an object of direct moral concern. The moral principles developed by these diverse theories are very often incompatible. I suggest that these seemingly intract-able differences over the scope of direct moral concern are the prod-uct of inadequate conceptions of individuality. Although nearly all contemporary moral philosophers have long since rejected modern philosophy's conception of individuals as isolated and independent substances mechanistically determined by inexorable laws of na-ture, few have replaced this worldview with an alternative that is adequate to the organic, processive cosmos in which we find our-selves. It is, for instance, increasingly difficult to find someone who would defend a Cartesian view of matter as static and lifeless in the face of developments in physics, biology, and ecology. Curiously, however, the failure and subsequent abandonment of these world-views, particularly dualism and materialism, have not meant the abandonment or even substantial revision of their ethical offspring. Rather, following a general trend away from speculative philoso-phy, moral philosophers seem simply to have abandoned meta-physics altogether.

The problem, I submit, is that it is not possible to divorce an ethical paradigm from the metaphysical assumptions upon which it was built. Thus, although most contemporary ethicists claim that metaphysical speculation is irrelevant to their theories, they are implicitly and often uncritically working within either a dual-istic or a materialistic conception of reality and these metaphysical presuppositions infect and distort the axiological commitments of their ethical theories. Our first step, therefore, must be to expose the axiological implications of these often uncritically perpetuated metaphysical presuppositions.

The Insidious Legacy of Modern Axiology

In his quest for apodictic certainty, René Descartes dramatically altered Aristotle's virtually unchallenged view of nature, wherein all living things have a teleologically oriented soul (*psyché*). For Descartes, nature is not an organic realm full of a multitude of different types of substances with corresponding functions and activities. As his famous analysis of wax in his second meditation is meant to demonstrate, the essence of material things is simply that they are extended; this quality alone is inseparable from them. Hence, essentially (or rather, substantially), a horse is no different from a daisy or a piece of granite. The ghosts of finality are exorcised from the natural world. Thus, Aristotle's ontologically rich and varied conception of the universe is reduced to three types of substances: extended things, thinking things, and God.[2]

Though natural things may vary in the complexity of the arrangement of their component parts, they are, according to Descartes, simply extended things mechanistically determined by the unflinching laws of nature. Thus, despite all appearances to the contrary, animals are not conscious of anything: they neither taste nor smell nor see nor feel pain or pleasure.[3] Accordingly, Descartes suggests in *Discourse on Method*, animals are like clocks: they may be able to do some things better than we are, just as a clock may be able to keep time more accurately than we can; however, like the clock, animals are neither conscious nor sentient.

> It is also a very remarkable fact that although many animals show more skill than we do in some of their actions, yet the same animals show none at all in many others; so what they do better does not prove that they have any intelligence, for if it did then they would have more intelligence than any of us and would excel us in everything. It proves rather that they have no intelligence at all, and that it is nature which acts in them according to the disposition of their organs. In the same way a clock, consisting only of wheels and springs, can count the hours and measure time more accurately than we can with all our wisdom.[4]

Animals are simply sophisticated machines created by the infinitely skilled artisan, God. *Qua* lifeless, passive "stuff," the extended world is merely a plenum of "facts." An extended substance simply is or it is not. But whether it is or is not, properly speaking, is not a good thing or a bad thing. According to this logic, the value of an extended thing is derived solely from its relation to an external valuer, rather than from its intrinsic nature. That is, the extended, material world is intrinsically valueless.

The consistency with which Descartes acted on this worldview can be seen in his repeated and disinterested use of vivisection in his biological investigations.[5] For example, in a letter dated February 15, 1638, Descartes encourages Plempius to attempt an experiment he has performed on the heart of a live rabbit. Descartes describes how he began by removing the rabbit's ribs to gain access to the heart and aorta, then after blocking the artery with a string and piercing the heart, he watched to see if blood flowed into the heart when the artery was blocked. Descartes notes that he then "cut away half the heart" remarking with much interest that the part of the heart that had been removed stopped beating at once, while the part within the rabbit "continued to pulsate for quite some time."[6] Similarly, in *Description of the Human Body*, Descartes mentions a "striking experiment" in which he "slice[d] off the pointed end of the heart in a live dog" and inserted his finger in order to feel the contraction of the heart.[7]

Descartes' experiments on live subjects were carried on by his followers, who were also interested in continuing Harvey's work on the circulatory system by means of vivisection.

> The (Cartesian) scientists administered beatings to dogs with perfect indifference and made fun of those who pitied the creatures as if they felt pain. They said the animals were clocks; that the cries they emitted when struck were only the noise of a little spring that had been touched, but that the whole body was without feeling. They nailed the poor animals up on boards by their four paws to vivisect them to see the circulation of the blood which was a great subject of controversy.[8]

For Descartes himself and his followers, the act of cutting open the chest of a live animal in order to study the circulation of its blood is not fundamentally different from lifting the hood to one's car to study the flow of oil. Extended substances, such as rabbits and dogs, can no more feel pain than a toaster or a footstool. They are machines, not subjects of lives. Thus, given such metaphysical commitments, the act of nailing a fully conscious animal to a board in order to cut it open and observe the flow of its blood is not a moral or immoral act at all.

Descartes' axiological dualism also has a dramatic effect on both the ontological and axiological status of humans. Regarding the former, Descartes' view of substance as that which requires nothing other than God in order to exist[9] fractures the world into a multitude of isolated, atomic agents ontologically dependent on no one and no thing, save God; human beings become, as Dewey puts it, "little Gods." Thus, Descartes' ontology not only isolates human beings from nature, it also isolates them from each other. Furthermore, in so doing, Descartes makes thinking things (and God) the sole loci of intrinsic value. In this way, Descartes' ontological dualism entails what may be called an invidious axiological anthropocentrism, resulting in the quite consistent behavior of Descartes and his followers. This conclusion can be seen very clearly in the axiology of another modern dualist, Immanuel Kant.

As the following passage from the *Groundwork of the Metaphysics of Morals* demonstrates, though Kant's metaphysics may differ considerably from that of Descartes, his axiology does not:

> Suppose . . . there were something *whose existence* has *in itself* an absolute value, something which as *an end in itself* could be a ground of determinate laws; then in it, and in it alone, would there be the ground of a possible categorical imperative—that is, of a practical law.
>
> Now I say that man, and in general every rational being, *exists* as an end in himself, *not merely as a means* for arbitrary use by this or that will: he must in all his actions, whether they are directed to himself or to other beings, always be viewed *at the same time as an end*. All the objects of inclination have only a conditioned value;

for if there were not these inclinations and the needs grounded on them, their object would be valueless. . . . Thus the value of all objects that can *be produced* by our action is always conditioned. Beings whose existence depends, not on our will, but on nature, have none the less, if they are non-rational beings, only a relative value as means and are consequently called *things*.[10]

In this passage, we see the axiology latent in Descartes gain its full and explicit expression. On the one hand, there are rational beings who, as authors of the moral law, are ends in themselves and have, as a result, "absolute value," while, on the other hand, there are nonrational entities that are only means to rational beings' ends and have therefore only "conditioned value." Hence, according to this view, it is not true that human beings have the highest degree of value out of a spectrum of values—as, for instance, human beings have the highest degree of goodness compared to animals and plants for a Neoplatonist such as St. Augustine. Having exorcised the Aristotelian ghosts of teleology from the nonhuman world, the ontological and axiological dualism at work in Descartes and Kant leads to the view that human beings have "absolute value" and that the value of everything else in the universe is dependent upon its relation to our needs.

Axiologically speaking, then, Kant's *phenomena* are no different from Descartes' *res extensa*; nonrational beings (or nonthinking beings, for Descartes) have no intrinsic value whatever. In this sense, their metaphysics establishes an invidious axiological anthropocentrism wherein human beings, as the sole loci of intrinsic value, are the only entities to which one can have direct duties. Indeed, Kant himself argues for such a view in his *Lectures on Ethics*:

So far as animals are concerned, we have no direct duties. Animals are not self-conscious and are there merely as a means to an end. That end is man. . . . Our duties towards animals are merely indirect duties towards humanity. . . . If a man shoots his dog because the animal is no longer capable of service, he does not fail in his duty to the dog, for the dog cannot judge, but his act is inhuman and damages in himself that humanity which it is his duty to show towards mankind.[11]

Simply put, since nonhumans only have "conditioned value," my duties to them can only be indirect.[12] Accordingly, one should, for instance, avoid despoiling nature's beauty not because it is replete with intrinsically valuable beings or because the world would be a poorer place if such beings were destroyed, but because such actions portray a lack of respect for oneself as the author of the moral law—that is, it damages humanity. For Kant, then, if I refrain from shooting my dog or nailing it to a board and cutting it open while it is still alive, it is in no way because of the complexity or richness of *its* experience.[13] Rather, I do so out of respect for myself. The dog, after all, is only a means to my ends, and consequently my duties to it are merely indirect.

To a certain extent, the metaphysics of materialism is already implicit within our analysis of dualism. For, in a sense, the materialist simply extends the notion of the material world established by dualists to include all of reality. According to materialism, the universe is composed of nothing but, in Descartes' terms, *res extensa*. Thus, along with God, Descartes' *res cogitans* and Kant's noumena are banished to "softer" sciences such as theology, sociology, and psychology. René Descartes' contemporary Thomas Hobbes provides an excellent example of modern materialism. Whereas Descartes insisted that reality is irreducibly divided between extended things and thinking things, Hobbes advanced the view that reality is composed exclusively of vacuous, material atoms. The axiological implications of this ontology are also a logical extension of the view of nature offered by axiological dualism: having finally banished the last vestiges of purpose from the universe, materialism conceives of the cosmos as an unending sea of facts marching in lockstep to nature's laws. Like our own subjective experience, values are simply a by-product of the motion of atoms through space.

For Hobbes, then, the atoms of which reality is composed can have no value in themselves. This has the result of eliminating any objective grounding for value. In a sense, then, the very concept of something with intrinsic value is unintelligible for the materialist. For, as with the dualist's conception of nature, facts simply are or are not, but whether this or that fact is or is not is not important; in a purely material world, there are no intrinsic values. Value's last tether to the objective structure of reality has been cut.

Having loosed value from its ontological mooring, axiological materialism sets out to develop an ethical theory that is independent from any analysis of how things are. Value is no longer something one finds in the world; it is something one places on the world. The disconnect between one's ethical judgments and one's rational understanding of the world is most lucidly developed by another modern materialist, David Hume. According to Hume, it is quite impossible to determine whether a given state of affairs is objectively valuable.

> An action, or sentiment, or character is virtuous or vicious; why? because its view causes a pleasure or uneasiness of a particular kind. In giving a reason, therefore, for the pleasure of uneasiness we sufficiently explain the vice or virtue. To have the sense of virtue, is nothing but to *feel* a satisfaction of a particular kind from the contemplation of a character. The very *feeling* constitutes our praise or admiration. We go no farther; nor do we enquire into the cause of the satisfaction. We do not infer a character to be virtuous, because it pleases: but in feeling that it pleases after such a particular manner, we in effect feel that it is virtuous. The case is the same in our judgments concerning all kinds of beauty, and tastes, and sensations.[14]

For Hume, virtue is not about doing something in accordance with or contrary to one's objective nature—as, for instance, it was for Aristotle. Hume's materialism eliminates any such grounding of value. Rather, virtue is "nothing but" feeling a certain satisfaction; this feeling "constitutes" the virtue. Hence, without an objective ground for value, questions of axiology become a matter of social and political convention; that is to say, the locus and scope of value is completely relative. After all, if value is not ontologically grounded, then it becomes simply a function of particular agents' interests.[15]

It is in this context that Hume made his famous claim that one can never move from what something "is" or "is not" to what it "ought" to be or what it "ought not" to be. For Hume, how something *is* tells us nothing about how it *ought* to be:

> In every system of morality, which I have hitherto met with, I have always remark'd, that the author proceeds for some time in the ordinary way of reasoning, and establishes the being of a God, or makes observations concerning human affairs; when of a sudden I am surpriz'd to find, that instead of the usual of propositions, *is*, and *is not*, I meet with no proposition that is not connected with an *ought*, or an *ought not*. This change is imperceptible; but is, however, of the last consequence. For as this *ought*, or *ought* not, expresses some new relation or affirmation, 'tis necessary that it shou'd be observ'd and explain'd; and at the same time that reason should be given, for what seems altogether inconceivable, how this new relation can be a deduction from others, which are entirely different from it.[16]

For a materialist such as Hume, the universe is composed exclusively of facts. Accordingly, outside of the aversions and adversions of a particular human subject, it simply doesn't make sense to ask whether some state of affairs ought to be affirmed over another or whether something is good independent of its being valued by a human agent. Overall, then, the inadequacy of the axiology of both dualistic and materialistic metaphysics is ultimately found in their distortion of the status of both human beings and nature, which makes of human beings a disconnected, atomic, and autonomous mass of individuals and of nature a vacuous material fact.

This conclusion brings to light a crucial conclusion regarding the relation between the scope of direct moral concern and the scope of intrinsic value. According to the analysis above, the scope of direct moral concern is a function of the scope of intrinsic value. To be more precise, the scope of direct moral concern and the scope of intrinsic value are coextensive; only those beings with intrinsic value are of *direct* moral concern. For instance, for both Descartes and Kant, this entails that only human beings are objects of direct moral concern, and that, therefore, morality is concerned only with those relations obtaining between human beings.

Part of the legacy of this logic can be seen throughout contemporary moral debates, particularly in the debate over abortion. It is no accident that, for some, the conflict over abortion primarily concerns whether a fetus is or is not a human being.[17] For if the fetus is a human being, then it has intrinsic value and must be considered in its own right. However, if it is not a human being, then the question of abortion is not truly a moral concern at all. That is, if a fetus is not a human being, then its destruction is no more reprehensible than the destruction of a dog or a tractor. One's duties to it would be merely indirect. Similarly, the debate over euthanasia for people who, either because of injury or to birth defect, exist only in a "vegetative state," is often waged over whether such individuals are still human in the full sense of the term. Dualistic axiologies have this binary quality about them: you either have intrinsic value or you don't. If you don't, my dealings with you are a matter of prudence, not morality. According to the axiology of the dualist, then, our relations to the extrahuman world are not, strictly speaking, moral relations at all.[18]

Peter Singer was one of the first to systematically expose the devastating consequences of this sort of logic.[19] For instance, while many would assume that, given what we now know about the complexity of nonhuman animals, animal experimentation has stopped or at least has diminished. Yet, according to some estimates, as many as 200 million animals are killed for use in scientific experiments each year in the United States. While more conservative estimates place the number between 15 and 25 million, the precise number of animal experiments is in fact impossible to determine because research institutes are not required to report them. The reason for this itself illustrates the influence of the mechanistic view of animals: often the animals used are not seen as being any different from the equipment used by researchers. Like a test tube or beaker, animals are just "tools for research." Lest one erroneously assume that these experiments are conducted without the infliction of unnecessary suffering, it may be helpful to briefly outline what takes place in some of these experiments.

For instance, in the Draize Test, in use since the 1940s, scientists test the toxicity of various substances to the eye. As Singer describes it:

> The animals are usually placed in holding devices from which only their heads protrude. This prevents them from scratching or rubbing their eyes. A test substance (such as bleach, shampoo, or ink) is then placed in one eye of each rabbit. The method used is to pull out the lower eyelid and place the substance into the small "cup" thus formed. The eye is then held closed. Sometimes the application is repeated. The rabbits are observed for swelling, ulceration, infection and bleeding. The studies can last up to three weeks. . . . Some substances cause so much serious damage that the rabbits' eyes lose all distinguishing characteristics—the iris, pupil, and cornea begin to resemble one massive infection.[20]

The gross infliction of unnecessary suffering is, sadly, more often the rule than the exception in animal experimentation. However, while I find such experiments troubling, my primary aim is to draw attention to the severe disconnect between how people treat non-humans and how they conceive of them.[21] At least Descartes was consistent; he held that vivisection was unobjectionable because animals are merely machines. Contemporary scientists have no such excuse. For all but the most hardened reductionists readily admit that animals are able to feel pain. In fact, the only reason the experiments take place is that the physiology of human and nonhuman animals are so similar. It seems that our axiological commitments are out of sync with our metaphysical presuppositions. These axiological and metaphysical presuppositions have justified treating nonhumans as mere resources to be used with impunity. Nonhuman animals, for instance, are not complex, feeling individuals; they are food machines and disease models. Whether consciously recognized or not, these presuppositions infect and distort the ethical offspring of these modern worldviews. Yet if we are to avoid the mistakes of our predecessors, it is not enough merely to recognize these shortcomings. To develop an ethical theory that is adequate to the value and beauty of all forms of actuality, we must seek new metaphysical and axiological shores. To this end, let us turn to that bold group of American philosophers who were among the first to reject dualisms and materialisms in all their forms.

American Pragmatists' Repudiation of Dualism and Materialism

At a time when idealism was prevalent on the Continent and in Great Britain, when materialism reigned in the still-Newtonian sciences, and when Cartesian or Kantian dualisms were taken as given by most philosophers, Charles Sanders Peirce set out to create a new metaphysical paradigm. Rather than reducing or bifurcating reality, Peirce began with the presupposition that reality is fundamentally continuous, referring to his theory as *synechism*.[22] In contrast to the prevailing metaphysics, which either reduced reality—that is, materialism and idealism—or bifurcated reality into mutually exclusive parts—that is, dualism—Peirce's synechism points toward an evolutionary cosmology "in which all the regularities of nature and of mind are regarded as products of growth, and to a Schelling-fashioned idealism which holds matter to be mere specialised and partially deadened mind."[23] For Peirce, then, the mental and the physical should not be understood as different *kinds* of existence. Rather, the mental and the physical are simply two different ways of looking at the same rich reality: "It would be a mistake to conceive of the psychical and the physical aspects of matter as two aspects absolutely distinct. Viewing a thing from the outside, considering its relations of action and reaction with other things, it appears as matter. Viewing it from the inside, looking at its immediate character as feeling, it appears as consciousness."[24] Reality is not merely mental or merely physical. There is just one continuous reality which, through eons of evolution, has developed into the various forms of experience we call mental and physical. Ultimately, for Peirce, both dualism and materialism are unable to explain the continuity that lies at the base of reality.

In *A Pluralistic Universe*, William James further lays siege to the walls of dualisms and reductionisms that threaten to separate us from nature. According to James, most philosophers conceive of entities as self-enclosed, wholly complete by themselves. Because of this, relations are external to the entity. However, James believes that this view of reality is misguided because it takes our linguistic constructions as designating ontological relations. For James, conceptual logic (such as Euclidean geometry or Newtonian physics) is useful in a certain limited context, but is not an adequate explanation of existence. Existence for James cannot be compartmentalized into conceptual blocks, each of which excludes every other.[25] James refers to the view that abstract notions designate existential limitations as "intellectualism."[26] He rejects intellectualism because it denies that "finite things can act on one another, for all things, once translated into concepts, remain shut up to themselves."[27] Thus, James rejects the emphasis in substance metaphysics on independence, emphasizing instead a view of individuality that puts relationality at its core. To be an individual is to be related, and to act on something is to "get into it somehow."[28] To exist is, *prima facie*, to be internally related to others. Thus, James concludes, conceptual logic ought not to be taken as prescribing metaphysical boundaries. "Reality, life, experience, concreteness, immediacy, use what word you will, exceeds our logic, overflows and surrounds it."[29] With Peirce, then, James denies that matter is simply lifeless stuff arrangable in different configurations by unflinching laws of nature: "The whole universe in its different spans and wave-lengths exclusions and envelopments, is everywhere alive and conscious."[30] Hence, for both James and Peirce, the lifeless matter of the materialists, the *res extensa* of the Cartesians, and the noumena of the Kantians are ultimately all fictions; there is no lifeless matter and no "matterless" psyche.

In his 1940 essay, "Time and Individuality," John Dewey takes James's relational view of individuality a step further by relating it to the question of time. According to Dewey, by divorcing individuality from temporality, classical notions of time conceived of individuals as static and impassive. Dewey cites Laplace as stating the logical outcome of the classical conception of time:

> "We may conceive the present state of the universe as the effect of its past and the cause of its future. An intellect who at any given instant knew all the forces of animate nature and the mutual positions of the beings who compose it . . . could condense into a single formula the movement both of the greatest body in the universe and of its lightest atom. Nothing would be uncertain for such an intellect, for the future, even as the past would be ever present before its eyes."[31]

By divorcing individuality from temporality, the classical view of time entails an absolute determinism. In contrast to this view, Dewey conceives of individuality as a career: "Individuality is the uniqueness of the history, of the career, not something given once for all at the beginning which then proceeds to unroll as a ball of yarn may be unwound."[32] In support of this view, Dewey turns to Heisenberg's principle of indeterminacy, according to which indeterminacy is an ontological aspect of nature. That is, reality itself is ontologically indeterminate.[33] The implication of this, according to Dewey, is enormous, for it "annihilates" the premises on which Laplace's conclusion is based.[34] For Dewey, Heisenberg's principle demonstrates that "the individual is a temporal career whose future cannot be *logically* deduced from its past." Thus, Dewey believes that the principle of indeterminacy is a way of "acknowledging the pertinency of real time to physical beings." Time is not simply a "measure of predetermined changes in mutual positions"; rather, time *enters into the being* of all individuals, both "physical individuals" and "human individuals."[35]

Thus, just as modern and classical notions of absolute time led to an absolute dualism between humans and nature, the notion of time as existence implies a conception of reality that calls into question the view of reality as bifurcated. Accordingly, we must count Dewey among the "few daring souls" willing to advance the view that "temporal quality and historical career are a mark of *everything*, including atomic events, to which individuality may [nay, *must*] be attributed."[36] Such a view affects a fundamental shift in our conception of humanity's place in the universe. According to such a view, humanity is different in degree, rather than in kind, from nature: "There is no fixed gap between them."[37] All things, inasmuch as they exist, are subject to the principle of a developing career and are, in this respect, individuals. "The difference between the animate plant and the inanimate iron molecule is not that the former has something in addition to physico-chemical energy; it lies in the *way* in which physico-chemical energies are interconnected and operate, whence different *consequences* mark inanimate and animate activity respectively."[38] The distinction between physical, psychophysical, and mental is thus one of levels of increasing intimacy and interaction among natural events. Like Peirce and James, then, Dewey affirms a view of reality that emphasizes continuity and, in so doing, advances a model of individuality that stresses interaction rather than independence: "Yet if man is within nature, not a little god outside, and is within as a mode of energy inseparably connected with other modes, interaction is the one unescapable trait of every human concern."[39] What is important here is that the realization that human beings are not an aberration or an exception to nature, that we are not a "little god outside" of nature, produces a fundamental shift in our axiological outlook. "When he perceives clearly and adequately that he is within nature, a part of its interactions, he sees that the line to be drawn is not between action and thought, or action and appreciation, but between blind, slavish, meaningless action and action that is free, significant, directed and responsible."[40] In a sense, my project is a systematic attempt to develop an ethical model that captures Dewey's insight. Once we repudiate our former conceit and realize that we are not a little god outside of nature but that we are thoroughly a part of the ongoing sweep of interacting and changing events, we must develop ways to act so that our actions are at once free, significant, directed, and responsible. As an example of, rather than an exception to, natural events, we must recognize that we are not responsible only to ourselves. The cosmos is not a lifeless sea of facts dotted by lonely islands of value; the cosmos is everywhere awash with value.

Though in different ways Peirce, James, and Dewey all steadfastly repudiate dualistic and materialistic attempts to bifurcate or reduce reality, they affirm a view of individuality that emphasizes interconnection over independence, community over individualism, and continuity over discontinuity. However, in the process, they also open the door to many further questions, none of which is systematically examined. For instance, once it is affirmed that individuals are not merely accidentally but essentially related to each other, it becomes critical to account for how these internal relations take place. How, for example, does one of James's individuals "get into another" in order to act on it? Because ethics is primarily concerned with achieving appropriate relations between individuals, this question is particularly important. The pragmatists' extension of individuality to atomic events also poses two further questions. First, how ought we to define "individual"? Second, what is the relationship between macroscopic individuals and the microscopic individuals of which they are composed? For instance, if I as a human being am an individual, and the atomic events of which I am composed are also individuals, how am I as a macroscopic individual related to my microscopic parts, which are also individuals? This question requires the pragmatist to address the question of questions: What is the relation between the one and the many?

These questions are not intended so much to point to errors committed by the pragmatists, but to highlight the need to push their analysis further. As a former mentor, Robert Spitzer, is fond of saying, "There are more sins of omission than commission." With an eye to these omissions, I turn to Alfred North Whitehead's "philosophy of organism," which is "mainly devoted to the task of making clear the notion of 'being present in another'" (PR, 50).[41] I contend that, given the social and environmental crises confronting the contemporary world, this move is not only appropriate, it is vital. To uproot the implicit hegemony of modern axiology's reduction of the natural world, we must systematically, though fallibly, develop an alternative worldview, one that explains *how* individuals are internally related to one another and that affirms the intrinsic value of every individual. Given the challenges that confront us, it is irresponsible not to pursue such a course.

Whitehead's Metaphysics of Creativity

Alfred North Whitehead is among the twentieth century's few daring souls to put forth a true metaphysical system. However, unlike the great metaphysical projects of the modern and medieval masters, Whitehead's "philosophy of organism" does not claim to arrive at a fully adequate, closed, apodictic system of truths. Though he aims at a fully logical, coherent, applicable, and adequate account of reality,[42] he does not claim that such an account is ever fully achievable. Like other pragmatists, Whitehead is a fallibilist.

The extent to which he embraced fallibilism as a foundation not only for his thought but also for his actions is captured beautifully in a letter written in response to the essays written in his honor for the Library of Living Philosophers Series. Rather than responding to the critics of his work by explaining how they had overlooked, misunderstood, or underappreciated this or that nuance of his thought, Whitehead writes, "The progress of philosophy does not primarily involve reactions of agreement or dissent. It essentially consists in the enlargement of thought, whereby contradictions and agreements are transformed into practical aspects of wider points of view. Thus my own reaction to this book should consist in devoting many years to rewriting my previous works."[43]

Unfortunately, Whitehead's failing health precluded such an endeavor. Nevertheless, the statement reveals his indefatigable commitment to the fallible pursuit of ever greater adequacy and coherence and illustrates Whitehead's conception of speculative philosophy. Philosophy in general and metaphysics in particular should not mean staking out and then defending to the death one's philosophical territory.[44] "A clash of doctrines is not a disaster—it is an opportunity" (SMW, 186). Speculative philosophy ought to involve a community of inquirers seeking an ever-fuller account of reality and of our place within it. In this context, Whitehead's allusion to "wider points of view" is particularly germane. For, as I will explain, the "width" of one's point of view is not only crucial for the adequacy of one's metaphysical speculation, but is also "inseparably conjoined" with the morality of one's point of view.[45] Because of this intimate connection between one's metaphysical and moral commitments, this first chapter takes a critical initial step toward elaborating an organic Whiteheadian ethic.

Whitehead starts "from the analysis of process as the realization of events disposed in an interlocking community. The event is the unit of things real" (SMW, 152). Thus, a fundamental tenet of the philosopher of organism is that the notion of an individual as the unchanging subject of change must be completely abandoned

(PR, 29). That is, Whitehead's philosophy of organism radically rejects the doctrine of "independent existence." "There is no such mode of existence; every entity is only to be understood in terms of the way in which it is interwoven with the rest of the Universe" (IM, 687).[46] As with James's rejection of intellectualism, Whitehead finds that to view individuals as independent itself implies that the subject-predicate form of statement "conveys a truth which is metaphysically ultimate," that is, that an individual substance with its predicates constitutes the "ultimate type of actuality" (PR, 137). The problem with taking the independence of individuals as one's primary metaphysical presupposition, Whitehead argues, is that it ultimately makes the relations between individual substances unintelligible.

Since Aristotle, "substance" has traditionally referred to the underlying substratum of change that does not itself change.[47] This is the notion of substance we receive from the *Categories*, wherein a substance is defined by its character of being "neither said of a subject nor in a subject."[48] Substances, then, are unchanging subjects of change that are defined by their characteristic of never being inside another. To be a substance is to be essentially unrelated and nondependent on others. That is, though substances must necessarily be related to others, these relations are irrelevant to the individual's essence. This is what we mean by saying an individual is essentially independent. Significantly, this notion of substance imports into the most fundamental level of reality the notion of the real (essential) independence of individuals. An individual is defined by its not entering into (that is, not being in) others and not requiring others in order to be what it is.

Exactly what is entailed in Whitehead's repudiation of substance philosophy's view of individuality? First, though he finds the substantial view to be inaccurate, Whitehead fully recognizes that human beings unavoidably and necessarily think of things in terms of substance and quality (SMW, 52). For, he says, "without these ways of thinking we could not get our ideas straight for daily

use" (SMW, 52). Things such as tables, dogs, and roses are not fictions, nor do their forms of order derive from the functioning of
our minds. Rather, Whitehead claims that part of what it is to be
the type of high-grade organism that we are is to be able to abstract
from, as James put it, the "blooming, buzzing confusion" that con-
stantly confronts us.[49] "We find ourselves," Whitehead says, "in a
buzzing world, amid a democracy of fellow creatures; whereas,
under some guise or other, orthodox philosophy can only introduce
us to solitary substances, each enjoying an illusory experience: 'O
Bottom, thou art changed! What do I see on thee?'" (PR, 50). For
Whitehead, our experience of the world, indeed the experience of
most animals, is the product of a complex physiological process
whose primary function is to attend to a focal foreground purchased
at the expense of a massive, neglected background. "There are other
elements in our experience, on the fringe of consciousness, and yet
massively qualifying our experience. In regard to these other facts,
it is our consciousness that flickers, and not the facts themselves.
They are always securely there, barely discriminated, and yet inescapable" (AI, 163). Put more simply, "Consciousness is the acme
of emphasis" (AI, 180).

Consequently, Whitehead claims, if we look closely at the concepts of substance and quality we will find that they are essentially
"elaborate logical constructions of a high degree of abstraction"
(SMW, 52).[50] They are complicated and highly useful abstractions,
but they are abstractions nonetheless. Thus, the problem is not the
fact that we perceive the world in terms of substantial individuals
—this is both unavoidable and practically important—but that we
fail to recognize "that we are presenting ourselves with simplified
editions of immediate matters of fact" (SMW, 52). This inappropriate substitution of the abstract for the concrete is the essence
of what Whitehead calls the "fallacy of misplaced concreteness."[51]
Ultimately, Whitehead explains, the violation of this fallacy does
not result from the mere employment of the word "substance," but

from taking, whether consciously or unconsciously, independence rather than interconnection as ontologically ultimate.[52] For the view of an individual substance as "complete in itself, without any reference to any other substantial thing" (AI, 133) not only violates the fallacy of misplaced concreteness, it also leads, as we saw in the analysis of dualism above, to the fracturing of the universe into a multitude of substantial things that only externally or "accidentally" relate to others and thereby renders the real interconnections between entities unintelligible (AI, 133). If we are to make the relations between individuals intelligible and meaningful, we must adopt a fundamentally different model of individuality, a model that presupposes the interrelatedness of individuals rather than their independence. Like the pragmatists above, Whitehead embraces a model of individuality that defines individuals in terms of their relations with others, rather than by their independence. However, unlike the pragmatists, Whitehead rightly speculates on exactly how these internal relations take place.

Whitehead envisions a cosmos that is pluralistically populated by individuals he refers to as "actual entities" or, equivalently, "actual occasions."[53] Actual occasions "are the final real things of which the world is made up. There is no going behind actual entities to find anything more real. They differ among themselves: God is an actual entity, and so is the most trivial puff of existence in far-off empty space" (PR, 18). This is Whitehead's "ontological principle," which insists that reasons or causes cannot simply float in from nowhere.[54] As he puts it in the eighteenth category of explanation of his categoreal scheme, "every condition to which the process of becoming conforms in any particular instance has its reason *either* in the character of some actual entity in the actual world of that concrescence, *or* in the character of the subject which is in process of concrescence" (PR, 24, author's emphasis). For Whitehead, then, every entity in the universe, including God, should exemplify the most basic metaphysical principles at work in the universe. Accordingly, unlike the systems of so many before him, Whitehead's God is the chief example of metaphysical principles, rather than that which is invoked to save them.

Though not in a crude building-block way, actual occasions are the atomic stuff of which the universe is made. Borrowing a phrase from James, Whitehead describes actual occasions as "drops" of experience; they come entirely or not at all.[55] Whitehead refers to the becoming of an actual occasion as *concrescence* (from the Latin *concrēscere*, to grow together). In concrescence, the actual occasion brings together or "prehends" past actual occasions or its "actual world." Past occasions that are prehended by a concrescing occasion are said to be functioning "objectively." However, unlike substance ontologies, the relationships obtaining between actual occasions are primarily internal, not external. Thus, as Whitehead explains in *Science and the Modern World*, "the relations of an event are internal, so far as concerns the event itself; that is to say that they are constitutive of what the event is in itself" (SMW, 104). Each actual occasion is, in this sense, its relationship to the universe. Therefore, Whitehead explicitly rejects Aristotle's dictum that a substance is never present in another. Indeed, according to Whitehead's principle of relativity, "an actual entity *is* present in other actual entities. In fact, if we allow for degrees of relevance, and for negligible relevance, we must say that every actual entity is present in every other actual entity" (PR, 50). In summary, Whitehead has taken substance ontology's "notion of vacuous material existence with passive endurance, with primary individual attributes, and with accidental adventures" (PR, 309) and replaced it with the notion of "atomic" yet internally related events. Thus, it is equally correct to refer to Whitehead's philosophy as one of continuity and one of atomism. But how can this be possible without contradiction? How can Whitehead affirm a thoroughgoing pluralism but also assert both the continuity and solidarity of the cosmos?

The answer ultimately lies in the nature of the actual occasions in question and in Whitehead's most basic category, creativity. If it were true that each actual occasion was a substance and was thereby essentially independent of everything else, then the simultaneous affirmation of the solidarity and the atomicity of the world would indeed be a contradiction. However, insofar as a substance view of reality is repudiated, individuality "does not mean substantial independence" (SMW, 70). Again, occasions are constituted by their relationship to their actual world; the occasion *is* its perspective on the whole. Hence, Whitehead's notion of individuality itself requires essential reference to others. This conclusion is embodied in what Whitehead refers to as the "category of the ultimate" or creativity: "'Creativity' is the universal of universals characterizing ultimate matter of fact. It is that ultimate principle by which the many, which are the universe disjunctively, become the one actual occasion, which is the universe conjunctively. . . . *The many become one, and are increased by one*" (PR, 21, emphasis added).[56] Our processive cosmos is the scene of a perpetual creative advance where the many past atomic individuals come together in the one new atomic individual, which thereby adds itself to the many. Thus, Whitehead does indeed mean to assert both the unity and plurality of the cosmos. This understanding of Whitehead's metaphysics of creativity is central to the development of a Whiteheadian ethics of creativity. Just as his metaphysics avoids the extremes of monism and atomism, the ethics of creativity deftly navigates between the extremes of classical liberal individualism and an all-consuming communitarianism.

Before proceeding to the axiological implications of Whitehead's novel conception of individuality, we should examine the phases of an actual occasion's becoming or concrescence. Throughout Whitehead's works, there are numerous accounts of concrescence. Though no two accounts are exactly the same, Whitehead usually delineates four phases in the becoming of an actual occasion: datum, process, satisfaction, and decision.

In the datum phase of concrescence, the incipient occasion arises out of a sea of intense feeling that surges up from its past. The budding event comes to this sea of feeling through a particular perspective toward the world, a world as already "settled." The settlement of the world is effected by the limitation of "received decisions" of past actual occasions that impose themselves on every future occasion. According to Whitehead, this "settled world" provides the "'real potentiality' that its many actualities be felt compatibly; and the new concrescence starts from this datum" (PR, 150).[57] Thus, the first phase concerns the reception of past, achieved occasions as "objects" or, equivalently, "superjects," which serve as the "real potential" for its own aesthetic self-determination.[58] From this datum the occasion will begin its process of self-determination. Whitehead explains, "Thus the primary stage in the concrescence of an actual entity is the way in which the antecedent universe enters into the constitution of the entity in question, so as to constitute the basis of its nascent individuality. If experience be not based upon objective content, there can be no escape from a solipsist subjectivism" (PR, 152). Notice that "objective content" entails that past occasions literally "enter into" the occasions that succeed them. Thus, this passage clearly delineates the importance of internal relations to Whitehead's system and the extent to which he does repudiate Aristotle's dictum that a substance is defined as something that is not in another. Without such internal relations, Whitehead believes that solipsist subjectivism is unavoidable. We should keep this conclusion in mind when examining the problem of subjectivism in chapter 3.

The passive reception of the given datum in the first phase is followed by the occasion's active synthesis of this datum in the process phase. In this second phase of concrescence, the nascent occasion renders determinate its relationship to each of the elements in its given datum. Specifically, the nascent occasion makes its relationship to each past occasion determinate either by affirming it through what Whitehead calls "positive prehension," thereby making it a part of itself, or by ignoring it through "negative prehension," thereby excluding it from itself. Therefore, "the 'process' is the addition of those elements of feeling whereby these indeterminations are dissolved into determinate linkages attaining the actual unity of an individual actual entity" (PR, 150). In explaining the process of self-determination in teleological terms, Whitehead is reversing modern philosophy's attempt to eliminate finality from nature. An actual occasion's process of self-determination is teleologically guided by its "subjective aim," an aim that is itself gradually shaped through the process of self-determination (PR, 212).

Note that an occasion's subjective aim is not limited merely to the "real potentiality" provided by past occasions in its "actual world." If this were the case, then new occasions would merely be a repetition of previous achievements, making novelty impossible and becoming inexplicable. To explain the infusion of novelty and aim into the universe, Whitehead makes an important distinction between the "real potentiality" provided by an actual occasion's objective datum and the "pure potentiality" of what he calls "eternal objects." As forms of definiteness, eternal objects share many similarities with Plato's Forms. However, eternal objects differ from Forms in at least one important respect: whereas Forms are supremely actual, eternal objects are only deficiently actual. In a way, then, Whitehead turns Plato's Forms on their heads.

Given the data received by a nascent occasion in the datum phase, a particular set of eternal objects (what Whitehead calls an abstractive hierarchy)[59] is relevant as a "lure" for feeling. However, as Whitehead himself notes, "effective relevance requires agency of comparison, and agency belongs exclusively to actual occasions" (PR, 31). Thus, if the ontological principle is to remain intact, there must be some actual occasion that accounts for the germaneness of particular eternal objects to the becoming of each actual occasion. For Whitehead, this actual occasion is God. "Apart from God," Whitehead explains, "eternal objects unrealized in the actual world would be relatively non-existent for the concrescence in question"

(PR, 31). Accordingly, the relevance of eternal objects is explicable only through God's "unconditioned conceptual valuation of the entire multiplicity of eternal objects" (PR, 31). Whitehead refers to this complete valuation or, equivalently, envisaging of the realm of eternal objects as the "primordial nature of God." Through God's primordial ordering of pure possibility, "the objectification of God in each derivate actual entity results in a graduation of the relevance of eternal objects to the concrescent phases of that derivate occasion" (PR, 31). In other words, it is through the decision of the primordial nature of God that novel forms of definiteness become relevant to process in the form of a particular "objective lure."[60] Thus, in this strict sense, "God is the principle of concretion; namely, he is that actual entity from which each temporal concrescence receives that initial aim from which its self-causation starts" (PR, 244).

In summary, the process phase involves an actual occasion's process of teleological self-determination whereby the occasion admits or rejects elements in its actual world and in its objective lure until it is rendered fully determinate. Paradoxically, then, in becoming itself, the entity resolves the question as to what it is to be (PR, 150). This is what Whitehead calls the principle of process: the determination of that which was indeterminate progressively constitutes *what* the entity is.[61] In a sense, then, the actual occasion creates itself out of its environment by rendering its relations to its actual world determinate. In this limited sense, it is *causa sui*.[62]

When all indetermination has been removed and the process of self-determination is complete, the entity achieves satisfaction. "It belongs," Whitehead explains, "to the essence of this subject that it pass into objective immortality. Thus its own constitution involves that its own activity in *self*-formation passes into its activity of *other*-formation. It is by reason of the constitution of the present subject that the future will embody the present subject and will reenact its patterns of activity" (AI, 193). In satisfaction, an occasion's subjective immediacy perishes, and it becomes "objectively immortal" in the sense that it becomes a "stubborn fact" that all future occasions must take into account. Accordingly, satisfaction marks the shift from the occasion as "subject" or actuality in attainment, to the occasion as "superject" or attained actuality.[63]

The transition from self-formation to other-formation marks the final stage of concrescence. For, *qua* satisfied, an entity becomes a "decision" that is then transmitted to succeeding actual occasions. "The final stage, the 'decision,' is how the actual entity, having attained its individual 'satisfaction,' thereby adds a determinate condition to the settlement of the future beyond itself" (PR, 150). This is the principle of relativity: that it is in the nature of every being that it is a potential for becoming. Thus the circle closes on itself; "the many become one, and are increased by one" (PR, 21). "The oneness of the universe, and the oneness of each element in the universe, repeat themselves to the crack of doom in the creative advance from creature to creature, each creature including in itself the whole history and exemplifying the self-identity of things and their mutual diversities" (PR, 228).

In affirming an organic model of individuality that takes the fact of interrelation and interdependence as primary, Whitehead challenges any worldview that seeks to ontologically bifurcate or otherwise reduce reality. Moreover, by reintroducing subjective aim at the heart of becoming and by leaving room for the novel response of an occasion to its circumstances, he avoids an undifferentiated monism. In this way, he presents a metaphysical system that affirms both the plurality and the solidarity of the universe. Individuality need not be purchased at the expense of community. In this sense, Whitehead's system is a metaphysics of creativity. As we will see in part 2, this provides a unique foundation for the development of a moral philosophy that affirms the intrinsic value not only of individuals, but also of the social environments in which these individuals are nested and on which they depend.

Vacuous Actuality Repudiated

While most scholars readily point out, as I have just done, that Whitehead had deep misgivings about the substantial view of individuality, few note that these misgivings stem as much from axiological considerations as ontological ones.[64] I contend that it is not possible to appreciate fully Whitehead's rejection of substance ontology without also examining his rejection of substance axiology and its notion of what he calls "vacuous actuality."

Whitehead defines vacuous existence in Cartesian terms as "a *res vera* devoid of subjective immediacy" (PR, 29). Thus, the rejection of the notion of a substance which, in its independence, is devoid of subjective immediacy, suggests that Whitehead extends subjective immediacy to all of reality. But what exactly is entailed by rejecting the notion of mere facts or of bodily substance? Does Whitehead then affirm that there are only mental substances? Is he an animist, a panpsychist, or an absolute idealist? From a certain perspective, it would seem that he is all of these. For he repeatedly affirms what he calls the reformed subjectivist principle: "that apart from the experiences of subjects there is nothing, nothing, nothing, bare nothingness" (PR, 167). According to this principle, process *is* the becoming of experience.

> The [reformed] subjectivist principle is that the whole universe consists of elements disclosed in the analysis of the experiences of subjects. Process is the becoming of experience. It follows that the philosophy of organism entirely accepts the subjectivist bias of modern philosophy. It also accepts Hume's doctrine that nothing is to be received into the philosophical scheme which is not discoverable as an element in objective experience. This is the ontological principle. (PR, 166)

Thus, far from repudiating the subjectivist bias of modern philosophy or Hume's insistence that nothing can be known apart from experience, Whitehead wholeheartedly embraces the subjectivist principle that "the whole universe consists of elements disclosed in the analysis of the experience of subjects" (PR, 166). However, we should note what the appellation "subjectivist" does not entail. Whitehead's *"reformed* subjectivist principle" does not hold that everything in the universe has a soul or that everything is conscious. There is no merely passive stuff, no lifeless bits of matter, but this does not mean that the walls literally have ears or that a brook literally babbles. Rather, by imputing experience and subjectivity to even the most trivial puff of existence, Whitehead is denying that there is anything that is absolutely determined by external forces. Even the most trivial puff of existence in some remote galaxy renders determinate a small window of relations that are not determined by its environment. Put in terms used above, insofar as each actual occasion is *causa sui*—that is, in the sense that every occasion to a greater or lesser degree (and this degree can make all the difference) renders determinate its relations to its actual world—it *cannot* be devoid of subjective immediacy or experience. Since experience and actuality are coextensive, the zero of experience is the zero of actuality. To lose sight of this is to commit what Charles Hartshorne terms the zero fallacy.[65] In this sense, rather than being a form of panpsychism or animism, David Ray Griffin suggests, a more appropriate term for Whitehead's metaphysics is "panexperientialism."[66] This conclusion effects a sea change in the conception of value: if everything is a subject of experience, there can be no mere facts.

As Whitehead himself states, "If we discard the notion of vacuous existence, we must conceive each actuality as attaining an end for itself. Its very existence is the presentation of its many components to itself, for the sake of its own ends" (FR, 30–31). If nothing is devoid of experience (vacuous actuality), then everything that exists must have some intrinsic value; there are no "sheer facts." "At the base of existence is the sense of 'worth.' It is the sense of existence for its own sake, of existence which is its own justification, of existence with its own character" (MT, 109). Given that, for Whitehead, to be an individual is to be essentially related to every other individual, the philosophy of organism embodies a rejection of any form of ontological dualism or bifurcation that might seek to carve reality into unrelatable pieces.[67] Unlike the systems of Descartes and Kant, for example, there is no absolute, ontological gap between human beings and nature, between the animate and the inanimate, or even between the universe and God. Thus, not only does Whitehead reject the ontological bifurcation or reduction of nature, he also rejects its axiological bifurcation or reduction. Like the pragmatists, Whitehead repudiates any dualism or materialism that makes of certain entities sheer facts, devoid of value. There is no longer such a thing as dead, lifeless, valueless stuff. In our processive cosmos, everything has value to some degree. "The zero of [value] intensiveness means the collapse of actuality. All intensive quantity is merely the contribution of some one element in the synthesis to this one intensiveness of value" (RM, 103). Accordingly, what is being affirmed is a form of ontological democracy; everything counts to some degree.[68] That is, to some degree, everything has value in and for itself. To be actual is to have value.

2

An Ecstatic Axiology

Everything has some value for itself, for others, and for the
whole. This characterizes the meaning of actuality. . . . Existence, in its own nature, is the upholding of value intensity.
Also no unit can separate itself from the others, and from
the whole. And yet each unit exists in its own right. It upholds value intensity for itself, and this involves sharing
value intensity with the universe.

Alfred North Whitehead, *Modes of Thought*

WHITEHEAD'S BOLD AFFIRMATION that actuality and value are coextensive introduces a potentially damaging problem for his axiology in general and for the development of an ethics of creativity
in particular: if actuality is coextensive with value, but actuality is
itself limited to subjects of experience, then the objective world
(that is, superjects or achieved occasions of experience) has no intrinsic value. This problem was first formulated explicitly by David
L. Schindler in a little-known essay entitled "Whitehead's Inability to Affirm a Universe of Value."[1] Schindler's thesis represents
the potentially damaging challenge that, rather than affirming an
ontology of generosity, Whitehead's system is essentially a form of

ontological subjectivism. That is, Whitehead's entire metaphysical project is in danger of collapsing into exactly what it was designed to overcome: a fractured universe of independent subjects each seeking their own ends.

The analysis of the challenge of ontological subjectivism is crucial in several respects.[2] First, if this argument is correct, it jeopardizes the very possibility of developing a meaningful moral philosophy from Whitehead's metaphysics. For if Whitehead is affirming a form of ontological subjectivism, then any ethical theory based on it will, at best, be a moral interest theory and, at worst, a form of psychological egoism.[3] Second, since its analysis will require the examination of the primary scholarly interpretations of Whitehead's metaphysics, responding to the problem of subjectivism will bring greater clarity and depth to the analysis of Whitehead's metaphysics presented in chapter 1 and will highlight the important relation between these metaphysical commitments and the locus and scope of value. Meeting the serious challenge presented by Schindler's argument requires us to seek an alternative to the classical interpretation of Whitehead's metaphysics. In the end, if we are to do justice to the relations between individuals, we must embrace an interpretation that can adequately account for the intrinsic value not only of the self, but of others and of the whole.

The Problem of Subjectivism

Initially, Schindler's criticism of Whitehead's axiology appears to proceed directly from the logic of Whitehead's ontology. As Schindler formulates it, the problem is that, in repudiating vacuous actuality, Whitehead limits actuality, and thereby value, to subjectivity. However, in limiting value to subjectivity he eliminates all ontological warrant for affirming "the value of what is given to us *as other*, that is, the value of what is given objectively."[4] In other words, if apart from subjects there is bare nothingness, as the reformed subjectivist principle states, then subjects are the sole loci and sole determinants of value. Accordingly, though he may have succeeded in eliminating vacuous and therefore valueless actuality, by limiting the scope of actuality to subjectivity, Whitehead simultaneously eliminates his ability to affirm the value of the objective world. Hence, Schindler asks, "If value is coextensive at any given instant with the immanent self-seeking which constitutes a subject, then how at any given instant can . . . what is given to the subject as other than the subject, be affirmed as having value—not simply for me, but in itself?"[5]

The viability of constructing an organic ethical theory based on Whitehead's metaphysics hangs on the answer to this question. For, as Schindler rightly argues, if the objective world has no value in itself, that is, no intrinsic value, "the universe of value fundamentally intended by Whitehead, given his account of actuality, collapses into what can be called at best a multiverse of individuals actively seeking their own self-realization. Whitehead's intended philosophy of generosity is undermined by an ontology of what can only be called selfish individualism."[6] If this claim is correct, Whitehead's system would be an unsuitable foundation for a moral philosophy that seeks to affirm the intrinsic value not only of the self, but of others and of the whole. We should begin to evaluate the problem of ontological subjectivism by examining how Whiteheadian scholars have traditionally drawn the scope of actuality. Since actuality and value are for Whitehead coextensive, if we find that the scope of actuality has been mischaracterized, we may conclude that Schindler is incorrect regarding the scope of value.

The Classical Interpretation

Leclerc and Christian

As it has long functioned (often unconsciously) as the basis for most commentators' understanding of Whitehead's system, we should begin with the "classical interpretation" of Whitehead's metaphysics. This interpretation has been principally defined by two highly influential works: Ivor Leclerc's *Whitehead's Metaphysics* and William Christian's *An Interpretation of Whitehead's Metaphysics*.[7] These works represent the first attempts at the systematic interpretation of Whitehead's metaphysics. My concern here is to examine how Leclerc and Christian circumscribe the extension of actuality and its relation to subjectivity.

For our purposes, the classical interpretation is defined primarily by a sharp ontological distinction between actual occasions as subjects (actuality in achievement) and as superjects (achieved actuality). Such a distinction leads to a view of the superject as devoid of actuality, activity, and creativity. As the following passages demonstrate, the classical interpretation goes to great lengths to emphasize that once an actual occasion has achieved satisfaction, once it is a superject, its subjective immediacy has perished and, furthermore, that the perishing of subjective immediacy entails the perishing of the *actuality* of the occasion. Leclerc writes:

> Whitehead is in full agreement with Aristotle, with Thomas Aquinas, Spinoza, and Leibniz, who had emphatically held this [that is, being,] to be act, action, agency. That is to say, being, existing, in the ultimate sense, is acting. To exist is to act; and to act is to exist. There is no being, in any sense, apart from, in separation from, acting, agency. . . . An "actual" entity is an acting entity.[8]
>
> Only concrescing, i.e. "acting" entities are actual in the full, proper sense. The acting of antecedent actualities is completed; as such they are, in the strict sense, no longer "actual." . . .
>
> An actual entity in the process of concrescence is a "subject," creating itself out of "data," its "objects." As we have seen, only those which are in the process of becoming are properly "actual" entities.[9]

Christian writes: "Thus when the satisfaction of an occasion exists objectively it no longer exists as an immediate feeling. That is to say *it is no longer actual*."[10] He continues, "But X can hardly be the reason for the fact that the datum *is* now given for A. Because X has now perished and is *no longer actual*, whereas the only 'reasons' according to the ontological principle are actual entities."[11] For the classical interpretation, then, subjects alone are actual in the full sense because only acting occasions are actual occasions.[12] This leaves us with the rather paradoxical conclusion that a past actual occasion is not really actual at all.[13] For both Leclerc and Christian, actuality is strictly limited to the actual occasion *qua* concrescence, that is, as subject.

The sharp ontological distinction introduced by Leclerc and Christian is given a systematic basis in the work of George L. Kline. In "Form, Concrescence, and Concretum," Kline meticulously sorts out ambiguities in Whitehead's use of certain key terms. Of particular interest is Kline's distinction between two perceived forms of actuality in Whitehead's thought, which he terms actual$_1$ and actual$_2$. According to Kline, an occasion is actual$_1$ when it is "active and self-significant but-not-efficacious," whereas an occasion is actual$_2$ if it is "efficacious and other-significant but-not-active."[14] Thus, Kline explains, "'actual$_1$' applies exclusively to concrescences, to subjects, to what is present; and 'actual$_2$' applies exclusively to completed past actual entities."[15] By carefully examining the different ways in which Whitehead uses key terms, Kline significantly mitigates the paradoxical nature of the classical interpretation's claim that past occasions are no longer actual; for Kline, past occasions are not actual$_1$, but they are actual$_2$. However, far from moving away from the classical interpretation's view of actuality, at the heart of Kline's interpretation is a "defense of a sharp ontological —as opposed to merely a functional—distinction between concrescence and concretum."[16] According to Kline, "The distinction between concrescence and concretum is a distinction . . . between different (types of) entities."[17] Although Kline is correct that Whitehead is often careless in his use of terms such as "actuality," his presupposition of a sharp ontological distinction between the past and the present blinds him to the possibility of an alternative explanation. The problem is that Kline and the other proponents of the classical interpretation argue from, rather than toward, the conclusion that there is a sharp ontological distinction between the individual as subject and the individual as superject, and this distinction eliminates all activity from the objective functioning of the superject. Because this distinction is central to the classical interpretation, this is a disturbing conclusion.

In that the classical interpretation limits all actuality to the concrescing subject, Schindler's interpretation of Whitehead's metaphysics is apparently not without precedent. In fact, the classic interpretation seems to encourage the view that only subjects are actual. And to the extent that the classic interpretation limits activity, creativity, and, most important, actuality, to subjectivity, to that extent it limits importance and value to the subject. Indeed, Kline himself says as much: "A concretum has significance—meaning and importance—not for itself but only for something other than itself: namely, the subsequent concrescences which causally objectified it."[18] All intrinsic value is limited to the concrescent subject. For, as John Goheen unabashedly puts it, "As a center of feeling the individual is the arbiter of all value, there is no other source of judgment with respect to satisfactory and dissatisfactory feeling."[19] Accordingly, given the classic interpretation, I contend that ontological subjectivism is in fact unavoidable.[20] Thus, to avoid these conclusions, we must seek out an alternative to the classic interpretation of Whitehead's metaphysics.

Ford's Temporal Interpretation

Lewis S. Ford is a prominent contemporary commentator on process thought and a self-described critic of the classical interpretation of Whitehead's metaphysics. In *Transforming Process Theism*, Ford boldly sets out to reorient the classical interpretation by reconceiving of actuality in terms of temporal modes. Ford contends that, because many process philosophers mistakenly assume that the univocity of actuality called for by Whitehead requires its restriction to one temporal mode, some have mistakenly argued that past actual occasions are no longer actual.[21] Ford notes, as we have done, that this creates the paradoxical situation whereby nascent occasions would arise out of an "*actual* world" of past occasions that are not themselves actual: "If concrescence is actual, and its outcome merely 'no longer actual,' what do we make of the longstanding tradition that identifies actuality with concrete determinateness? Whitehead is not willing to regard past determinateness as nonfactual; they serve as perfectly good reasons according to the ontological principle."[22]

In suggesting that an achieved actuality is no less actual than an actuality in attainment, Ford would seem to be in direct opposition to the classical interpretation. But the relationship between Ford's interpretation and the classical interpretation is not as straightforward as this might suggest. In one sense, Ford claims to extend actuality to include not only the past, but also the future. Thus, explicitly breaking with Whitehead's own view of the future as real but nonactual and of the past as the source of creativity, Ford argues that the future should be conceived not only as actual, but as the locus both of creativity and the ultimate source of subjective aim.[23] Accordingly, Ford affirms three modes of actuality coinciding with the three modes of time: "the past as determinately actual, the present as the activity of determination, and the future as activity, transferring the power of creativity to the present."[24] Hence, rather than defining actuality in terms of activity, like Leclerc and Christian, Ford defines actuality as what has primacy in a given temporal mode.[25] The question is, does Ford's temporal interpretation of actuality avoid the problem of subjectivism?

Given that Ford's temporal interpretation claims to extend actuality not only to the present, but also to the past and the future, he might seem to have avoided affirming a form of ontological subjectivism. For if actuality is not coextensive with subjectivity, then neither is value, and egoism is avoided, right? Unfortunately, the situation is a bit more complex. The heart of the problem of sub-

jectivism is not merely that actuality is coextensive with subjectivity
—this is what might be called its ontological basis. Although it
rests on this ontological claim, the problem of subjectivism is essentially axiological. That is, it concerns the axiological status of
the past vis-à-vis the present—or, in other words, the status of the
other vis-à-vis the self. Thus, for instance, although Schindler's
objection rests on the ontological claim that actuality extends only
to the subject, his primary objection concerns "how at any given
instant can . . . what is given to the subject as other than the subject, be affirmed as having value—not simply for me, but *in itself*?"[26]
That is, how can the objective world be seen to have more than just
instrumental value for subjects of experience? Interpreted in this
light, Ford's temporal interpretation ultimately leads to the same
undesirable axiological implications as the classical interpretation.

The problem with Ford's temporal interpretation is that, as the
following passage demonstrates, because it adheres to the classical
interpretation's strong ontological distinction between the subject
and the superject, it is precluded from truly affirming the actuality and value of the past: "All present becoming is subjective; all
past being (the outcome of becoming) is objective, here understood
in terms of ontological categories."[27] This sharp ontological distinction is also clearly seen in Ford's definition of past actual occasions. Like the classical interpretation, Ford claims that the past is
"devoid of creativity" and "lacks all active power."[28] Hence, according to Ford, "While the past is in many ways substantial, it is
impotent. No past actuality can influence any other past actuality,
and it can only influence present actualities insofar as present actualities actively appropriate the past."[29] In fact, Ford goes so far as
to claim that past actual occasions are essentially nothing more
than the material cause of the present:

> While each occasion is actual for itself, it is also potential for every
> supervening occasion. . . . This is the concrete particularity the
> past can provide, and it is the potentiality traditionally associated
> with proximate matter in Aristotelian thought. On this interpre-

tation, the concrete particularity is neither abstract form nor the activity of creativity.[30]

Thus the past serves as the data for the future unqualifiedly, and for present actualities from their limited standpoints. The past is potential for the future (and the present), but differently from the way they are potential with respect to creativity. The future and the present possess the activity, the past the material for actualization. The past is primarily potential for the future, and secondarily (as mediated by the future) for the present.[31]

When Whitehead introduces a theory whereby concrescing occasions are derived from past actualities, these past actualities severally contribute their particular achieved values to the new concrescence. In this sense they contribute matter for the form supplied by the subjective aim.[32]

Note that in the last quotation Ford argues that "past actualities severally contribute their particular achieved *values* to the new concrescence." But wouldn't this refute my claim that Ford only extends instrumental value to past actual occasions and therefore does not avoid axiological subjectivism? To answer this question, we must first know in what sense past occasions can be said to "contribute their value." Do they have value merely for the subject (instrumental value) or do they also have value in and for themselves (intrinsic value)? Here Ford's descriptions of past actualities as "material for actualization" and "proximate matter" are particularly germane. If past actual occasions are merely the passive, impotent, and inactive material out of which nascent occasions create themselves, and if past actual occasions "can only influence present actualities insofar as present actualities actively appropriate the past,"[33] then they could only "contribute themselves" as instrumentally valuable. Hence, in conceiving of past occasions as actual but wholly impotent and passive, Ford ultimately drains them of all intrinsic value.

Upon closer examination, then, although Ford's temporal interpretation appears to refute the ontological basis of the problem

of subjectivism by extending actuality beyond the subject to include both the objective world and future creativity, because this
reinterpretation retains the sharp ontological distinction that renders the objective world wholly passive, it does not alter the axiological status of achieved actual occasions and consequently fails to
avoid the axiological implications of the problem of subjectivism.
The subject is still the sole determinant and therefore the sole locus
of intrinsic value. Hence, although Ford's reformulation of Whitehead's ontology may have much to offer, in the final analysis, its
axiological implications are not distinguishable from those of the
classical interpretation.[34]

This conclusion brings to light a crucial discovery: if Whitehead is truly to affirm a universe of value, if intrinsic value is not
to be limited merely to concrescing subjects, we must affirm not
only that the objective world is actual, but also that it is not wholly
impotent and passive. Only in this way can the intrinsic value of
the objective world be meaningfully affirmed. What is needed,
then, is an interpretation of Whitehead's metaphysics that makes
past actual occasions both actual and in some sense active. Only in
this way can we avoid an axiological subjectivism and solipsism.

The Ecstatic Interpretation

The pervasiveness of what I call the classical interpretation is difficult to calculate. However, I suspect that it unconsciously infects
much of Whitehead scholarship, particularly analyses that seek to
apply Whitehead's work to specific topics, such as physics, psychology, education, political science, ethics, and so on. If so, this is a very
disturbing trend. Luckily, however, a growing number of scholars,
among them Jorge Luis Nobo, Nancy Frankenberry, Elizabeth
Kraus, and Judith A. Jones, provide the basis for a radically new
understanding of Whitehead's metaphysics that challenges the classical interpretation's preeminence. Borrowing a phrase from Jones,
I refer to their collective interpretations of Whitehead's system as

the ecstatic interpretation, or an interpretation that is willing to challenge the sharp ontological distinction between past and present. The word *ecstasy*, derived from the Greek *ex* ("out") and *histanai* ("to stand"), literally means to stand outside oneself. This term, familiar in existentialism and phenomenology, appropriately describes those interpretations of Whitehead that emphasize the unity of the subject-superject and therefore insist that the past in some sense plays an active role in causing subsequent occasions. Let us examine these authors' interpretations, focusing particularly on the status of the superject. We may then evaluate their success in responding to the problem of subjectivism.

Like Ford, defenders of the ecstatic interpretation of Whitehead's metaphysics argue that the classical interpretation is mistaken in restricting actuality to the concrescent subject.[35] However, in addition to affirming the actuality of both subjects and superjects, the ecstatic interpretation repudiates the sharp ontological distinction between the subject and superject that is at the heart of the classical interpretation. Instead, it emphasizes those passages, like the following from *Process and Reality*, in which Whitehead insists on the unity of the actual occasion: "The theory of 'prehensions' embodies a protest against the 'bifurcation' of nature. It embodies even more than that: its protest is against the bifurcation of actualities" (PR, 290). Significantly, the theory of prehension manifests this "protest" by denying the existence of merely public or merely private facts. It contends that the distinction between an occasion's public life (*qua* superject) and its private life (*qua* subject) is only "a distinction of reason, and is not a distinction between mutually exclusive concrete facts. . . . Prehensions have public careers, but they are born privately" (PR, 290). Thus, the theory of prehensions reverses the bifurcation not only of nature, but of actualities as well. "An actual entity is at once the subject experiencing and the superject of its experiences. It is subject-superject, and neither half of this description can for a moment be lost sight of" (PR, 29).[36] Hence, the ecstatic interpretation insists that we take seriously Whitehead's claim that "to be actual must mean that all things are alike objects . . . and that all actual things are subjects" (PR, 56). Insofar as something is actual, it "has two sides, namely, its individual self and its signification in the universe [and] either of these aspects is a factor in the other" (PR, 120). Subjectivity is an aspect of actuality, but in no way exhausts it.

What truly defines the ecstatic interpretation, however, is its affirmation that the objective world is not only actual, but also active. Nancy Frankenberry and Elizabeth Kraus were two of the first process philosophers to suggest such a view. They argue that, far from being impotent, the past is active and has the power to influence the present *as itself.*[37] As Frankenberry puts it, "The energy of this process has been transformed into the energy of a fully formed object that will play its causal role in the creating of later occasions of experience. Satisfaction spells the death of the process of unification but not the end of the creative energy involved."[38] Once it has achieved its satisfaction by rendering determinate its relations to the elements in its actual world, an actual occasion's subjectivity (process of self-determination) perishes, but the emotional energy achieved in that process does not. Far from being dead, impotent, or passive, for Frankenberry and Kraus superjects are throbbing pulses of energy that are active in forming occasions beyond themselves.[39] "Thus, perishing [that is, satisfaction] is not so much a tragedy an entity falls passive victim to, but its self-initiated shift to a new mode of activity. It is a beginning, not an end; an existential culmination, not an existential frustration. It marks the subject's entrance into objective immortality as a functioning agent."[40] Of course, this is not to say that the activity of the superject is the same as that of the subject. As Frankenberry convincingly argues in the following passage, subjects are active in the process of self-creation, whereas objects are active in other-creation:

> To be sure, subjects are active in self-creation, but objects are active in other-creation. The activity of subjects is teleological self-

determination, while that of objects is efficient causation. Both activities are conjointly constitutive of the subjects. Without the past creative energies, no new present self-creativity could come about; without the private creativity, no new public energy could come about. Each is for the sake of the other and neither has any meaning apart from their dialectical unity.[41]

Accordingly, *qua* efficient, not only is the past actual, it must also be active.

Jorge Nobo's colossal *Whitehead's Metaphysics of Extension and Solidarity* illuminates the sense in which objects are efficient causes by focusing on Whitehead's concept of "transition." Nobo's primary difficulty with the classical interpretation—what he calls the "received interpretation"—is that, in placing all activity solely in the concrescent subject, it effectively collapses the process of transition into the process of concrescence and, in so doing, it unknowingly destroys Whitehead's theory of genuine efficient causation. According to Nobo, genuine efficient causation is

> causation which *really produces* its effect; causation which *really determines* its effect in part, though not in whole; and causation which—*in addition, and not merely*—conditions the subsequent self-determining phases of the effect it has produced. In place of Whitehead's theory of efficient causation, but still under the same, if now undeserved, title, most received interpretations give us what in the end is no more than a theory of *material causation*, a theory where the already-attained actualities are the material, but in no sense the efficient, causes of the actualities in attainment.[42]

Though it is not possible to examine in depth Nobo's very nuanced interpretation of the phases of concrescence, the following quotation helps clarify how Nobo conceives of the crucial relationship between transition and concrescence:

> The newborn subject itself, as well as each of its initial feelings, is an *effect produced by the attained actualities in its actual world*. In

other words, in the conformal phase of its existence, an occasion is entirely the product of the efficient past, and is not in any way the cause of itself. Accordingly, each subject, through no choice of its own, is *thrown* into existence as conformally feeling its given actual world. The actual world both produces and conditions it.[43]

Accordingly, in sharp contrast to the classical interpretation, which limits all activity to the nascent subject, in the "conformal" or "datum" phase of an occasion's existence, it is past, already achieved occasions that are active in producing the nascent occasion. At the heart of Nobo's interpretation, then, is the view that past actual occasions are not merely the dead matter out of which nascent occasions create themselves, like logs used to build a cabin. Past occasions actively impose themselves on every future occasion; they demand to be reckoned with.[44]

There is a crucial piece of the ecstatic interpretation that has not yet been unearthed. While Kraus and Frankenberry persuasively argue for the active power of the past, and while Nobo thoroughly develops an interpretation of transition and concrescence that does not reduce the one to the other, to respond successfully to the problems of ontological and axiological subjectivism, we must develop a positive account of the nature of the individuals that are achieved in these processes.

In her ground-breaking work *Intensity: An Essay in Whiteheadian Cosmology*, Judith A. Jones expands on the insights of Frankenberry, Kraus, and Nobo by developing an account of Whitehead's metaphysics based on her notion of "ecstatic individuality" or "ecstatic existence."[45] By focusing on the constitution of actuality in terms of intensities of contrast, Jones finds that, contrary to the classical interpretation, "*qua* actual, there is no distinction between the agentive decisions and contrasts effected in those decisions; the decision *is* the contrast."[46] If there is no difference between the decisions of subjects and the contrasts achieved by those decisions, Jones concludes, "an entity exists with the ontological status of *its* subjectivity to *some* degree in every subject in which it comes to have influence (and, to an extent, in every subject from which it originally derived)."[47] Hence, whereas most commentators focus on the differences between the subject and the superject, Jones begins by examining the aim of process, rather than its morphology. Focusing on Whitehead's eighth Categoreal Obligation, the category of subjective intensity, Jones notes that "Whitehead ties the ultimate teleological concerns of process—subjective aim—to the concept of intensity."[48] Accordingly, insofar as the aim of process is at intensity, what is achieved in satisfaction is an intensity of contrast, not a static product. But if we look "at the 'constitution' of an actuality in terms of its status as an intensity of contrast, we would note that, *qua* actual, there is no distinction between the agentive decision and the contrasts effected in those decisions; the decision *is* the contrast."[49] Taken in this sense, it becomes impossible to describe an actual occasion's objective functioning in another as passive, static, or dead. Thus, for Jones, "The only thing in Whitehead's scheme that is bereft of inherent activity is an eternal object."[50] As an intensity of contrast, a satisfied occasion is irrevocably active.

However, Jones reminds us that this aesthetic achievement is not completely independent or private. Rather, it is by definition "'self-retentive,' 'infectious,' requiring for its very essence the presence, internal to it, of former aesthetic achievement."[51] Therefore, even as objectified, occasions are "yet themselves, in the ontologically significant sense of individuality of existence."[52] In this way, the notion of ecstatic existence greatly problematizes the sharp ontological distinctions imputed to them by the classical interpretations:

> I contend that the effort to attach ontological status to anything in the Whiteheadian system—objective datum, satisfaction, subjective form, feeling, character, actuality, and so on—as if anything else were being discussed except the achievement of aesthetic intensity, will inevitably produce a picture of Whiteheadian atomism as cryptosubstantialist, when in fact such an effort is itself the

cryptosubstantialism infecting the subject matter with its presuppositions about the nature of individuality.[53]

Hence, central to Jones's project is the view that the internal relatedness of one individual in another entails the real repetition of
the past, *as itself*, in the present nascent occasion. Like Kraus,
Frankenberry, and Nobo, Jones achieves this by denying the classical interpretation's ontologizing of the subject and the superject
because, in so doing, she finds that it essentially repeats the metaphysical errors that Whitehead's system was explicitly developed
to avoid. According to Jones,

> Some sense may be made of Whitehead's atomism, which does
> not require the sharp ontological distinction that seems to lurk
> behind the verbal ambiguities. Such a distinction seems to me to
> participate in a major error identified by Whitehead in philoso-
> phies of substance: it asserts a kind of independence—the inde-
> pendence of agency—which isolates each individual as such in its
> own ontological "space," if you will. We recall it was precisely this
> isolation, *not* the fact of persistence, of substance that Whitehead
> deplored.[54]

For Jones, then, if Whitehead's metaphysics is to be the exposition
of how all actual occasions are internally related, then any ontological form of independence must be out of bounds. To truly
affirm the internal relatedness of one individual in another, there
can be no independence, even of agency. That is, the subject and
the superject are "existentially of a piece."[55] The implication of this
stance cannot be overstated. For if the subject and the superject are
one, then "to assert the 'objective' functioning of the superject of
satisfaction in the becoming of other entities need not require that
subjectivity in all senses wholly perish, nor does it necessitate a
view of an entity as a 'closed-up' individuality."[56] Insofar as subjectivity does not wholly perish, the superject is *not* a static product, a
dead datum, or a passive object. In this way, Jones's notion of ec-

static individuality eliminates the sharp ontological bifurcation of the subject from the superject introduced by the classical interpretation. Inasmuch as Whitehead's metaphysics is an attempt to account for the organic relations between occasions, Jones's notion of ecstatic individuality dramatically captures the elusive balance between the one and the many at which Whitehead aimed.

By reorienting the locus of value to include the actual occasion as a whole, as subject-superject, the ecstatic interpretation put forth by Kraus, Frankenberry, Nobo, and Jones avoids the twin problems of ontological and axiological subjectivism. For since such an interpretation requires that we affirm the unity, actuality, and activity of actual occasions as a subject-superject, then at any given moment what is given to the subject as other has value not simply for the subject, but in itself, intrinsically. As I will argue next, such an approach to axiology is as unique as it is promising.

A Triadic Theory of Value

Over the last thirty years, many of the battles waged among environmental philosophers have been over the definition of "intrinsic value."[57] To enter this briar patch of competing theories, I ask this question: What does it mean to say that something has value in itself or intrinsically? The problem is that, as John O'Neill argues in "The Varieties of Intrinsic Value," the term "intrinsic value" is not used univocally.[58] First let us examine which, if any, of the three forms of intrinsic value distinguished by O'Neill could be affirmed by a Whiteheadian moral philosophy.

The first, intrinsic value$_1$, is simply a synonym for noninstrumental value whereby something has instrumental value insofar as it is a means to some other end. Thus, with intrinsic value$_1$, "an object has intrinsic value if it is an end in itself."[59] Intrinsic value$_2$, on the other hand, is modeled after G. E. Moore's notion of intrinsic value wherein the value of an object is solely by virtue of its "intrinsic properties." According to intrinsic value$_2$, the intrinsic properties of an object are defined as those properties of an object that are *not* derived from its relations. Thus, intrinsic value$_2$ depends solely upon an entity's nonrelational properties or what it is independent of anything else. Finally, according to O'Neill, intrinsic value$_3$ is a synonym for "objective value" or the value an object possesses independently of the valuations of valuers.[60] The question is, which of these forms of intrinsic value, if any, does Whitehead affirm?

Proceeding in reverse order, let us ask whether Whitehead's notion of intrinsic value corresponds to intrinsic value$_3$ or objective value, which was most famously and systematically defended by Holmes Rolston. In one sense, Whitehead seems to be saying that an actual occasion's value is objective in the sense that it does not depend upon the valuations of other valuers. In this way, Whitehead would heartily join Rolston in rejecting the common view that value is anthropogenic or created by human beings.

> An interlocking kinship suggests that values are not merely in the mind but at hand in the world. We start out valuing nature like land appraisers figuring out what it is worth to us, only to discover that we are part and parcel of this nature we appraise. The earthen landscape has upraised this landscape appraiser. We do not simply bestow value on nature; nature also conveys value to us.[61]

For both Rolston and Whitehead, value does not mysteriously appear on the scene with the arrival of human beings; value is not conferred by a human valuer or anything else. Taken in this sense, it seems correct to say with Rolston that the intrinsic value$_3$ of an entity is the value it has independent of its being valued by another. However, this point of agreement obscures a more fundamental point of tension. The problem is that Rolston's position is founded on a distinction that Whitehead goes to great lengths to refute, namely, the distinction between the subject and object. The starting point for both Whitehead and the pragmatists was to repudiate any such dualism. "To be actual must mean that all actual

things are alike objects, enjoying objective immortality in fashion-
ing creative actions; and that all actual things are subjects, each
prehending the universe from which it arises" (PR, 56). Thus,
Whitehead's project begins from the premise that Rolston rejects,
that "there is no value without an experiencing valuer."[62] For
Whitehead, because there is nothing but the experience of subjects, to exist is to be a valuer and to be a valuer is to have value.
Furthermore, inasmuch as an entity *is* its relations to everything in
its world, it is incoherent to refer to the value something has independent of other valuers. The value that is achieved in the actualization of an occasion is what it is because of its relations to the
other values in its world. The problem with intrinsic value$_3$, then, is
that it appears to presuppose a notion of individuality that Whitehead rejects.[63]

This analysis also gives us our answer regarding intrinsic value$_2$,
according to which something has value solely in virtue of those
properties that are nonrelational. But, as the previous analysis
should make evident, Moore's very notion of a purely nonrelational
property is unintelligible within a processive cosmos as described by
Whitehead. According to the organic model being defended, since
there are no independent, substantial individuals, there can be no
properties that could inhere in these substances, whether relational
or nonrelational. This also entails the repudiation of Moore's so-
called naturalistic fallacy. For, as we have seen, at the heart of the
philosophy of organism is the rejection of the view that there is
such a thing as a mere fact or a vacuous actuality. Thus, as I will
contend in part 2, the problem is not arguing from facts to values,
but properly acknowledging and respecting the values that are
present.[64]

We are now left with intrinsic value$_1$. But is Whitehead's conception of intrinsic value synonymous with noninstrumental value,
as O'Neill's distinction requires? Again, it seems safe to agree that
this is the form of intrinsic value to which Whitehead is referring.
Actual occasions have value as ends, not simply as means, because

they are unique, self-determining, acts of togetherness. However, we must be cautious before accepting intrinsic value$_1$. To argue that intrinsic value$_1$ is not merely a means but is an end in itself potentially brings with it the atomic individualism of classical liberalism. To repeat, although the ethics of creativity defends the notion of an individual as an end in itself, the notion of individuality requires essential reference to others. In the end, although Whitehead's conception of intrinsic value is similar to intrinsic value$_3$ and to intrinsic value$_1$, it is strictly speaking without a precedent in contemporary moral and environmental philosophy. The reason is that most conceptions of intrinsic value rest on an inadequate conception of individuality. Hence, to understand the unique conception of intrinsic value being advanced, we must understand it through the lens of Whitehead's organic conception of individuality.

In a processive cosmos, individuality does not imply independence. An actual occasion begins from and is partially constituted by the achieved values of the past and completes itself by rendering its relationship to each of these past values determinate either by eliminating them (negative prehension) or by incorporating them by repeating their felt value intensity (positive prehension). Hence, an individual is what it is *because* it is internally and essentially related to other achieved values. "Thus an event is a matter of fact which by reason of its limitation is a value for itself; but by reason of its very nature it also requires the whole universe in order to be itself" (SMW, 194). This process constitutes the ultimate fact of existence: the many become one and are increased by one. Accordingly, the answer to the question "What does it mean to say that something has intrinsic value?" is ultimately to be found in the perplexing category of creativity. But what does this oft cited, but rarely understood, category really mean? Do many discrete individuals come together to form a single monistic unity in which all individuality is lost, or is there truly a multiplicity of atomic individuals? In the following passage, Whitehead qualifies the still enigmatic category of creativity:

The fundamental *basis* of this description is that our experience is a value experience, expressing a vague sense of maintenance or discard; and that this value experience differentiates itself in the sense of many existences with value experience; and that this sense of the multiplicity of value experience again differentiates it into the totality of value experience, and the many other value experiences, and the egoistic value experience. There is the feeling of the ego, the others, the totality. (MT, 110, author's emphasis)

Initially, this passage simply reiterates our earlier conclusion that self-worth is at the base of experience. But here we see that this fundamental value experience differentiates itself into the recognition of the value of the diverse individuals of the world for each other. Accordingly, and this is fundamental, the value experience at the base of existence is not solipsistic; self-value essentially involves the real presence (objective functioning) of other values as themselves. This thesis is at the heart of Jones's version of the ecstatic interpretation:

The functioning of an existent in another existent must be ascribed to the internal account of the first existent, as much as it is to be ascribed to the present self-constitution of an entity in concrescence. The fully determinate feeling characterizing the "satisfaction" of any occasion includes elements whose sources lie in *other* entities that to some significant extent retain their character as determinate unities of feeling *in themselves* even as they are objectified in a present concrescence. The objective functioning of one thing in another, in other words, never completely loses the subjective, agentive quality of feeling that first brought it into being.[65]

Put differently, the individual's egoistic upholding of value intensity for itself cannot be taken apart from its sharing its value intensity with the universe. Hence, when an actual entity functions objectively it still has intrinsic value. Whitehead writes in *Modes of Thought*, "There must be value beyond ourselves. Otherwise every thing experienced would be merely barren detail in our own solipsist mode of existence" (MT, 102). As I will argue below, recognition of this fact is the essence of morality.

However, the analysis does not stop here. This recognition of a multiplicity of values in the world is further differentiated into the sense of the value of the whole objective world, which is both a community derivative from the interrelations of its component individuals and necessary for the existence of each of these individuals (RM, 59). Interestingly, as we see in the following passage from *Religion in the Making*, Whitehead characterizes this sense of the value of the whole as a religious intuition: "The moment of religious consciousness starts from self-valuation, but it broadens into the concept of the world as a realm of adjusted values, mutually intensifying or mutually destructive. The intuition into the actual world gives a particular definite content to the bare notion of a principle determining the grading of values" (RM, 59–60). The religious intuition, then, is this recognition of the value of the whole, which includes, but does not devour, the value of others and of the individual.

At its core, therefore, value is neither monistic nor solipsistic. Rather, in keeping with the organic conception of individuality being advanced, self-value is always intertwined with the value of others and with the value of the whole. The true import of this crucial conclusion begins to become clear in this passage, part of which opens this chapter:

> The basis of democracy is the common fact of value experience, as constituting the essential nature of each pulsation of actuality. Everything has some value for itself, for others, and for the whole. This characterizes the meaning of actuality. By reason of this character, constituting reality, the conception of morals arises. We have no right to deface the value experience which is the very essence of the universe. Existence, in its own nature, is the upholding of value intensity. Also no unit can separate itself from the others,

and from the whole. And yet each unit exists in its own right. It upholds the value intensity for itself, and this involves sharing value intensity with the universe. (MT, 111)[66]

In one form or another, many elements of a Whiteheadian moral philosophy can be found in this passage. For the immediate context, what is important is, first, that the very meaning of actuality is characterized by this triad of self, other, whole. Each actual entity has self-value, is self-important, but this realization does not entail (as it all too often does in ethical theory) that the individual is the sole locus of value that must be protected at all costs. What debates over moral considerability often miss is that each individual, *qua* value experience, has value not only for itself, but also for others and for the whole. In politico-ethical terms, this is to say that every individual is a locus of value, but each individual also has value for its community and even for the whole cosmos. Classical liberal atomic individualism is not, on this interpretation, an option, nor is simplistic communitarianism. Every entity "exists in its own right" and "upholds value intensity for itself," but this upholding of value intensity for oneself *necessarily* involves "sharing value intensity with the universe" (MT, 111). Every entity is self-important *and* important to the universe. In more familiar terms, everything that in any sense exists has intrinsic value$_4$ (heretofore, simply intrinsic value), which includes having instrumental value, and religious value. This axiological triad of self, other, and whole captures the essence of Whitehead's unique sense of intrinsic value. To have intrinsic value is (1) to have incorporated the values of others (concrescence), (2) to subsequently become a (instrumental) value for others (principle of relativity), and (3) thereby to contribute to the value experience of the whole, that is, for God. According to Whitehead, each of these divisions is "on a level. No one in any sense precedes the other" (MT, 117).[67]

This triadic structure not only characterizes the meaning of actuality, but also is the stimulus for the conception of morals (MT,

111). For if each entity were understood only in terms of egoistic self-value, the conception of morals would not arise. For in such a world, each entity would simply strive for its own selfish ends, like Adam Smith's invisible hand demands. This would be egoism and even solipsism on an ontological level. If solipsism were true, the conception of morality would not even arise. However, because every entity has some value not only for itself but also for others and the whole universe, the conception of morality becomes possible. Again, if each entity's own value essentially involves the values of others, solipsism and egoism become impossible, at least ontologically speaking. With this conclusion, we acknowledge that Whitehead does indeed affirm a true universe of value.

In the end, the important question is not whether others have intrinsic value, but whether the intrinsic value of others and of the whole is recognized, appreciated, and affirmed. Actuality is intrinsically valuable, and it is the obligation of each individual to recognize that value. Accordingly, to be adequate, a moral philosophy must be able to give an account of responsibility that acknowledges that every individual—no matter how fleeting or seemingly insignificant—has value not only in and for itself, but also for its community and for the whole.

Though he does not explicitly distinguish them, Whitehead seems to understand responsibility in both an ontological sense and in a moral sense. According to Whitehead, given their complex organization, human beings are capable of significant novelty of experience and therefore are morally responsible for their actions.[68] In Ferré's words, "Persons, on this understanding, are living beings complex enough to be conscious and free enough to be responsible."[69] However, because of their insufficient level of complexity, the vast majority of individuals—from microscopic events to complex organisms such as plants—lack the potential for significant novelty of experience and therefore cannot be said to be morally responsible for their decisions. However, Whitehead also uses the notion of responsibility in a more basic, ontological sense to refer to a subject's responsibility for its process of self-determination. According to Whitehead, "The subject is responsible for being what it is in virtue of its feelings. It is also derivatively responsible for the consequences of its existence because they flow from its feelings" (PR, 222). That is, every subject is responsible for being what it is by virtue of the "decisions" it makes in its process of self-determination. This is the principle of process: "that the actual entity, in a state of process during which it is not fully definite, determines its own ultimate definiteness" (PR, 255). In this sense, every entity is ontologically responsible for what it becomes, for how it conditions the creativity beyond itself.

3

An Organic Model
of Individuality

> Of course, Plato was right and Aristotle was wrong. There
> is no clear division among genera; there is no clear division
> among species; there are no clear divisions anywhere. That
> is to say, there are no clear divisions when you push your
> observations beyond the presuppositions on which they
> rest. It so happens, however, that we always think within
> limitations.
>
> Alfred North Whitehead, *Modes of Thought*

GIVEN WHITEHEAD'S FOCUS ON microscopic process, many
commentators on Whitehead's philosophy contend that a process
metaphysics is unable to capture adequately the unity and self-
identity of macroscopic individuals and therefore cannot support a
robust conception of moral responsibility. For if the world is composed exclusively of microscopic events called actual occasions that
neither endure nor have histories,[1] and if "there are no clear divisions among species," then how is meaningful, personal moral responsibility possible for enduring, macroscopic individuals such as
ourselves? First, these critics correctly affirm the value of acknowledging the very real differences among the various "things" that

we (human beings) experience. The differences between a stone and a wildflower, or between the desk upon which I write and myself, are very real and even morally significant. However, what critics do reject is that these differences are properly understood in terms of fundamentally different ontological kinds or species. One goal of this chapter is to demonstrate that difference may be real without the multiplication either of ontological kinds or (what is more important) of the statuses that attach to them.[2]

The challenge confronting an organic model of individuality is to provide a conception of macroscopic individuality that, on the one hand, avoids committing the fallacy of misplaced concreteness or violating the ontological principle and, on the other hand, is robust enough to do justice to the undeniable unity that we experience of ourselves and of other macroscopic individuals. In other words, how can Whitehead meaningfully, not just metaphorically, refer to macroscopic wholes as "individuals" when the actual occasions of which they are made do not endure? How can we account for a world that seems to be full of enduring, substantial individuals, given the flux at the base of reality? This chapter will develop a detailed account of macroscopic individuality that is adequate both to our experience of the world and to the organic metaphysics presented in chapters 1–2. Accordingly, chapter 3 concerns not only the adequacy of Whitehead's metaphysics, but also the possibility of constructing an ethical theory based upon it. For if the organic model of individuality being defended cannot adequately account for the unity of macroscopic individuals, it is impossible to conceive of moral responsibility at this level in any meaningful way.

Process and Order

To ask how Whitehead does or does not affirm different types of macroscopic individuality, we may turn to one of the most long-standing and ostensibly the clearest divisions of reality: that between a living body and a nonliving body. In a way, given Whitehead's affirmation of the reformed subjectivist principle that there is nothing apart from the experience of subjects, even this traditional division is no longer safe if it is taken as ontologically basic. If the last century's revolutionary discoveries in quantum physics, chemistry, biology, physiology, and ecology have taught us anything, we must acknowledge that there are no absolute divisions in nature. Ferré provides several compelling examples from contemporary science that illustrate this point: "Postmodern science is finding the 'line' between complex forms of matter and simple forms of living things hard to identify. This . . . is exactly as it should be. There is no fixed line. Liquid crystals and polymers act in fascinating, mysterious, and beautiful ways; viruses act a lot like crystals. Viruses cannot reproduce—cannot be what they are—without a living host. Are they 'dead' matter? Are liquid crystals 'alive'? The philosophy of organism rejects these dichotomies."[3]

According to the organic view of individuality being defended, then, there is a single genus of actual occasions that includes everything from the "lowliest actual occasion" to God (PR, 110). The ontological fabric of the universe contains no true gaps. Thus, for example, the difference between a wildflower and a boulder is ultimately found not in an appeal to different ontological kinds but in the difference in the degree of "coordination" achieved in the satisfactions of the actual occasions of which each is composed: "It seems that, in bodies that are obviously living, a coördination has been achieved that raises into prominence some functionings inherent in the ultimate occasions. For lifeless matter these functionings thwart each other, and average out so as to produce a negligible total effect. In the case of living bodies the coördination intervenes, and the average effect of these intimate functionings has to be taken into account" (AI, 207). In that, according to such a view, macroscopic individuality is a function of "order," to truly understand the nature of macroscopic individuals we must first understand the complex social relations between the actual occasions of which they are composed.

Our earlier analysis of concrescence included the revelation that actual occasions involve each other through their mutual immanence or prehensions of each other. However, what was omitted from this account was that these prehensions form "real individual facts of . . . togetherness of actual entities, which are real, individual, and particular, *in the same sense* in which actual entities and the prehensions are real, individual, and particular. Any such particular fact of togetherness among actual entities is called a 'nexus'" (PR, 20, emphasis added). Thus, the macroscopic objects that we experience—such as desks, birds, trees, rocks—are "nexūs" (Whitehead's plural form of nexus) of actual occasions that are real, individual, and particular "in the same sense" in which their constituent occasions are real, individual, and particular. To be more precise, entities such as birds and trees are particular types of nexūs that Whitehead refers to as "societies." While all societies are nexūs, not all nexūs are societies. For Whitehead, societies and nexūs, not actual occasions, are the "things" that endure and have adventures.

> The real actual things that endure are all societies. They are not actual occasions. It is the mistake that has thwarted European metaphysics from the time of the Greeks, namely, to confuse societies with the completely real things which are the actual occasions. . . . Thus a society, as a complete existence and as retaining the same metaphysical status, enjoys a history expressing its changing reactions to changing circumstances. But an actual occasion has no such history. It never changes. It only becomes and perishes. Its perishing is its assumption of a new metaphysical function in the creative advance of the universe. (AI, 204)

Whitehead defines a society as a nexus that enjoys "social order." By this, he means that a society is a nexus with (1) a common form or defining characteristic shared by each member of that nexus, wherein (2) this defining characteristic arises in each member of the nexus because of the conditions imposed upon it by its prehensions of other members of the nexus, and (3) these prehensions impose that condition of reproduction by reason of their inclusion of positive feelings involving that defining characteristic (AI, 203). Accordingly, it is crucial to note that societies are not mere collections or aggregates of entities to which the same class-name applies: "To constitute a society, the class-name has got to apply to each member, by reason of genetic derivation from other members of that same society. The members of the society are alike because, by reason of their common character, they impose on other members of the society the conditions which lead to that likeness" (PR, 89). Members of a society of occasions aren't simply grouped together because they happen to share similar characteristics. Rather, as the ecstatic interpretation suggests, the common characteristic possessed by a society's present nexus of actual occasions is genetically imposed by past members of the society.[4] In this sense, a society creates the conditions of its own continuation, or as Whitehead puts it, "it is its own reason" (AI, 203).

However, to be properly understood, this claim must be qualified. The notion of a society must not be taken from its larger context. Like its constituent actual occasions, a society must always be understood as nested within a larger environment of actual occasions (PR, 90). Hence, taken together, a society and its environment form a larger nexus and, perhaps, a larger society: the electron is within the molecule; the molecule is within the cell; the cell is within the body; the body is within its ecosystem, and so on, until we arrive at the universe as a whole. The whole order of nature, therefore, consists of nests of social environments.[5] A complex society that includes subordinate societies and/or nexūs is referred to as a "structured society."[6] A notable feature of structured societies is that they provide a favorable environment for the' subordinate societies that they harbor. Of course, every structured society is itself set within a wider environment that permits its (the structured society's) continuance.[7] Ultimately, there is no independence of existence.

With this analysis, we are in a position to explain more fully how Whitehead characterizes the difference between a living and a nonliving individual. First, for Whitehead, a natural body is not an independent, static, enduring substance. Rather, a natural body is a complex, structured society nested within many environments. That is, natural bodies are societies that likely include many subordinate societies and/or nexus. Second, according to the organic conception of individuality, "there is no absolute gap between 'living' and 'non-living' societies" (PR, 102). Life is not a binary quality that is either switched on or off. For Whitehead, a society is referred to as "living" if it includes actual occasions that are themselves living. Thus, a society is living to a greater or lesser degree depending on the prevalence of living occasions in it. Furthermore, just as societies can be more or less living depending on the prevalence of living occasions within them, actual occasions themselves can be living to a greater or lesser degree "according to the relative importance of the novel factors in its final satisfaction" (PR, 102). Whitehead explains, "A single occasion is alive when the subjective aim that determines its process of concrescence has introduced a novelty of definiteness not to be found in the inherited data of its primary phase" (PR, 104). That is, an occasion is alive to a greater or lesser degree depending upon the novelty afforded to it by its subjective aim.[8] Once again, however, there is no absolute gap between the living and the nonliving. There is always a degree of novel adaptation, no matter how slight; everything is alive to some degree. This conclusion brings us once again to the repudiation of vacuous existence and the affirmation of value as inherent in the act of existence. There are no mere facts; there is no lifeless matter. Every occasion, and by extension every society, seeks an end for its own sake and is therefore intrinsically valuable.

Given this blurring of the division between a living and a nonliving society, one may fairly ask how Whitehead accounts for the differences between different types of societies? For instance, how would an organic conception of individuality account for the difference between a plant and an animal?

For Whitehead, both plants and animals are complex, living, structured societies. The difference between them is ultimately explained by a greater degree of coordination in a particular subordinate society within the animal such that this subordinate society is "personal." A personal society is one in which "each stage of realization . . . consists of a set of contiguous occasions in serial order" (AI, 205). That is, a society is personal if its nexūs are "purely temporal and continuous" (205). Accordingly, what differentiates an animal from a plant is that the complex organization of the animal body is able to support the dominance of a personal society. A plant, on the other hand, is unable to support such a "regnant" society and is therefore more like a "democracy."[9]

> When we survey the living world, animal and vegetable, there are bodies of all types. Each living body is a society, which is not personal. But most of the animals, including all the vertebrates, seem to have their social system dominated by a subordinate society which is "personal." . . . But the lower forms of animal life, and all vegetation, seem to lack the dominance of any included personal society. A tree is a democracy. Thus living bodies are not to be identified with living bodies under personal dominance. (AI, 205–6)

In this way, Whitehead is able to account for the very real differences between different types of occasions without committing the fallacy of misplaced concreteness or violating the ontological principle. Though there is a real difference between a tomato plant and a cougar, for instance, this difference is ultimately traced to the differences in the complexity of their organization and the greater intensity of satisfaction that this organization brings.

The affirmation of a single continuum of actuality does not amount to the elimination of difference. Though there is only one genus of actuality, Whitehead is a pluralist, not a monist. As John Dewey reminds us, the repudiation of any ontological gaps in the fabric of reality "does not mean that physical and human individuality are identical, nor that the things that appear to us to be nonliving have the distinguishing characteristics of organisms. The difference between the inanimate and the animate is not so easily wiped out. But it does show that there is no fixed gap between them."[10] Difference is very real, but it is ultimately a matter of degree rather than kind. Thus, given an organic conception of individuality, the language of "kind" is to be treated like the language of "substance": both are useful abstractions in everyday life, but they do not fully explain the structure of reality.

This analysis should make it evident that there also can be no absolute gap between human beings and the rest of nature. As mentioned above, animals (both human and nonhuman) are different from plants because they can support a personal society that permits a high degree of novel functioning.[11] However, although "the distinction between men and animals is in one sense only a difference in degree . . . , the extent of the degree makes all the difference. The Rubicon has been crossed" (MT, 27). Critics of process thought often overlook passages such as this one and claim instead that Whitehead's system fails to appreciate the truly new capacities of human beings. However, Whitehead makes it quite clear that although there are no fundamentally (ontologically) different "kinds" of beings in the world, there are different kinds of organization with accompanying differences of functioning. In this way, arguing for the emergence of novel functioning is completely compatible with the rejection of ontologically distinct "kinds" or "types." The difference between human and nonhuman animals, then, is not ultimately found in some rational capacity in the former that is wholly absent in the latter. Every animal is capable of significant novelty of experience. Yet, in particular species such as humans, the intensity of coordination is so great that conceptual entertainment of possibilities becomes feasible. "The central activity of enjoyment and expression has assumed a reversal in the importance of its diverse functionings. The conceptual entertainment of unrealized possibility becomes a major factor in human mentality. In this way outrageous novelty is introduced, sometimes beatified, sometimes damned, and sometimes literally patented or protected by copyright" (MT, 26).

With the emergence of the conceptual entertainment of unrealized possibility, the concepts of importance and morality become relevant.

> The animal grade [of actuality] includes at least one central actuality, supported by the intricacy of bodily functioning. Purposes transcending (however faintly) the mere aim at survival are exhibited. From animal life the concept of importance, in some of its many differentiations, has a real relevance. The human grade of animal immensely extends this concept, and thereby introduces novelty of functioning as essential for varieties of importance. Thus morals and religion arise as aspects of this human impetus towards the best in each occasion. (MT, 27–28)

Though the difference between human and nonhuman animals may ultimately be only a matter of degree, this degree makes all the difference. The Rubicon has indeed been crossed.

This important conclusion is further clarified by making a distinction between moral agents and moral patients.[12] A moral patient is defined as someone or something that, owing to its intrinsic value, is an object of direct moral concern. Accordingly, another way of saying that every form of existence has intrinsic value is to say that everything that exists is a moral patient; everything is an object of direct moral concern. On the other hand, the technical vocabulary of Whitehead's organic model of individuality defines a moral agent as a particularly complex, personally ordered, structured society that, because of the complexity of its organization, has a capacity for significant novelty of experience. Put differently, moral agents are macroscopic individuals who possess a degree of complexity that makes it possible to conceive of unrealized possibilities. Although this is a useful distinction, we should avoid the temptation to ontologize it. Just as an individual (macroscopic or microscopic) may be alive to a greater or lesser degree, as noted earlier, it may also have a greater or lesser degree of freedom and, therefore, be a moral agent to a lesser or greater degree. Although there are no absolute gaps between moral agents and moral patients, we must recognize that "when we come to mankind, nature seems to have burst through another of its boundaries" (MT, 26).

With an organic conception of individuality, the language of "kind" and "type" has real moral footing without being ontologically basic. That is, given such an interpretation, we can appreciate the very real and potentially morally significant differences between individuals without introducing ontological gaps in the fabric of reality. Given this organic conception of individuality, let us examine exactly how individuals are to be categorized.

Constructing a Functional Taxonomy

Though the ontological principle requires that everything shall ultimately be explicable in terms of actual occasions, there are many different types of occasions. To be more precise, there are differences between the "satisfactions" achieved by different occasions. "An actual entity must be classified in respect to its 'satisfaction,' and this arises out of its datum by the operations constituting its 'process'" (PR, 111). In other words, how an occasion is classified depends upon what it is. In keeping with the ecstatic interpretation and particularly with Jones's focus on intensity, Whitehead argues in *Process and Reality* that occasions are to be classified by the intensity of their satisfaction: "'Satisfaction' is a generic term: there are specific differences between the 'satisfactions' of different entities, including gradations of intensity" (PR, 84). Hence, a complete understanding of the classification of an occasion would require the analysis of the conditions that provoke a more or less intense satisfaction. However, for present purposes, it is sufficient to recognize that nature's divisions are a function of the differences in intensity among the satisfactions achieved by actual occasions.[13]

Rather than trying to cobble together Whitehead's various and not always consistent accounts of the most basic types of individuals, I lean heavily on Frederick Ferré's division of entities, which, though equal in number to Whitehead's, are significantly more developed. In *Being and Value*, Ferré takes up the task of distinguishing between "types" of individuals by reexamining the very notion of an "entity." According to Ferré, anything that can support properties of its own is potentially an entity.[14] Thus, for instance, he contends that species are a kind of entity because they can support properties of their own. "Only a species, not its members, can evolve. Likewise, while individual exemplars of a species may be variously endangered (by predators, disease, etc.), they are not endangered in the same way a species is endangered. Animals die. Species go extinct."[15] With this basic criterion in mind, let us proceed to Ferré's sixfold division of entities.

Ferré begins his investigation with rather simple questions, such as, "What kind of entities are mountains and boulders?" According to Ferré, these are "aggregate entities." They are enduring, made up of many "lesser things," and are capable of supporting some of their own properties, but they are primarily externally related to both their components and their surroundings.[16] This last characteristic, externally related parts, principally defines aggregate entities.[17] Thus Ferré concludes that a boulder's status as an entity is "largely dependent on human interests, to group the aggregated facts into a unity capable of taking a name or becoming an object of attention. In the mixture of fact and decision, the larger share for aggregate entities comes from decision."[18] Though the unity and identity of aggregate entities are largely functions of humanity's level of functioning, interests, and definitions, aggregate entities are in no way fictitious.

Ferré next looks at "systematic entities." Unlike aggregate entities, systematic entities "are characterized by at least some strong internal relations between parts that vary with one another and together perform a common function. The entity as a whole is what it is because of the interplay of these parts, and without them it would cease to be an entity of that kind."[19] Ferré offers an ecosystem as a paradigmatic example of a systematic entity. According to Ferré, an ecosystem "is more than an aggregate of many parts. What distinguishes an ecosystem from a mountain as such is the presence within the former of many feedback loops which provide the system as a whole relative (stochastic) stability over time."[20] Thus, as a systematic entity, an ecosystem is what it is because of the constitutive interplay of its parts; without this interplay it would cease to be an entity of that kind. For instance, just as "a heap of airplane parts on a hangar floor—even a complete set of parts—is not an airplane,"[21] a collection of entities in close proximity does not make a system.

I mentioned previously that Ferré believes that, in some sense, species are entities because they are able to support properties of their own. But what type of entity are they? Are they aggregates or systems? As Ferré explains, "Species are not aggregate entities. . . . They are not at all like mountains or glaciers or boulders. Species are not like ecosystems, either. Individual animals of the same species may group themselves in herds or flocks or nests, all of which may have systematic properties, but this does not make the species, as such, a system. . . . Species constitute a third, distinct, type of entity, which I suggest we call *formal* entities."[22] Unlike aggregates and systems, "formal entities" are "constituted entirely by internal relations to specified possibilities."[23] A species is real, but it is not fully actual. Ferré distinguishes between two kinds of formal entities: temporal and nontemporal. Nontemporal formal entities correspond to Whitehead's eternal objects, which are at the opposite end of the ontological spectrum from actual occasions.

Thus, as in Plato, eternal objects serve as forms of determinateness but, unlike Plato's view, an eternal object is the least actual type of entity. According to Ferré, however, there are also forms of definiteness, like species, that have a temporal career. Ferré explains them in the following manner:

> Formal entities like animal or plant species are . . . not fictitious; rather, they are historical processes to which we give a name, in which identifiable patterns of characteristics are replicated across time through internal relations with many individuals who relate to one another. They are not, however, in any meaningful sense "agents." And, like aggregate entities, they are highly [though certainly not entirely] dependent on our interests and definitions for their delimitation.[24]

Ferré is careful to note, however, that, as forms of definiteness, temporal formal entities, like species, do not have interests of their own. "Formal entities, including even temporal ones, are not of that ilk."[25] To suggest that they are would be to violate the fallacy of misplaced concreteness. Only the individuals that exhibit this form of definiteness have interests, goals, or value.

The entities that actually populate ecosystems and are instances of species are what Ferré calls organic entities. In keeping with the previous analysis of societies, Ferré suggests that organic entities are simply systematic entities that "show significant degrees of spontaneity."[26] Another name for this spontaneity is "life." Thus, the defining characteristic of organic entities is that they include a "living system." In Ferré's words, "In manifesting these two traits, *holism* and *homeostasis*, they are no more than systematic entities. But living systems have one more essential characteristic that sets them apart from nonliving systems: they are capable of [significant] novelty, improvisation, evolution, growth—in a word, creativity. This is their defining characteristic."[27] Note that organic entities are not fundamentally different from systematic entities; there are no absolute gaps. In keeping with what was suggested above and unlike substance ontologies, the novelty and spontaneity that characterize living entities is a function of their complexity of organization. As I argue above, though in the inanimate it may be so low, on our macroscopic level of functioning, as to be practically negligible, the degree of novelty is never zero. And, as Charles Hartshorne reminds us, "The difference between zero and a finite positive quantity makes *all* the difference when we are seeking the general principles of reality."[28]

What about the status of artifacts such as tables and hammers? Are they entities too? Such questions present a central problem that has plagued philosophy since the time of Plato and Aristotle. The problem is that their status as objects of a certain type is almost exclusively a function of our (human) interests. The proper metaphysical level of analysis of entities such as artifacts is not at the macroscopic level at which we experience them, but rather at the molecular level: "Molecules are not simply *aggregates* although whether they represent chemical compounds or elements, they are comprised of many smaller parts. Since concrete, they are not *formal* processes. They are not in any obvious way *systems* made up of differentiated interactive parts and are certainly therefore not living *organic* systems. For molecules, then, I suggest the term *compound* entities."[29] Compound entities, Ferré explains, are nonliving, nonsystematic entities that are constituted by strong internal relations. In fact, these internal relations may be so strong that they cannot be broken without special or nuclear methods.[30] A good example of a compound entity is water, which remains the same all the way down to a single molecule.[31] Water's level of organization, whether it be liquid, gas, or solid, is at the molecular level, not at the level at which we visually experience it. However, the very definition of a compound suggests that these entities cannot be the most metaphysically basic form of entity. Thus, Ferré's sixth type of entity is what he calls "fundamental entities." With this we are back to Whitehead's actual occasions, already examined at length. These are the finally real things beyond which we cannot go. In outline form, here are the six main divisions in our functional taxonomy:

1. Aggregate entities
2. Systematic entities
3. Formal entities
   a. Temporal formal entities
   b. Nontemporal formal entities
4. Organic entities
5. Compound entities
6. Fundamental entities

To avoid potential misunderstandings, I will qualify these divisions. First, as Ferré himself indicates, this list is not meant to be exhaustive.[32] As our knowledge and our needs advance, it may be necessary to elaborate additional types of entities. Differentiation is a function of the complexity of the organization of a nexus's constituent entities and of our explanatory practices. It is equally important, because of the ontological continuity at the base of reality, not to take the distinctions elaborated by Ferré as metaphysically absolute. Rather, they are functional distinctions, or what Whitehead calls in *Modes of Thought* six "rough divisions" of occurrences (MT, 157).

This last qualification brings us to a third point. Though the divisions outlined above refer to objective facts of togetherness, to a certain extent they are also a product of our (human) mode of perception and our interests. In this sense, the divisions are "rough." How we divide up the world has always had as much (perhaps too much) to do with how we perceive the world as with how the world actually is. Some of what we pick out as individuals has more to do with "our habits of human life" than with the objective structure of the universe. Is a clod of dirt an individual? What about a finely cut diamond? As Whitehead notes, a primary determinant of what we choose to pick out has to do with scale. "Each scale of observation presents us with average effects proper to that scale" (MT, 158). In other words, if we were small enough to fit inside a single cell or large enough to fit the galaxy in our hand, we would denote very different objects as constituting the basic divisions of nature. This is not to say that nature's structures are simply a matter of the interests of the percipient, though some interpret Whitehead in this way. Rather, Whitehead is noting that how we "carve up" reality at our abstract level of functioning does not always coincide with, or exhaust, its objective structure.[33] In a sense, then, the differences between the occasions that we experience may ultimately be explained in both epistemological and metaphysical terms. "From the metaphysical standpoint these types are not to be sharply discriminated; [but] as a matter of empirical observation, the occasions do seem to fall into fairly distinct classes" (PR, 110). Metaphysically, actuality is seamless; epistemologically, it falls into neat categories.[34] As Whitehead succinctly puts it, "Nature suggests for our observation gaps, and then as it were withdraws them upon challenge" (AI, 206–7). Because of this, the above taxonomy can never be more than "functional." That is, it may be employed as a useful generalization but should never be taken as metaphysically adequate or exhaustive.

Clarke's Neo-Thomist Challenge to Process Thought

Now that I have presented Whitehead's organic model of macroscopic individuality, the question is, "Will it work?" Is his conception of macroscopic individuality robust enough to ground a moral philosophy? To test the adequacy of the organic model of individuality, let us examine the work of the contemporary neo-Thomist W. Norris Clarke, who gives voice to arguments that are commonly leveled against such a system. Clarke provides a clear challenge to this model of individuality by explicitly formulating and defending the objection that Whitehead's system allows for only an attenuated conception of macroscopic individuality that is unable to ground meaningful, personal moral responsibility. Moreover, Clarke's own dynamic interpretation of the classical notion of substance seriously questions the very need for Whitehead's "process turn" toward what Clarke sees as a misguided metaphysical atomism.[35] Thus, engaging Clarke's ideas not only provides an opportunity to justify the need for the "process turn" toward an organic model of individuality, but also allows us to respond to the criticism that Whitehead's system does not do justice to the unity of macroscopic individuals.

Substance as Dynamic?

In *The One and the Many* (2001), Clarke characterizes Whitehead's system as a metaphysical atomism in which "process itself is made up of many discretely distinct, tiny entities, 'actual occasions' or 'actual entities,' following each other in ordered sequence."[36] Clarke's understanding of Whitehead's account of macroscopic individuals follows directly from this interpretation of process as composed of discrete entities:

> The macroscopic objects we call things—plants, animals, humans, chairs, etc.—are really societies or collections of many actual entities bound together by various relations, causal connections, etc., existing at any one time. Down through time there is no actual entity that remains the same, unchanged, but only a series of successive entities that we call one being because the series is closely connected by a chain of "inheritance" of properties one from the other. Thus what we call the human "self," the "I," is really only a succession of selves bound together by a common chain of inheritances.[37]

From this understanding of Whiteheadian macroscopic objects as "only a series" or "collection" of "discretely distinct" actual entities, Clarke criticizes Whitehead's system for not adequately accounting for the experienced unity of macroscopic individuals. Simply stated, Clarke's objection is that a mere succession of entities, no matter how closely connected, could never account for how we experience ourselves or others. As Clarke puts it, a society of "discrete, non-identical selves linked in a temporal and spatial chain is not nearly strong enough to do justice to these powerful experiences of perduring unity and self-identity. . . . The unity of a society, founded on external relations, not on the inner unity of the being itself, is again not strong enough to do justice to the evidenced facts."[38] It is primarily this problem—the unity of macroscopic individuals—that makes Clarke unable to embrace process metaphysics.

Thus, in summary, Clarke finds that because Whitehead insists that the most basic ontological units of reality are not the macroscopic entities that we experience in everyday life, but rather "discretely distinct" microscopic entities, he fails to capture adequately the undeniable unity of macroscopic individuals. This objection, if correct, would be particularly troubling for the present project. For if Whitehead indeed affirms that macroscopic individuals are merely a succession of "selves," then the possibility of meaningful, personal moral responsibility is seriously jeopardized. As Clarke himself notes, it is one thing to take responsibility for a predecessor's action and quite another to take responsibility for having personally committed an action oneself.[39] If Whitehead's system cannot "do justice to the evidenced facts" of macroscopic individuality, then any ethical theory based on it is doomed to fail.

For Clarke, the source of what he sees as Whitehead's misguided metaphysical atomism is his repudiation of the doctrine of substance. From his point of view, what is particularly tragic about this error is that Whitehead's repudiation of substance was itself the result of a flawed understanding of Aristotle and St. Thomas Aquinas's notion of substance.[40] Clarke has devoted much of his career to advancing what he calls a "creative retrieval" of Aquinas that interprets substance dynamically. In contrast to the traditional depiction of substances as independent, unchanging subjects of change, Clarke conceives of every being as inherently active or "self-communicating." "A non-acting, non-communicating being is for all practical purposes . . . *equivalent* to no being at all. To be *real* is to *make a difference*."[41] This emphasis on being active and self-communicating also brings Clarke to refute the notion that substances are independent and unrelated. "To have a universe, a community of real existents, its members would have to communicate with each other, be linked together and all communication requires some kind of action."[42] In fact, Clarke goes so far as to state that a completely unrelated, unchanging entity would not only be "totally pointless"; it "could not be the work of a wise creative God. And so we live in a universe where all the real beings that count, that make a difference, are dynamically active ones, that pour over through self-manifesting, self-communicating action to connect up with other real beings, and form a community of interacting existents we call a 'universe.'"[43] Clearly, this is not the notion of vacuous existence that Whitehead had in mind when he used the term "substance."

Far from joining Whitehead in repudiating substance, Clarke steadfastly affirms the supremacy of substance as "the principle of continuity and self-identity throughout the whole spectrum of accidental change open to a particular being."[44] Clarke is quick to point out, however, that being self-identical is not the same as being unchanging or immutable, as Whitehead (among others) has charged.[45] Clarke reminds us, "The authentic meaning of self-identity through change is this: 'In an accidental change, the substance itself changes, but not substantially or essentially, only accidentally.' Thus the subject that changes retains its essential self-identity through the spectrum of accidental change open to it in terms of its natural potencies."[46] A substance is something that actively maintains self-identity over time, but this self-identity does not signify something static or self-enclosed. On the contrary, Clarke insists, "Self-identity is not immutability but the active power of self-maintenance in exchange with others. Thus the best way to maintain psychological self-identity is not by not changing, doing nothing, but by stability of goals, perseveringly pursued." "You could not," Clarke retorts, "find a more dynamic notion [of substance] than this."[47] In this way, Clarke believes that he can at once affirm the traditional concept of substance as well as capture the dynamic, processive nature of reality in systems such as Whitehead's. Accordingly, given his dynamic interpretation of substance, Clarke seems to be arguing that Whitehead's complicated account of process is not only inadequate, but also unnecessary.

Clarke and the Process Turn

Ironically, just as Clarke finds that Whitehead misinterprets Aristotle and St. Thomas's notion of substance, in participating in misleading aspects of the classical interpretation, Clarke fails to recognize the adequacy of Whitehead's system. Thus, before turning to analyze Clarke's "creative retrieval" of the doctrine of substance, let us first examine certain serious flaws in Clarke's interpretation of Whitehead.

Because Clarke recognizes that Whitehead's emphasis on interrelatedness is "one of the most fertile of all the Whiteheadian insights into what it means to be in our world,"[48] it is surprising that he characterizes process as "made up of many discretely distinct, tiny entities."[49] Though it is true that Whitehead believes that experience comes in "drops" and that I referred in chapter 1 to actual occasions as the "atomic stuff of which the universe is made," we must also recall that this atomism is *not* purchased at the expense of the unity of the universe. The relations obtaining between actual occasions are primarily internal, not external, wherein these internal relations "are constitutive of what the event is in itself" (SMW, 104). In this sense, each actual occasion is its relationship to the universe. Hence, for Whitehead, the concept of individuality (both macroscopic and microscopic) itself requires essential reference to others. This emphasis upon interrelation and interdependence is inherent in seeing Whitehead's model of individuality as "organic." Furthermore, in this way Whitehead sees himself explicitly rejecting Aristotle's dictum (which Clarke affirms) that a substance is never present in another. Again, according to Whitehead's principle of relativity, "an actual entity *is* present in other actual entities. In fact, if we allow for degrees of relevance, and for negligible relevance, we must say that every actual entity is present in every other actual entity" (PR, 50). Since every actual occasion is present in every other, actual occasions are anything but "discretely distinct," as Clarke contends. As a matter of fact, given the principle of relativity, they are more nearly the opposite.

Because of the constitutive relation between them, the proper understanding of actual occasions as organically interrelated has a significant impact on how to conceive of societies, Clarke incorrectly depicts a society as "an aggregate of many distinct beings held together in an extrinsic unity based on external relations."[50] As my previous analysis of societies should demonstrate, this interpretation of Whitehead's concept of "society" is incorrect on virtually every point. A society is not an "aggregate" of "discrete," "externally related" beings held together in an "extrinsic unity." Rather, a society is a socially ordered nexus of internally related occasions that form an intrinsic unity. Societies are not mere collections or aggregates of entities to which the same class-name applies. This is the difference between a nexus and a society. Whereas a nexus is simply any real fact of togetherness, including extrinsic unities such as what were classified above as aggregate entities (such as boulders and mountains), a society is a particular type of nexus that enjoys "social order." That is, a society's constituent occasions share a common, defining characteristic because of their *internal* relatedness with previous members of that society. Hence, unlike aggregate entities, complex structured societies such as plants and animals are organic entities that, like systematic entities, are characterized by "strong internal relations between parts that vary with one another and together perform a common function. The entity as a whole is what it is because of the [constitutive] interplay of these parts, and without them would cease to be an entity of that kind."[51]

This reveals a crucial difference in the role of "interrelation" in Clarke's and Whitehead's systems. Whereas for Whitehead the relations between individuals are constitutive of their very character, for Clarke, although it is essential to the nature of substances that they be related to "some other beings and systems of them," it is merely "accidental to which particular beings and systems [they] are related."[52] That is, according to Clarke every substance or real being is nested within and depends upon various kinds of order or systems, although to which others and to which systems a substance is related or is not related is purely accidental; that is, it does not affect its essence. For Whitehead, on the other hand, every individual is just its relationships to every element in its world. Though some relations may be more central in the constitution of an entity than others, there are no purely accidental relationships.[53] Thus, although he may affirm a notion of substance as dynamically interrelated with its environment, insofar as these interrelations are only external and accidental to what that substance is, Clarke still adheres to the notion of "independent existence." According to Whitehead, this is the "misconception which has haunted philosophic literature throughout the centuries. . . . There is no such mode of existence; every entity is only to be understood in terms of the way in which it is interwoven with the rest of the Universe" (IM, 687).

In sum, Clarke is incorrect in his interpretation both of process as involving discrete entities and of societies as collections of externally related entities. Far from being "discretely distinct," actual occasions are in fact constituted by their internal relations with others. Similarly, rather than being mere "extrinsic unities" composed of "collections" or "aggregates" of "externally related" entities, societies are intrinsic unities of socially ordered actual occasions that, by reason of the conditions imposed upon them by their internal relatedness to previous members of the society, share a common characteristic, what is traditionally called the essential form.

Both of these misinterpretations, I suspect, stem largely from Clarke's misunderstanding of why Whitehead felt compelled to reject the doctrine of substance. While he is correct in seeing that, at least in part, Whitehead developed his metaphysics of process in response to the inadequacies he perceived in substance ontologies, Clarke is mistaken in claiming that Whitehead's motivation was primarily to "banish any notion of a unitary subject perduring through time."[54] As I suggest in chapter 1, it is simply false that Whitehead denies that we experience the world in terms of substantial, perduring individuals. With Clarke, Whitehead believes that the experienced unity of macroscopic individuals is an undeniable fact. The problem with the idea of an enduring substance, Whitehead claims, is that "whenever we try to use it as a fundamental statement of the nature of things, it proves itself mistaken" (PR, 79). What Whitehead denies, then, is not the unity of macroscopic individuals, but the notion that these macroscopic, perduring individuals are the most basic ontological units of explanation. Accordingly, the question at stake is not whether Whitehead seeks to "banish" the idea of perduring individuality, which he does not, but rather how perduring individuality is to be explained.

It may be helpful to formulate this claim by means of Bernard Lonergan's distinction between description and explanation, to which Clarke himself subscribes.[55] According to Lonergan, it differs from an explanation in that a description derives from relating objects of inquiry to the percipient, whereas an explanation derives from relating objects of inquiry to one another. For instance, while a descriptive account of a sunrise, by relating the data to the percipient, would claim that the sun literally rises over a stationary earth, an explanatory account, by relating the data to each other, would claim that the sun only appears to rise because the earth rotates on its axis as it revolves around the sun.

Taken in these terms, Whitehead is rejecting substance as an adequate explanation of the nature of things, not as an adequate description. It is Clarke's account of experience in terms of substantial, perduring individuals that is insufficient because it arrives at its most basic ontological units—i.e., macroscopic, perduring individuals—by means of how the world appears to human beings. In Whitehead's terms, this means that in taking our perception of the world as delineating the most basic ontological units, substance ontology violates the fallacy of misplaced concreteness. "It is the mistake that has thwarted European metaphysics from the time of the Greeks, namely, to confuse societies with the completely real things which are the actual occasions" (AI, 204). Beyond this criticism, which applies to substance ontologies in general, Clarke's dynamic account of substance is uniquely lacking in explanatory force.

According to the traditional account, a substance provides unity by being the static, unchanging subject of accidental changes. The substance is what remains unchanged throughout accidental changes. Both Clarke and Whitehead agree that such a concept of substance is unable to account for the dynamic, energetic nature of reality and is in fact contradicted by experience. However, if Clarke is to avoid the conception of substance as a static cabinet of accidental changes, if active self-maintenance is not achieved by "not changing, doing nothing," he must explain how this active self-maintenance takes place. In *Adventures of Ideas*, Whitehead eloquently captures this challenge:

> Consider our derivation from our immediate past of a quarter of a second ago. We are continuous with it, we are the same as it, prolonging its affective tone, enjoying its data. And yet we are modifying it, deflecting it, changing its purposes, altering its tone, re-conditioning its data with new elements.
>
> We reduce this past to a perspective, and yet retain it as the basis of our present moment of realization. We are different from it, and yet we retain our individual identity with it. This is the mystery of personal identity, the mystery of the immanence of the past in the present, the mystery of transcience [*sic*]. (AI, 163)

It is not sufficient to say that substance or essential form is simply that principle that provides unity and links the accidental attributes of a being. What is needed is an explanation of how the active maintenance of self-identity takes place from moment to moment. To do so Clarke must ultimately appeal to some doctrine of internal relations. For if an individual is not essentially the same by *not* changing, but by changing at each moment, by actively responding to changing circumstances in its environment, then at each successive moment, from its creation until its destruction, its self-identity must be continually reaffirmed. Unfortunately, Clarke does not provide any such account of how this active reassertion of a given character at each successive moment takes place. Because self-identity must be continually reasserted and maintained, the internal relatedness of each moment to the one before it cannot be taken for granted. To demonstrate that Whitehead's organic model has greater explanatory power than Clarke's, let us examine the ontological status of systems in each.

Building on advances in fields such as ecology and biology, Clarke recognizes that he must break with Aristotle and St. Thomas and affirm that a system is "a new mode of unity existing between and binding together individual substances, which is not merely the sum of many different accidental relations but forms a *new unity* with its own properties that is not reducible merely to the sum of all the individual relations, but is a new mode of unity that resides in all the members at once."[56] Clarke recognizes that "things" such as ecosystems are not simply aggregates of externally related substances. A system is a mode of unity with properties of its own. However, this introduces a problem. While systems have properties of their own and are therefore more than a mere aggregate of entities, they have insufficient unity to be considered a substance in their own right. Within Clarke's system, it is invalid to claim that a system is "partially" or "sort of" a substance; something is either a substance or it is not. Given the constraints of his substance ontology, Clarke takes the only option open to him. Namely, he argues that a system "belongs to the order of accidents, but it is a unique kind of accident that inheres in many subjects at once—a form of one-in-many—and so deserves a name of its own because of its special properties."[57] Clarke appeals to a distinction that in fact makes no difference; referring to systems as a type of accident, even a unique type, cannot do justice to the real form of unity that a system is.

Interestingly, Clarke flirts with a model very similar to the one being defended when he examines systems that so strongly dominate their constituents that "their individuality becomes almost submerged or wiped out, e.g., the ants in an ant colony or bees in a beehive are so powerfully governed by the 'psychic field' of the whole that they surrender themselves instinctively and totally to the good of the whole, and will die soon if removed from it, even though they have adequate food, water, etc. The system has almost totally absorbed them; it so dominates them that they can be almost said to compose one being, but not quite."[58]

What is particularly noteworthy in this passage is that Clarke has his finger on the difference between a structured, living society and a personally ordered, structured, living society. That is, human experience is characterized by the dominance of a single, serially ordered, continuous society that governs its structured society. Whereas on Clarke's model of substance such a relation is problematic, for Whitehead it is simply a matter of analyzing the types of order achieved by a particular nexus of actual occasions. All macroscopic individuality is a matter of order. If there is a high degree of order and novelty is introduced, then it is a living society. If it is higher still it may be a personal society. The question is not *whether* a particular form of order is or is not a substance, as it is for Clarke. Though systems, such as ecosystems, may not have the same degree of intrinsic unity as a plant or animal, they are nonetheless real forms of togetherness with properties of their own. By taking only the macroscopic units that we perceive at our scale of experience as the ontologically basic units, Clarke is unable to affirm that there are degrees of coordination, each of which is a form of togetherness that is real, particular, and individual.[59] Thus, it is Clarke who must ultimately make the process turn if he is to truly explain, not merely describe, the fact of dynamic self-identity.

Though Clark's interpretation of Whitehead is mistaken in several important respects, and Clarke's own system is insufficiently explanatory, a Whiteheadian ethic could still be subject to Clarke's basic criticism. The question that must be addressed is: "Can a societal model of macroscopic individuality ever adequately account for the undeniable unity that we ourselves experience and that we perceive in other macroscopic objects?" If this question cannot be answered, not only is the *metaphysics* of creativity being advanced in jeopardy, but any hope of developing a meaningful *ethics* of creativity is doomed before it starts. In the remainder of this chapter, I intend not only to demonstrate that a Whiteheadian organic model of individuality can account for the unity experienced by macroscopic individuals, but also explain how this continuity takes place.

Society and Self-Identity

At the heart of Clarke's objection to Whitehead's societal account of macroscopic individuals is the idea that a society's actual occasions do not endure. "Down through time there is no actual entity that remains the same, unchanged, but only a series of successive entities that we call one being because the series is closely connected by a chain of 'inheritance.'"[60] First, since Clarke himself repudiates the notion that immutability is needed for self-identity, it is ironic that he criticizes Whitehead's account because "no actual entity . . . remains the same, unchanged."[61] However, this claim also portrays a crucial misunderstanding regarding the proper level of comparison between Clarke's system and Whitehead's. Although in the philosophy of organism actual occasions are indeed the most basic ontological units, it is societies, not actual occasions, that endure and change and therefore should be compared with substances.

The importance of adopting the proper level of comparison becomes evident in light of Clarke's conclusion drawn from the fact that actual entities do not endure. Since, unlike substances, no actual occasion endures, Clarke concludes that "what we call the human 'self,' the 'I,' is really only a succession of selves bound together by a common chain of inheritances."[62] However, insofar as the proper comparison is between societies and substances, the affirmation that actual occasions do not endure no more implies that a society is a succession of selves than does the affirmation that substances are composed of subatomic particles that do not endure. That is, the human "self" is no more a succession of actual occasions than a substance is a succession of material particles. The society is the ground of the perduring unity and self-identity of macroscopic individuals, not its constituent occasions. Furthermore, by definition a society is not something that can happen at an instant. Although a set of contemporary actual occasions may belong to a society, the genetic conditions of a society cannot be satisfied by a set of contemporaries alone (AI, 204). In other words, whereas an actual occasion "only becomes and perishes," as a "complete existence and as retaining the same metaphysical status" a society "enjoys a history expressing its changing reactions to changing circumstances" (AI, 204). That is, since a society is a career, not just a nexus of contemporary occasions, it is always adding to itself. "For example, the man adds another day to his life, and the earth adds another millennium to the period of its existence. But until the death of the man and the destruction of the earth, there is no determinate nexus which in an unqualified sense is either the man or the earth" (AI, 204).

Accordingly, the proper question is: "Are societies and nexus, not actual occasions, able to adequately account for the self-identity of macroscopic individuals?" To answer it, let us examine how

Whitehead specifically characterizes human beings such that they are more than a mere succession of discrete, nonidentical selves. For if an organic model of individuality can do justice to the unity of human beings, which are the most complex natural entities known, then in principle his system will be able to account for other less complex forms of unity as well.

In *Adventures of Ideas*, Whitehead describes human consciousness as a society in which "the successive nexus of its progressive realization have a common extensive pattern in which each such nexus is purely temporal and continuous" (AI, 205). This, as we saw above, is the definition of a personal society. Hence, all healthy human beings are persons.[63] Yet, given this definition of consciousness as a succession of occasions of experience, Whitehead would seem to be subject to Clarke's criticism that he defines the human "self" as a series of discrete, nonidentical selves. However, this is not the case. "For," as Aristotle reminds us, "one swallow does not make a spring, nor does one day."[64] Although consciousness may be a purely temporal and continuous succession of nexūs, as Whitehead notes,

> a man is more than a serial succession of occasions of experience. Such a definition may satisfy philosophers—Descartes, for example. It is not the ordinary meaning of the term "man." There are animal bodies as well as animal minds; and in our experience such minds always occur incorporated. Now an animal body is a society involving a vast number of occasions, spatially and temporally coordinated. It follows that a "man," in the full sense of ordinary usage, is not a "person" as here defined. He has the unity of a wider society, in which the social coordination is a dominant factor in the behavior of the various parts. (AI, 205)

Accordingly, like Aristotle and in contrast to Descartes, Whitehead argues that a human being is a complex, structured society encompassing both an animal body, which is itself a society involving vast arrays of subordinate societies and nexus, as well as a "soul" or a regnant, personally ordered subsociety that makes self-consciousness possible. Whitehead's reference to a "wider society" that becomes a "dominant factor" in the behavior of its parts introduces two very important themes: (1) the role of a society's defining characteristic in constituting its self-identity and its "nature," and (2) the sense in which societies exercise agency as a whole.

Many commentators on Whitehead's system, including Clarke, give insufficient attention to the crucial role of a society's "defining characteristic" and its very close resemblance to the classical notion of "essential form."[65] Just as the essential form is the "intelligible, qualitative pattern or constitutive structure within the being that makes it to be this kind of being,"[66] for Whitehead, "a society has an essential [or defining] character, whereby it is the society that it is, and it has also accidental qualities which vary as circumstances alter" (AI, 204).[67] Thus, an organic model of individuality holds that a macroscopic individual is the type of individual that it is because of its defining characteristic or essential form. In addition, just as the essential form is the principle of continuity that maintains the self-identity of a substance, it is the defining characteristic of a society that grounds its self-identity (AI, 204). However, as with Clarke's dynamic interpretation of substance, the defining characteristic of a society does not retain self-identity by not changing. Self-identity is not immutability; it is active self-maintenance in exchange with others. Thus, according to an organic model of macroscopic individuality, owing to the particularly complex, genetic relation and social coordination of its subordinate societies, the human body is able to support a society that becomes a "dominant factor in the behavior of the various parts" (AI, 205). In other words, the human being as a particularly complex structured society is able to act *as a whole*.

This introduces the second point: namely, the sense in which an organic account of macroscopic individuality is able to exercise agency. Although, in the strictest metaphysical sense, the ontological principle limits agency to actual occasions, with Joseph A.

Bracken I find that to make sense of the experience of complex structured societies such as ourselves, we must affirm some meaningful sense in which societies exercise what Bracken calls "collective agency." According to Bracken, "Whitehead's statement that agency belongs exclusively to actual occasions is not wrong but merely incomplete. Whitehead simply failed to mention that these individual agencies fuse into a collective agency for the structured society as a whole."[68] Though I would not go as far as Bracken and argue that societies are "equiprimordial" with actual occasions, I do agree that in complex, structured societies such as animals, the "soul" or regnant personally ordered subsociety allows the structured society as a whole to be a subject of experience and to make decisions in a way that is not possible in organisms lacking a central nervous system.[69] Bracken writes:

> For, in virtue of the central nervous system, the dominant actual occasion at any given moment can communicate its "decisions" to all the subordinate living and nonliving occasions in the body; and they, in turn, can communicate their response to its successor in the dominant subsociety. But it is still the structured society as such, the organism as a whole, that exists and exercises activity.[70]

In this way, Bracken believes that Whitehead's organic model can account for a type of macroscopic agency that does not violate the ontological principle. In the strictest sense, ontological agency is reserved for the actual occasions that in each successive generation repeat the defining characteristic of a given society. However, macroscopic individuals are agents in a second, collective sense. "Hence," as Bracken puts it, "the structured society as a whole is the ontological agent even though it exercises that agency principally (though not exclusively) through one of its constituent actual occasions."[71]

This distinction brings to light the very important difference between the classical notion of essential form and Whitehead's notion of defining characteristic. Whereas traditionally the essential form imposes and is the cause of the unity and self-identity of a substance by imposing its activity, as it were, from "above," for Whitehead, the defining characteristic arises out of the mutual immanence of the genetically related nexus of actual occasions that comprise a society. For Clarke, the essential form is "that central unifying force in a material being that binds all its elements together into an intrinsic unity of being and action, not a mere aggregate. It functions as the abiding center of characteristic actions."[72] However, given the organic model being defended, the defining characteristic of a society is, as Bracken puts it, "derived moment by moment from the genetic interrelatedness of the actual occasions making up a given society."[73] Thus, whereas for Clarke and the substance tradition the form is active and the material constituents are passive, given the organic model being advanced, in an important sense both the defining characteristic and the so-called material constituents (that is, actual occasions) are active. The defining characteristic is what provides the environment in which a higher degree of functioning is possible, but it is the actual occasions that perpetuate the defining characteristic.[74] This should clarify the argument that the difference between types of entities is ultimately not of different ontological kinds but lies in the *degree* of "coordination" in satisfying the actual occasions comprising a given nexus or society. This gives the organic model an advantage over the doctrine of substance.

Whereas it is a mystery how a substance's essential form ultimately gives it unity in the present and over time, the organic model can be explained in another way: the unity of macroscopic individuals arises out of the intense, organic interrelation and coordination of actual occasions. In Whitehead's words, "The organic starting point is from the analysis of process as the realization of events disposed in an interlocking community. The event is the unit of things real. The emergent enduring pattern is the stabilization of the emergent achievement so as to become a fact which retains its identity throughout the process" (SMW, 152). In this way, the organic model can better explain the unity of experience possessed by perduring macroscopic individuals. The most basic difference between a traditional substance account of individuality and the organic model being advanced is ultimately to be found in the level of explanation open to each. Whereas Clarke's and other traditional substance ontologies stop with macroscopic agents, Whitehead's organic model accounts for how macroscopic agency arises and how it is perpetuated. In this way, Whitehead's organic model of individuality not only provides an adequate account of the experienced unity of macroscopic individuals, but does so with greater explanatory depth. And in so doing, it establishes a foundation upon which an ethics of creativity can be built.

I have shown how an organic model of individuality can meaningfully, not just metaphorically, refer to macroscopic wholes as "individuals" in a way that not only meets Whitehead's metaphysical requirements by avoiding the fallacy of misplaced concreteness and not violating the ontological principle, but also does justice to our experience of ourselves and of other macroscopic individuals. Further, I have shown that the organic model of individuality being defended is, in principle, able to support meaningful, personal moral responsibility. Yet we must address a final component of Whitehead's metaphysics of creativity before we can turn directly to his ethics of creativity. We must look at what drives this inexhaustible quest for the achievement of value intensity; we must examine the very aim of process itself: beauty.

4

Process as Kalogenic

Our ability to perceive quality in nature begins, as in art,
with the pretty. It expands through successive stages of the
beautiful to values as yet uncaptured by language.

Aldo Leopold, *A Sand County Almanac*

AT THE HEART OF Whitehead's philosophy of organism is the view
that every form of existence aims at and achieves an end for its
own sake. In so doing, it has value for itself, for others, and for the
whole. Yet what is the end toward which actuality strives? This
question introduces one of the more novel (and for some, troubling)
elements of Whitehead's philosophy. The following passages reflect
Whitehead's belief that the telos of the universe, and therefore of
every actual occasion, aims at the achievement of beauty:

> The final actuality has the unity of power. The essence of power
> is the drive towards aesthetic worth for its own sake. All power is
> a derivative from this fact of composition attaining worth for it-
> self. There is no other fact. . . . It constitutes the drive of the uni-
> verse. (MT, 119)

> The teleology of the Universe is directed to the production of

Beauty. Thus any system of things which in any wide sense is beautiful is to that extent justified in its existence. (AI, 265)

Creativity, the dynamic process of the universe, is not aimless. Rather, every process of becoming aims at the achievement of beauty. To use a term coined by Ferré, actuality is inherently kalogenic.[1] In bringing together the diverse elements in its world, he writes, "every pulse of actualizing energy represents in itself an act of kalogenesis."[2] In a sense, in that it attempts to give a consistent, adequate, coherent, and applicable account of process, a process that is an achievement of beauty, Whitehead's metaphysics *is* an aesthetics.[3]

A Multidimensional Continuum of Beauty

In *Modes of Thought,* Whitehead warns that "in the history of European thought the discussion of aesthetics has been almost ruined by the emphasis upon the harmony of the details" (MT, 62). Although it is not altogether clear from this statement alone what precisely he finds objectionable in the emphasis upon the harmony of the details, the statement that follows it gives us a clue as to how Whitehead positively conceives of aesthetics: "In the greatest examples of any form of art, a miraculous balance is achieved. The whole displays its component parts, each with its own value enhanced; and the parts lead up to a whole, which is beyond themselves, and yet not destructive of themselves" (MT, 62).[4] This miraculous balance, which not only achieves a harmonious whole, but simultaneously enhances its parts without sacrificing their individuality, is the key to Whitehead's conception of beauty. In a sense, it is the notion of creativity itself. Just as creativity is the universe's drive toward a complex unity that does not devour individuality, beauty is the achievement of a whole that enhances the value of each part while not being destructive of them. The jagged rocks of monism and solipsism are equally to be avoided. "There is one whole, arising from the interplay of many details. The importance arises from the vivid grasp of the interdependence of the one and the many. If either side of this antithesis sinks into the background, there is trivialization of experience, logical and aesthetic" (MT, 60). Remembering Whitehead's warning regarding overemphasizing harmony, let us turn to the treatment of beauty in *Adventures of Ideas*.

Here, Whitehead concisely defines beauty as "the mutual adaptation of the several factors in an occasion of experience" (AI, 252). The first component of this definition of beauty is that adaptation implies an end and that this end is twofold. The first aim of this adaptation is at the "absence of mutual inhibition among the various prehensions" (AI, 252). Chapter 1 discussed how in concrescence actual occasions bring together elements in their actual world. Hence, concrescence achieves the first aim of beauty when the data prehended do not inhibit each other. However, Whitehead suggests that this is merely the "minor form" of beauty, which he described in *Modes of Thought* as the mere harmony of details. Therefore, this form of beauty would seem to be inadequate or deficient by itself. There is, however, a second aim of the adaptation toward beauty. According to Whitehead, the major form of beauty

> presupposes the first form, and adds to it the condition that the conjunction in one synthesis of the various prehensions introduces new contrasts of objective content with objective content. These contrasts introduce new conformal intensities of feelings natural to each of them, and by so doing raise the intensities of conformal feeling in the primitive component feelings. Thus the parts contribute to the massive feeling of the whole, and the whole contributes to the intensity of feeling of the parts. (AI, 252–53)

Since this account of the major form of beauty involves a number of technical terms, we should treat the parts of this account one by one. First, the major form of beauty presupposes the absence of mutual inhibition involved in the minor form of beauty. But in addition to the lack of mutual inhibition, the major form of beauty also involves the achievement of intensity through the introduction of new contrasts. For Whitehead, "contrast" is a technical term that refers to the positive relation of two or more elements involved in experience such that those elements are not only mutually compatible but also mutually enhancing.[5] The introduction of new contrasts enables the parts to "contribute to the massive feeling of the whole, and the whole contributes to the intensity of feeling of the parts" (AI, 252). In this way, the perfection of beauty involves two elements: (1) "massiveness," which concerns the greatest possible variety of detail with effective contrast, and (2) "intensity," which concerns the comparative magnitude or depth of the contrasts achieved. This is the "miraculous balance" referred to in *Modes of Thought* wherein "the whole displays its component parts, each with its own value enhanced; and the parts lead up to a whole, which is beyond themselves, and yet not destructive of themselves" (MT, 62).

By defining beauty as a form of unity in diversity, Whitehead places himself within a long tradition of aesthetics. However, one should not conclude too much from this similarity. Although Whitehead's conception of beauty is similar to the traditional formulations of beauty, taken in conjunction with his reformed subjectivism, which holds that there is nothing apart from the experience of subjects and the complex process of concrescence it involves, Whitehead's aesthetics is more complex than may first appear. For greater access to Whitehead's rich conception of beauty, let us turn to the work of Charles Hartshorne, who brings greater clarity to Whitehead's basic insights.

Hartshorne develops a diagram that is helpful in explaining the complex notion of beauty Whitehead advanced (see figure 1).[6] Consider a large circle, in the middle of which is a smaller circle. The small circle represents beauty in the truest and most complete sense. The larger circle includes aesthetic value in the most comprehensive sense. Since everything has some value, there is nothing

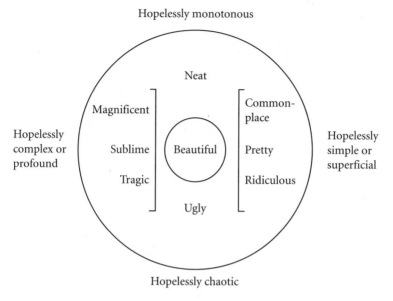

Figure 1. Aesthetic Circle

outside the larger circle. Thus, although we may call an experience unaesthetic if its degree of harmony and intensity is low, this negation cannot be absolute. In rejecting the zero of actuality, we must also reject the notion that there is an "absolutely unbeautiful object or unaesthetic experience."[7] The zero of aesthetic value is the zero of actuality.

The Dimension of Harmony

A helpful way to conceive of the Aesthetic Circle is as a two-dimensional version of Aristotle's conception of virtue as a mean. However, rather than a one-dimensional relation between a single pair of extremes, the Aesthetic Circle is two-dimensional and therefore entails two opposing pairs of extremes. Let us begin with the vertical dimension. The vertical axis lies between the poles of unity and diversity, corresponding to the minor form of beauty that is concerned with harmony. The ideal of this dimension is maximum diversity in unity. The upper region of the larger circle represents those forms of beauty that are very orderly but, lacking diversity, are merely "neat" or "tidy," rather than beautiful. An example would be an orchestra that plays a single note over and over again. The "music" played would be very orderly and possess a degree of harmony, but, lacking all diversity, the unity achieved is overly simple, monotonous, and, at the extreme, bordering on absolute order. The ideal of beauty, therefore, is not one that aims at absolute order; there must be sufficient diversity and variety for an experience to be beautiful.

However, too much diversity means the deterioration of unity. At the opposite extreme of the undiversified unity of monotony lies the un-unified diversity of chaos. Specifically, the lower region of the larger circle represents those forms of beauty that, because of an excess of diversity, lack unity and are what Hartshorne labels "ugly." Since "ugliness" popularly refers to any form of aesthetic deficiency, a better term would be "chaotic." What is important here is that this form of experience misses the mean of beauty because its excess of variety undermines the formation of significant unity and, at the extreme, borders on absolute disorder or chaos. If one has ever had the misfortune of hearing a primary school orchestra warm up, then one has an idea of the chaos of excessive diversity.

In this way, just as Aristotle's notion of courage is the mean of fear and rashness, this conception of beauty involves, though is not limited to, the mean of unity and diversity. Hartshorne explains, "Beauty is the blessed escape from the opposite evils of monotonous or mechanical repetition and an equally meaningless succession of unrelated novelties. . . . It is the mean between extremes. On one side are mere disorder, confusion, chaos, unexpectedness, unintegrated diversity, on the other, mere order, regularity, predictability, unity without diversity."[8] However, Hartshorne recognizes that the extremes of absolute order and absolute disorder (chaos) are purely verbal entities to be found nowhere in reality. "Any state of affairs that can be definitely conceived without contradiction has some degree of order. A hopelessly discordant entity is not *an* entity, nor can an experience be without some minimal degree of concord among its aspects. There is always some 'satisfaction,' to use Whitehead's term."[9] Accordingly, if absolute order and absolute disorder are equally unrealizable, then every experience has some degree of order and some degree of disorder. Thus some degree of disorder or conflict is an unavoidable part of the creative advance.

> All realization is finite, and there is no perfection which is the infinite of all perfections. Perfections of diverse types are among themselves discordant. Thus the contribution to Beauty which can be supplied by Discord—in itself destructive and evil—is the positive feeling of a quick shift of aim from the tameness of outworn perfection to some other ideal with its freshness still upon it. Thus the value of Discord is a tribute to the merits of Imperfection. (AI, 257)[10]

For both Whitehead and Hartshorne, then, not only is discord unavoidable, it is in fact necessary for the achievement of deeper forms of beauty. Although the loss resulting from the conflict between two individuals is tragic, this discord helps avoid tameness or "anesthesia" by introducing uncertainty, unpredictability, and freedom. Discord plays an essential role in the procurement of beauty.[11] "Thus chaos is not to be identified with evil; for harmony requires the due coordination of chaos, vagueness, narrowness, and width" (PR, 112). Or, as Jones puts it, "The discord of intensities breathes life into a processive universe, forcing a constant adjustment of aesthetic achievement."[12] This point is illustrated clearly by predation in nature. Although the discord between a bald eagle and a trout is itself destructive and evil, such predation is necessary for the healthy functioning of the ecosystem and the multitudes of organisms that depend upon it.

The Dimension of Intensity

Whereas the vertical dimension concerns the degree of harmony achieved, the horizontal dimension concerns the relation of complexity and its contrary, simplicity. The relation of complexity and simplicity determines the intensity of experience. The region to the right of the larger circle represents experience which, because of its lack of significant complexity, is merely "pretty." For instance, played by a novice, the song "Greensleeves" is pretty rather than beautiful because its chords lack sufficient complexity. The song is too trivial; it fails to introduce effective contrast. On the other hand, the region to the left represents experience that is too complex or too profound to grasp. Thus, continuing the music metaphor, though stretching the limits of it, one might think of a symphony requiring 10,000 parts as being so complex that it is impossible to grasp.[13]

Given the four poles of unity, diversity, complexity, and simplicity, we may also fill in the diagonal extremes that represent minor deficiencies in both harmony and intensity. For instance, whereas a profound disorder is tragic, a trivial disorder is comic. Similarly, while a profound experience lacking in diversity is superb, a trivial experience lacking in diversity is merely commonplace.[14] In this way, Hartshorne's diagram of aesthetic value provides a powerful tool for conceiving of Whitehead's rich and complex notion of beauty. This diagram particularly highlights the importance of effective contrast, which, as we have seen, is crucial to the major form of beauty. Beauty depends upon the optimal contrast between diversity and unity, on the vertical dimension, and complexity and simplicity, on the horizontal dimension. "On both dimensions, (1) chaos versus monotony, (2) the profound versus the superficial, beauty is the golden mean, balanced between excess of unity and excess of variety, between excess of depth and excess of superficiality."[15] Thus, an occasion is more or less beautiful depending on its success in achieving the most effective contrast between maximally diversified unity and the maximum balanced complexity. Put more simply, an individual is beautiful to a greater or lesser degree depending on the depth of its harmony and intensity.

Comparative Beauty

This analysis suggests that, in addition to the vertical dimension of harmony and the horizontal dimension of intensity, we need also to distinguish a third dimension of beauty that enables us to compare the relative intensity and harmony of the beauty achieved across individuals. That is, we can say that an individual is not only more or less beautiful than it could have been, but also more or less beautiful than another. This conclusion may be understood in terms of Aristotle's statement that the mean of virtue is not a fixed, mathematical mean, but a mean relative to the individual. There is the famous example of Milo the wrestler who needs to eat more than the average adult. As Hartshorne notes in "The Aesthetic Matrix of Value," this same logic can be applied to Whitehead's conception of beauty. He notes that the scope or "diameter" of the inner circle will be greater or lesser relative to the level of organization of the individual involved.[16] The greater the level of organization, the wider the circle. Hartshorne gives the example of the difference in the beauty achieved by a bird song and a symphony. Because of a symphony's greater level of organization and the greater scope of beauty that this opens, it potentially has a greater depth of beauty than even the most complex of bird songs (see figures 2 and 3). Thus, Hartshorne concludes, "For a bird, a symphony is hopelessly profound; for a human being, some bird songs are almost hopelessly superficial."[17]

Whitehead provides a very different example to illustrate this second point. He suggests that an electron that resides inside a living organism has the potential for a greater depth (scope) of beauty, than an electron outside an organism. "The electron blindly runs

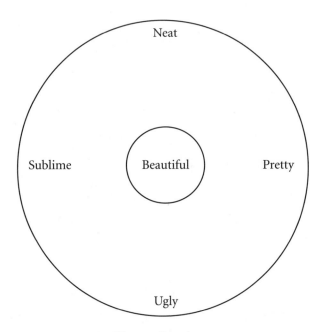

Figure 2. Symphony

within or without the body; but it runs within the body in accordance with its character within the body; that is to say, in accordance with the general plan of the body, and this plan includes the mental state" (SMW, 79). It may help to explain this example in terms of Whitehead's notion of subjective aim outlined in chapter 1. The subjective aim represents the ideal of what each occasion could become. The scope of the subjective aim varies according to the social environments in which the individual finds itself. Thus, an electron that is nested within a living body has a subjective aim with a greater breadth of possibility than one in a less complex environment. Thus the intensity of the beauty experienced by the occasions that comprise an electron outside a living body would be of a lesser degree than that of the occasions that comprise an electron within a living body. Thus, the "scope" of an individual's potential

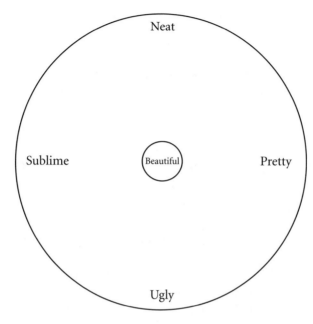

Figure 3. Bird Song

is largely a function of its environment. The truth of this relation is known all too well by the tens of millions of starving people around the world who, due to material want, are unable to realize even a fraction of their potential.

The point is that just as for Aristotle the mean of virtue is relative to the individual, for Whitehead the depth of beauty and value open to an individual (its real potentiality) is relative to its level of organization, and this organization depends on the social environments in which it finds itself. In this way, Whitehead affirms what Ferré aptly refers to as a "multidimensional continuum of aesthetic value."[18] Whitehead's aesthetic axiology is a continuum in that there are no absolute gaps. Beauty and value may be more or less, but never zero. But it is not a flat continuum. Rather, it is complex and multidimensional.[19] Strictly speaking, the kinds and types of beauty are as numerous as the modes of togetherness. Thus, along the third dimension of beauty runs a multidimensional continuum of beauty and value ranging from the exceedingly trivial and simple to the profoundly complex.

From this notion of grades of beauty and value, Whitehead draws an important (and for some, troubling) conclusion regarding the "ranking" of individuals. Whitehead contends, "Perfection at a low level ranks below Imperfection with higher aim. A mere qualitative Harmony within an experience comparatively barren of objects of high significance is a debased type of Harmony, tame, vague, deficient in outline and intention" (AI, 264). Interestingly, in *Science and the Modern World*, Whitehead says that this interplay of lower success and higher failure is essentially the problem of evolution:

> The problem of evolution is the development of enduring harmonies of enduring shapes of value, which merge into higher attainments of things beyond themselves. Aesthetic attainment is interwoven in the texture of realisation. The endurance of an entity represents the attainment of a limited aesthetic success, though if we look beyond it to its external effects, it may represent an aesthetic failure. Even within itself, it may represent the conflict between a lower success and a higher failure. The conflict is the presage of disruption. (SMW, 94)[20]

The problem of evolution, of course, is the development of the more complex from the less complex. In this sense, Whitehead means that the endurance of an entity, say, a boulder, represents the attainment of a limited aesthetic success—that is, it achieves the beauty open to it—but, taken in a wider context, it may represent an aesthetic failure. If boulders were the highest form of organization, the earth would be a much less beautiful place. Evolution aims at higher, more organized forms of beauty and experience. However, the aim at higher forms of experience is not without its perils, for such flights of novelty greatly increase the possibility of failure. Endurance and repetition are safe; life and novelty are precarious. For Whitehead, a higher failure may rank above a lower success. However, note that the "failure" and "success" to which Whitehead refers is ontological, not moral. As I will argue in part 2, according to the ethics of creativity as I construe it, an individual's ontological status does not directly constitute its moral worth. Accordingly, although, ontologically speaking, an imperfection at a higher level may rank above a perfection at a lower level, this may not be true morally speaking. I will illustrate this by means of a simple comparison between two macroscopic individuals: say, a pine tree and a boulder.

In general, because of its greater level of organization, the subjective aims of the occasions comprising a pine tree have a greater depth of beauty and value open to them than the occasions comprising a boulder. Accordingly, Whitehead would conclude that, in general, a pine tree represents a higher grade of beauty and value than the boulder, which, in terms of the functional taxonomy outlined in chapter 3, is essentially an aggregate entity. However, let us say that because our pine tree is struggling to grow between two boulders on the side of a steep cliff, its growth has been severely stunted. Thus, its environment has inhibited it from achieving its potential. Yet, even in this example, Whitehead would contend that the imperfect achievement of the pine tree "ranks above" the perfection achieved by the boulders that surround it. That is, Whitehead is claiming that even if the pine tree is unable to fully realize its potential beauty, the beauty it does achieve is still greater than a boulder that fully realizes all of the beauty open to it. Put in terms of the Aesthetic Circle, this is to say that, compared to the pine tree, the inner circle of beauty available to the boulder would have a relatively small diameter.

However, both critics and Whiteheadians alike often forget that although Whitehead affirms that entities may be graded by the depth of beauty they achieve, contrary to many traditional ontological hierarchies, an individual's position in this abstract hierarchy does not directly translate into moral worth. As we will see in part 2, whether one individual's interests are to be preferred over another's is not simply a function of their ontological complexity. Rather, for Whitehead what is preferable is a state of affairs that achieves the most harmonious and intense beauty in the situation *taken as a whole*. The potential depth of an occasion's beauty does not neatly translate into its moral worth. Hence, those individuals with greater complexity and beauty should not necessarily be given preference over those individuals with less complexity and beauty.

> The hermit thrush and the nightingale can produce sound of the utmost beauty. But they are not civilized beings. They lack ideas of adequate generality respecting their own actions and the world around them. Without doubt the higher animals entertain notions, hopes, and fears. And yet they lack civilization by reason of the deficient generality of their mental functionings. . . . Civilization is more than all these; and in moral worth it can be less than all these. (MT, 3–4)[21]

I leave a fuller defense of this conclusion to later chapters. What is important here is that, although we are advancing a multidimensional continuum of value and beauty, this scale does not have the same relation to morality as it does in, for instance, natural law theory. This is not to say that aesthetics plays an insignificant role in the ethics of creativity. Indeed, insofar as every form of process, including the actions of moral agents, aims at the achievement of beauty, the world is good only when it is beautiful (AI, 268). In this sense, aesthetics can act as a bridge from the metaphysics of creativity to the ethics of creativity.

First let us turn to an analysis of how and why achievements of beauty are so often maimed and destroyed. That is, we must investigate the role of ugliness and evil in the world. Such an analysis is necessary not merely because of the logical symmetry that it would bring, but also because a degree of discord or tragedy is integral to the achievement of a truly beautiful experience.

Ugliness and Evil

Anesthesia and Violence

Whitehead's conception of ugliness is a direct result of his view that the ideal of every process is the attainment of the greatest beauty possible. Accordingly, to the extent that an individual falls short of achieving the beauty of experience open to it relative to what it could have been, it is ugly and evil. In *Adventures of Ideas*, Whitehead distinguishes between two types of ugliness, both of which stem from a form of inhibition or frustration: (1) "anesthesia," which involves the frustration of greater possibilities by the interposition of lesser achievements, and (2) "aesthetic destruction," which involves the active destruction and inhibition of past achievements of beauty.[22] Since in a certain sense anesthesia is also a form of aesthetic destruction, I will refer to the latter form of ugliness as "violence."

Anesthesia results from an individual's failure to act on opportunities that would increase the depth of its beauty.[23] The problem of anesthesia arises because, as Ferré notes, it "embraces the status quo too tightly. It may do so in the name of protecting its own sort of beauty, but compared to what it prevents, its beauty is relatively ugly. Such grosser beauty stands in the way of finer beauty, something 'better,' either morally or nonmorally understood."[24] Thus, anesthesia is that form of ugliness that inhibits or frustrates greater forms of beauty from being achieved by the interposition of lesser forms. Of course, because every form of experience has some degree of beauty and value, an attenuated achievement is evil in comparison to what might have been achieved. This does not diminish the inherent tragedy of such loss.

Whereas anesthesia involves the squandering of higher forms of beauty owing to inaction, the ugliness of violence involves the active destruction or defacement of achieved forms of beauty.[25] "It is the violence of strength against strength" (AI, 276). Interestingly, however, Whitehead notes that violence is not an evil for the actual occasions destroyed. For having been destroyed, they are strictly speaking no longer in existence. The evil of violence, Whitehead explains, "lies in the loss to the social environment" (RM, 97). This interpretation of violence brings Whitehead to an interesting conclusion: "Evil in itself leads to the world losing forms of attainment in which that evil manifests itself. . . . Thus evil promotes its own elimination by destruction, or degradation, or by elevation. But in its own nature it is unstable" (RM, 96). Whitehead's insight is that violence and force tend to be self-defeating in that they undermine the very social structures that make them possible. For instance, in *Science and the Modern World*, Whitehead gives an example of a species of microbes which, in killing its host, ultimately destroys itself. A more dramatic example of Whitehead's point may be humanity's wanton destruction of the environment. For by undermining those very systems that make higher forms of order possible, such violence will, if left unchecked, surely result in the destruction of most higher forms of life on this planet. Whitehead's point, then, is that "in the history of the world, the prize has not gone to those species which specialised in methods of violence, or even in defensible armour. . . . There is something in the ready use of force which defeats its own object" (SMW, 206).[26] The ugliness of violence is inherently unstable and in the end self-defeating. This claim takes on a special urgency in this post–September 11 world of instability and violence, where scores of individuals willingly sacrifice their lives for a cause and governments wage preemptive wars.

Given the destructive force of violence, one may be surprised to find that Whitehead suggests that violence is often preferable to anesthesia. "Harmony is bound up with the preservation of the individual significance of detail, and Discord [or violence] consists in its destruction. In Discord there is always frustration. But even Discord may be preferable to a feeling of slow relapse into general anæsthesia, or into tameness which is its prelude" (AI, 264). Why might this be? For Whitehead, since the creative advance aims at achieving beauty through the unending process of the many becoming one and being increased by one until the "crack of doom" (PR, 228), the static maintenance of perfection or beauty that anesthesia seeks is not possible. That is, in a processive cosmos, the only live options are advance or decay (AI, 274). Hence, the conservativism of general anesthesia is even more objectionable than violence because, in frustrating the introduction of greater forms of beauty, "the pure conservative is fighting against the essence of the universe" (AI, 274). Note, however, that Whitehead is not attacking all forms of conservativism. A healthy conservativism is essential to provide the stable environments necessary for great forms of beauty. Thus Whitehead rejects only obstructionist forms of conservativism.[27] Nevertheless, it is ironic that this sort of obstructionist conservativism often attempts to justify itself as a defender of morality. "Of course," Whitehead notes in an uncharacteristically harsh passage, "it is true that the defense of morals is the battle-cry which best rallies stupidity against change. Perhaps countless ages ago respectable amœbæ refused to migrate from ocean to dry land —refusing in defence of morals. One incidental service of art to society lies in its adventurousness" (AI, 268). Indeed, as we will see in later chapters, the ethics of creativity does not aim at a static or abstract moral law; moral philosophy must be as dynamic and fluid as the cosmos itself.

Whitehead's construction of the two forms of ugliness as being evil relative to what could have been achieved (anesthesia) on the one hand, and what has been achieved (violence) on the other, is surprisingly similar to St. Augustine's conception of evil. A brief comparison between Whitehead's conception of evil and Augustine's will begin to reveal the role of the divine in Whitehead's aesthetics and ethics.

In his attempt to counter the Manichaean conception of evil as an independent reality, Augustine argues that every form of being is good to some degree and that, therefore, evil arises from those things that "suffer privation of some good."[28] Whitehead's conception of evil as a relative frustration of beauty is surprisingly similar to this formulation.[29] For both Augustine and Whitehead, evil does not exist in its own right, but is relative to what should have been achieved. Furthermore, both contend that defining evil as a relative lack does not mean that evil does not have positive consequences. Augustine could have written the following passage from Whitehead's *Religion in the Making*: "Evil, triumphant in its enjoyment, is so far good in itself; but beyond itself it is evil in its character of a destructive agent among things greater than itself. In the summation of the more complete fact it has secured a descent towards nothingness, in contrast to the creativeness of what can without qualification be termed good. Evil is positive and destructive" (RM, 95).[30]

Whitehead's reference to "the summation of a more complete fact" introduces a further similarity between himself and Augustine. For in addition to his theory of evil as privation, Augustine also employs an aesthetic theory of evil. According to this view, what appears to be evil when seen in isolation or seen from a narrow perspective is, in fact, a necessary element in a universe that, viewed as a totality from the divine perspective, is wholly good. Hence, lower forms of existence are not evil. Rather, all contribute in different ways to the perfection of the universe. For Augustine, this conclusion applies to both natural entities and moral entities. That is, it applies to natural evil and moral evil. According to Augustine's aesthetic theory of evil, natural evil, such as disease or natural disasters, which may seem evil from a limited human perspective, is from the divine perspective ultimately a necessary part of a maximally beautiful universe. Similarly, in the context of moral evil, Augustine argues that the universe is better or more beautiful in its inclusion of free beings, even if this freedom leads to actions that are evil.[31]

It is important to qualify to what extent Whitehead subscribes to the classical distinction between moral and natural evil. Although he never does so explicitly, Whitehead could have employed the distinction between moral evil and natural evil. For those individuals that lack sufficient complexity for meaningful freedom, the inhi-bition and frustration caused by cross-purposes could accurately be labeled natural evil. On the other hand, for those individuals who, owing to the presence in them of a personally ordered struc-tured society, are sufficiently conscious and free to choose between various possible courses of action, to the extent that such an indi-vidual's actions are violent or anesthetic, these actions are, relative to what could have been achieved, morally evil. This helps to clar-ify the following passage from Whitehead's *Religion in the Making*:

> Good people of narrow sympathies are apt to be unfeeling and unprogressive, enjoying their egotistical goodness. Their case, on a higher level, is analogous to that of the man completely degraded to a hog. They have reached a state of stable goodness, so far as their own interior life is concerned. This type of moral correcti-tude is, on a larger view, so like evil that the distinction is trivial. (RM, 98)

Egoistic people who focus only on their own "narrow sympathies" are not purely evil; they have achieved a sort of "stable goodness, so far as their own interior life is concerned." But, in comparison to the level of beauty they could and should have achieved, their level of experience is evil.

> A hog is not an evil beast, but when a man is degraded to the level of a hog, with the accompanying atrophy of finer elements, he is no more evil than a hog. The evil of the final degradation lies in the comparison of what is with what might have been. During the process of degradation the comparison is an evil for the man himself, and at its final stage it remains an evil for others. (RM, 97)

Though he may validly employ the distinction between moral and natural evil, Whitehead would not embrace the ontological pre-supposition on which this distinction rests. As with the distinction between moral agents and moral patients, Whitehead would not affirm that there is an absolute gulf between beings with a free and eternal soul and those without. Unlike Augustine, Whitehead understands difference in a kalogenic cosmos in terms of degrees of beauty, value, and organization, rather than degrees of being; though undoubtedly more complex, human beings are just as natural as anything else. Thus, like the concepts of "substance" and "kind," the distinction between natural and moral evil is a useful abstraction, not an ontological distinction.

Peace and the Role of the Divine

This conclusion introduces a further level of contrast between Whitehead's and Augustine's views of evil: namely, the role of the divine. One of the most significant differences between Whitehead and Augustine is the final status of evil in relation to the divine. According to Augustine's aesthetic theory, the evil of fragmentary purposes is ultimately not seen as evil from the divine perspective. Hence, for instance, disease and disaster only *seem* to be evil from our limited perspective, but, from the divine perspective, they are necessary for the achievement of the most beautiful whole. For Whitehead, on the other hand, the loss of aesthetic attainment due to cross-purposes is irrevocably tragic. Perhaps for this reason Whitehead chooses very different images to describe God. In contradistinction to Augustine and much of classical theism, Whitehead conceives of God not as the ultimate judge but as "the great companion—fellow-sufferer who understands" (PR, 351). Significantly, this image of God effects an important change in the role that God plays in world process.

Whereas, according to Augustine and classical theism, beauty and goodness are primarily explained by God's role as creator, in process thought it is the individual occasions of experience that are responsible for the achievement of beauty. However, this is not to say that God plays no role in world process. For Whitehead, God affects the world in the capacity of a lure toward the ideal coordination of harmony and intensity. Put differently, God is the individual responsible for the universe's aim at the achievement of

beauty.[32] In *Science and the Modern World*, Whitehead characterizes God's role as a lure toward perfection: "It is always there, and
it has the power of love presenting the one purpose whose fulfill-
ment is eternal harmony. Such order as we find in nature is never
force—it presents itself as the one harmonious adjustment of complex detail" (SMW, 192).[33] God is efficacious in the world, therefore, by being a lure toward ever greater, more beautiful forms of
order. In *Adventures of Ideas*, Whitehead refers to God's role as the
vision of "eternal harmony" in terms of "peace" or the "Harmony
of Harmonies" (AI, 285–86). In the context of moral agents, the intuition of peace acts as an impetus to move away from the evils of
egoism and narrow sympathies. Accordingly, in inspiring the intuition of peace, God is efficacious in the lives of moral agents:

> God is that function in the world by reason of which our purposes
> are directed to ends which in our own consciousness are impartial
> as to our interests. He is that element in life in virtue of which
> judgment stretches beyond facts of existence to values of exis-
> tence. He is that element in virtue of which our purposes extend
> beyond values for ourselves to values for others. He is that ele-
> ment in virtue of which the attainment of such a value for others
> transforms itself into value for ourselves. (RM, 158)

The intuition of peace takes us beyond our own "narrow sympathies" to an understanding of the immensity of things. Peace is
"the removal of the stress of acquisitive feeling arising from the
soul's preoccupation with itself. Thus Peace carries with it a surpassing of personality" (AI, 285).[34] The power of the divine, then,
is in being "persuasive toward an ideal coordination" (IM, 694).
Although we have no infallible access to this divine perspective,
with James I would argue that the very postulation of God serves
to "let loose" in us what James calls the "strenuous mood" or "moral
energy."[35] Thus, God affects world process by inspiring us to reject
our own narrow, egoistic commitments and strive instead for the
most inclusive perspective possible. This is what Whitehead calls

in *Religion in the Making* the moment of "religious consciousness," which "starts from self-valuation, but it broadens into the concept of the world as a realm of adjusted values, mutually intensifying or mutually destructive" (RM, 59–60).[36]

This introduces a final point that has up to now been largely omitted: while we have examined at length the value an individual has for itself (intrinsic value) and for others (instrumental value), we have not explicitly discussed an individual's value for the whole. For Whitehead, the individual's value for the whole is its religious value. This may be understood in two interrelated senses. First, the value an individual has for the whole corresponds to the value experience that each individual adds to the "consequent nature of God" or that aspect of God that is in ongoing temporal relationship with the world. But an individual's value for the whole also concerns the ideal relative to each individual that would achieve the perfection of beauty and value open to it. In *Religion in the Making*, Whitehead refers to this as "world-loyalty." "This principle is not a dogmatic formulation, but the intuition of immediate occasions as failing or succeeding in reference to the ideal relevant to them. There is rightness attained or missed, with more or less completeness of attainment or omission" (RM, 61–62). Thus, the individual's value for the whole corresponds to the ideal relative to it or its subjective aim. Note, however, that an individual's value for the whole is not, properly understood, opposed to its value for itself and for others. The moment of religious consciousness is the recognition that the value of the individual and the whole are not truly opposed. It is a recognition of the world as "a community derivative from the interrelations of its component individuals, and also necessary for the existence of each of these individuals" (RM, 59). It is in this sense that I understand Whitehead's statement, "Morality of outlook is inseparably conjoined with generality of outlook. The antithesis between the general good and the individual interest can be abolished only when the individual is such that its interest is the general good, thus exemplifying the loss of the minor intensities in order to find them again with finer composition in a wider sweep of interest" (PR, 15).

Thus, God and the ideal of peace play crucial roles in my project. Far from inert abstractions, they instill within us the strenuous mood and the moral energy needed to face the tragedy of the world not with skepticism, but with the constancy of character needed to "seek incessantly, with fear and trembling, so to vote and to act as to bring about the very largest total universe of good which we can see."[37]

2

A Genuine Ethical Universe

5

A Whiteheadian Aesthetics
of Morals

The metaphysical doctrine, here expounded, finds the foundations of the world in the aesthetic experience, rather than
—as with Kant—in the cognitive and conceptive experience. All order is therefore aesthetic order, and the moral
order is merely certain aspects of aesthetic order. The actual world is the outcome of the aesthetic order, and the
aesthetic order is derived from the immanence of God.

Alfred North Whitehead, *Religion in the Making*

THE VIEW THAT world process is inherently kalogenic or beauty
creating has a profound effect on the shape of any would-be Whiteheadian moral philosophy.[1] As we see in the passage above, insofar
as aesthetic experience is the foundation of world process, all order,
including the moral order, is ultimately an aspect of aesthetic order.
It is in this sense that we should understand Whitehead's claim
that "the real world is good when it is beautiful" (AI, 268). The relation between what is good and what is beautiful provides an important clue as to how to develop a Whiteheadian moral philosophy.
Insofar as something is only as good as it is beautiful, the complex
conditions of a beautiful experience are also the conditions of a

moral experience. In a sense, then, ethics must, as Hartshorne put it, "lean upon aesthetics." For "the only good that is intrinsically good, good in itself, is good experience, and the criteria for this are aesthetic."[2]

The aim of this chapter is to establish the ideal of the ethics of creativity by examining the kalogenic structure of reality as the source and foundation of moral obligation. However, before beginning to develop such an ethic, we must first confront two related criticisms that arise because of the constitutive relation between beauty and goodness: (1) in founding reality on value experience, any Whiteheadian moral philosophy is ultimately a subjectivistic moral interest theory; and (2) in reducing ethics to aesthetics, such a theory is guilty of a vicious aestheticism. Both of these objections were first advanced in 1941 by Paul Arthur Schilpp in "Whitehead's Moral Philosophy," a contribution to the Library of Living Philosophers volume dedicated to Whitehead. Schilpp's essay is an apt point of departure for our investigation because it set the tone for nearly all subsequent analyses of the moral dimension of Whitehead's thought. (I will limit my exposition of Schilpp's arguments to those that serve as the context for those analyses.)

Morality as a Species of Process

Schilpp's argument is twofold. First, in grounding his ethics in the psychic processes of value judgments, which are themselves largely emotionally dominated and controlled,[3] Whitehead not only establishes a foundation for morals that is "treacherously thin,"[4] but also makes importance equivalent to "interest."[5] For this reason, Schilpp suggests, "Whitehead's moral philosophy could well be classed among the so-called 'moral interest theories.'"[6] Second, although Schilpp agrees that both ethics and aesthetics "fall into the field of value-judgments and value-experience, and that both make use of ideal abstractions,"[7] this similarity is not a sufficient reason for subsuming the one (ethics) under the other (aesthetics). There are "sufficient differences, both of kind and in number, between the two types of value judgment and value experience to warrant a rather precise method of differing analysis, procedure, and conclusion for the two areas."[8] Because Schilpp conceives of substantial differences between ethics and aesthetics, it would be a "disastrous reduction" to subsume ethics under aesthetics. "After all," Schilpp argues, "morality is not beauty, though the moral life—like a lot of other things—may be beautiful; but it is not the fact that it is beautiful which makes it moral."[9]

Before examining Schilpp's claims directly, I will first introduce Lynne Belaief's attempt in *Toward a Whiteheadian Ethics* to circumvent Schilpp's objections.[10] Belaief insists that Whitehead's use of aesthetic categories in ethical contexts is merely metaphorical. She writes, "I suggest that the apparent identity of ethical concepts with the basic aesthetic analysis is only apparent, Whitehead [is] being intentionally metaphorical when using the language of aesthetics to apply to ethical phenomena, except in the justifiable case when he is discussing the generic origin of moral experience."[11] This attempt to defuse Schilpp's arguments by claiming that Whitehead's references to aesthetics are merely rhetorical is greatly problematic. I intend to demonstrate to the contrary that Whitehead's use of aesthetic categories in reference to ethics is an extension of the fundamental metaphysical principles at work in the universe. To make ethics anything other than a species of aesthetics is to make it into an inexplicable aberration. Both Belaief's and Schilpp's positions ultimately fall short because of their uncritical acceptance of and dependence on the classical interpretation's reading of the nature and aim of process.

Let us begin with Schilpp's first contention that Whitehead's conception of importance results in a subjectivistic moral interest theory. He derives this argument from Whitehead's definition of morality as "the control of process so as to maximize importance"

(MT, 13). However, in a passage that occurs several pages before this definition, Schilpp misinterprets both the scope and depth of Whitehead's notion of importance in limiting it to interest: "Importance is a generic notion which has been obscured by the overwhelming prominence of a few of its innumerable species. The terms *morality, logic, religion, art*, have each of them been claimed as exhausting the whole meaning of importance. Each of them denotes a subordinate species. But the genus stretches beyond any finite group of species" (MT, 11).[12] First, insofar as he sees morality, logic, religion, and art as merely a handful of the "innumerable species" of importance, it is evident that Whitehead uses the term in a much wider and more fundamental sense than mere "interest." Whitehead explicitly states as much: "There are two aspects to importance; one based on the unity of the Universe, the other on the individuality of the details. The word *interest* suggests the latter aspect; the word *importance* leans toward the former" (MT, 8). Given critics' claims to the contrary, it is ironic that Whitehead intentionally chooses the term "importance" *because* it emphasizes the unity of the universe. Moreover, it is crucial to note that Whitehead defines importance by reference to both the "unity of the Universe" and "the individuality of the details." This directly contradicts Schilpp's claim that Whitehead's emphasis on importance limits morality to the interests of individuals alone. Consequently, it is inappropriate to classify it as a subjectivistic moral interest theory.

This conclusion clarifies the sense in which morality is a species of process, as well as Schilpp's misinterpretation of Whitehead. Indeed, what most commentators miss is that Whitehead defines morality as the control of process so as to maximize importance: "The generic aim of process is the attainment of importance, in that species and to that extent which in that instance is possible" (MT, 12). Morality, then, is but one species of the process of the universe, the whole of which aims at the attainment of importance. With this conclusion, the relation of Whitehead's aesthetics and ethics also begins to become clear.

In my initial presentation of Whitehead's conception of aesthetics and its relation to metaphysics, I argued that because every process aims at the achievement of beauty, Whitehead's metaphysics is also an aesthetics. If we juxtapose the above passage with earlier statements on aesthetics, we also see that importance and beauty are essentially equivalent. For both importance and beauty are appealed to as the ultimate aim of world process. Recall that the discussion of Whitehead's aesthetics in chapter 4 included the claim that the teleology of the universe is directed toward the production of beauty. Now we find Whitehead making the claim that the general aim of process is the attainment of importance in that species and to whatever extent is possible in each situation. Hence, both importance and beauty are described at different times as the ultimate aim of the universe. In this context we should understand Whitehead's claim that "all order is therefore aesthetic order, and the moral order is merely certain aspects of aesthetic order. The actual world is the outcome of the aesthetic order, and the aesthetic order is derived from the immanence of God" (RM, 105). Whitehead's statement that the aesthetic order is derived from the immanence of God should not be interpreted as implying that all experience is only about achieving value experience for God. Every achievement of value is for the entity itself, for others in its community, and, ultimately, for the whole. (We should keep this in mind when examining Clare Palmer's criticisms of process theology's doctrine of contributionism in chapter 7.)

However, by making morality a species of process, a process that aims at the achievement of beauty, do we not agree with those critics who suggest that Whitehead is guilty of aestheticism? That is, if every process aims at the achievement of beauty, if importance and beauty are equivalent, and if morality is but a species of process, then doesn't Whitehead thereby reduce morality to aesthetics, as Schilpp contends?

As with the problem of subjectivism, the answer to these questions ultimately lies in how one interprets Whitehead's metaphysics.

Like most commentators, Schilpp examines Whitehead's definition of morality by focusing almost entirely on what he means by importance, to the nearly complete neglect of his notion of process. However, insofar as the "maximization of importance" aimed at in morality is made possible only by the "control of process," we must return to our examination of Whitehead's notion of process. If we interpret his metaphysics properly, the relation of Whitehead's ethical theory to his aesthetico-metaphysics will be made apparent. Thus, let us again examine Whitehead's definition of morality in terms of the two competing interpretations of Whitehead's metaphysics: the classical interpretation and the ecstatic interpretation.

As we established in chapter 2, for the classical interpretation, activity, creativity, and actuality are limited to concrescence, to subjectivity. Insofar as this interpretation limits actuality to the subject, it also limits importance and value to the subject. "A concretum has significance—meaning and importance—not for itself but only for something other than itself: namely, the subsequent concrescences which causally objectified it."[13] How does this interpretation of process and importance affect our understanding of Whitehead's definition of morality as the control of process so as to maximize importance? If, following the classical interpretation, process is cast in terms of an ontologized distinction between the subject and the superject, and if the maximization of importance is solely a matter of the decision of the subject, it is no wonder that Schilpp concludes that Whitehead's is a moral interest theory that reduces ethics to aesthetics. In fact, as argued in chapter 2, if all importance is relative solely to the subject, an ethics of creativity is not only a moral interest theory, it is more nearly a moral solipsism.

What are the implications for a Whiteheadian moral philosophy under the ecstatic interpretation, particularly as it is defended in Jones's ontology of intensity? It would seem that, by making the aim of process the attainment of aesthetic intensity, Jones would be forced to affirm a subjectivist form of ethics and aesthetics. However, as the following passage suggests, not only is Jones aware of

the subjectivist and even solipsistic flavor often given to Whitehead's moral philosophy, she believes that her own ecstatic interpretation avoids these problems:

> The standard problem of subjectivism is held to be particularly
> acute in a scheme such as Whitehead's, since the scheme founds
> reality on subjects whose immediate aims suggest the extreme pos-
> sibility of the most vicious and aestheticist moral solipsism. I hope
> that the concept of ecstatic individuality, founded on a thorough
> understanding of intensity, has already begun in the reader's mind
> to circumvent such a subjectivism, solipsism, or egoism. Since the
> subject is wherever its effects are, and in a nonderivative ontolog-
> ical sense, subjectivism in the solipsistic or egoistic sense is not an
> option, or at least not the primary form of moral experience de-
> rivable from the atomism.[14]

While the ecstatic interpretation undermines the axiological assumptions of Schilpp's position, one may still ask why, if the ecstatic
interpretation grants that the aim of process is the attainment of
aesthetic intensity, is it not subject to a "vicious and aestheticist
moral solipsism"?

To answer this question, let us examine the definition of morality in light of the ecstatic interpretation. Recall that because the
classical interpretation limits all activity, and thereby all control of
process, to the subject, it also restricts all importance to the "interests" of the concrescing subject. Proponents of this view would cite
in their defense this statement by Whitehead: "Actuality is the
self-enjoyment of importance" (MT, 117). The classical interpretation focuses on passages such as this because they seem to limit both
actuality and importance to the subject. But is this really the case?
Is Whitehead limiting self-enjoyment, and thereby actuality and
importance, to the concrescing subject alone? According to the
ecstatic interpretation, this cannot be true. In stark contrast to the
classical interpretation, the ecstatic interpretation contends that
we cannot isolate the subject from the superject and, therefore, we

cannot limit activity or importance solely to the subject. Everything, including the superject's objective functioning in another, is in some sense active and self-important.[15] Thus, the ecstatic interpretation extends importance to the actual occasion as a whole, as subject-superject. Interestingly, if we take the above statement in its larger context, we find corroboration for this interpretation: "But the sense of importance is not exclusively referent to the experiencing self. It is exactly this vague sense which differentiates itself into the disclosure of the whole, the many, and the self. . . . Actuality is the self-enjoyment of importance. But this self-enjoyment has the character of *self-enjoyment of others* melting into the enjoyment of the one self" (MT, 117–18, emphasis added). Contrary to the classical interpretation, to which Schilpp seems to adhere, importance is not exclusively referent to the subject or experiencing self. Rather, self-enjoyment is marked by the fusing of the self-enjoyment of others into the "enjoyment of the one self." Thus, the "others" to which this refers are past actual occasions that are themselves in some sense self-enjoying. Every individual has value for itself, for others, and for the whole. This conclusion brings us to an important point: namely, the relation between importance and value.

As with importance and beauty, which we have found to be co-extensive, importance and value are also ontologically equivalent. This equivalence is clearly demonstrated by juxtaposing several key passages from Whitehead's *Modes of Thought*. First, Whitehead uses both importance and value to describe what is attained by actuality. Compare, for instance, the following statements: "Our enjoyment of actuality is a realization of worth, good or bad. It is a value experience" (116); and "Actuality is the self-enjoyment of importance" (117). Second, both importance and value have the same triadic structure of self, other, whole: "But the sense of importance is not exclusively referent to the experiencing self. It is exactly this vague sense which differentiates itself into the disclosure of the whole, the many, and the self" (117); and "Everything has some value for itself, for others, and for the whole. This characterizes the meaning of actuality" (111). Third, Whitehead describes morality in terms of both value and importance: "Morality is the control of process so as to maximize importance" (13–14); and "Everything has some value for itself, for others, and for the whole. . . . By reason of this character, constituting reality, the conception of morals arises" (111). Thus, value and importance have the same structure and equally characterize morality and actuality. I therefore contend that value and importance are ontologically interchangeable.[16] Consequently, if morality aims at maximizing importance and importance is equivalent to value, it is valid to conclude that morality aims at maximizing value.

This conclusion is significant because if morality aims at the maximization of value, but value is understood to extend not merely to the self but to others (the past actual occasions in an occasion's actual world) and to the whole (the totality of achieved occasions), it becomes impossible to interpret Whitehead's moral philosophy as affirming a form of subjectivistic moral interest theory. The subject is not the arbiter of all value, as the classical interpretation suggests. Actual occasions have value for themselves, but in having self-value they also become a value for others and the whole. In Whitehead's words, "There must be value beyond ourselves. Otherwise every thing experienced would be merely barren detail in our own solipsist mode of existence" (MT, 102). As we saw in our discussion of the concept of peace, the perfection of beauty and importance at which every individual aims involves surpassing an individual's narrow self-interests. Thus, the very ideal and aim of process conflicts with Schilpp's theses.

This argument also reveals the true relation between Whitehead's moral philosophy and his aesthetics. Because the aim of the universe itself is at the attainment of beauty, importance, and value, morality must be a species of aesthetics, but in a nonreductive sense. For inasmuch as morality is simply a specialized species of process, it follows that the aim of morality is the same as that of process in general; again, the world is good only when it is beautiful (AI, 268). At this point my reasons for disagreeing with Belaief become most apparent. For if one were to suggest, as Belaief does, that Whitehead's use of aesthetic categories with ethical phenomena is merely metaphorical, then either one must deny that the universe aims at the achievement of beauty, or one must argue that the aim of ethics is different from the aim of process in general. Both of these conclusions are unintelligible, given Whitehead's project.

Moreover, given the rich and complex conception of beauty being defended, the fact that ethics is a species of aesthetics is in no way reductive. Let us pose this question to the critics, "Why is it reductive to make ethics a species of aesthetics?" I believe that the crux of arguments regarding the so-called reduction of ethics to aesthetics lies in Schilpp's simple objection, "After all, morality is not beauty, though the moral life—like a lot of other things—may be beautiful; but it is not the fact that it is beautiful which makes it moral."[17] Thus, it seems that it is reductive to subsume ethics under aesthetics because what is moral is broader than, or at least different from, what is beautiful. However, this statement portrays a greatly attenuated notion of aesthetics, wherein the independent subject is the arbiter of all value and importance. Yet, as I have taken great pains to suggest, Whitehead's aesthetics is not a matter of subjectivistic or solipsistic considerations. He is defining beauty, importance, and value in a far broader and richer way. Again, since the aim of the universe itself is at the attainment of beauty, importance, and value, morality must be a species of aesthetics, but in a nonreductive sense. Indeed, given such a view, it is not possible for something to be moral but not beautiful; for everything is beautiful to some degree.

Therefore, the ecstatic interpretation of Whitehead's aesthetic metaphysics, which requires that beauty, importance, and value be extended to the entire life of the actual occasion—as both subject and superject—makes it possible to affirm that Whitehead's ethics is a species of his aesthetics in a nonreductive sense. For to do so is simply to affirm that morality is a process that is continuous with the creative advance of the universe as a whole. Accordingly, in stark contrast to contemporary trends in moral philosophy, Whitehead seeks to reestablish the role of metaphysics (and by extension aesthetics) as the ground of morality. This conclusion has a dramatic, transformative effect on both the nature and limits of moral philosophy.

The Limits of Moral Philosophy

It had been less than thirty years since Lee surrendered to Grant, ending the Civil War, when William James delivered "The Moral Philosopher and the Moral Life" to the Yale Philosophical Club. In this provocative essay, James contends that the moral philosopher is ultimately distinguished from the skeptic, the relativist, and the absolutist by the ideal at which the philosopher aims and the strenuous mood instilled by that aim. For James, the aim of moral philosophy is to "find an account of the moral relations that obtain among things, which will weave them into the unity of a stable system, and make of the world what one may call a genuine universe from the ethical point of view."[18] However, the moral philosopher does not have the luxury of surveying the moral landscape from some elevated position; there is no Archimedean ethical point. The problem, as James was well aware, is that we are in a world where "every one of hundreds of ideals has its special champion already provided in the shape of some genius expressly born to feel it, and to fight to death in its behalf."[19] The force of this point was made brutally clear by the events of September 11, 2001. Given such a world, an ethic that is situated, but not grossly relativistic, is more important than ever. In this spirit, I am interested in investigating what James's ideal of a genuine ethical universe would look like through the lens of Whitehead's kalocentric panexperiential-ism. Since James himself embraced a form of panexperientialism at the end of his career, this comparison is particularly germane.[20]

In keeping with the fallibilistic stance toward truth and certainty that characterizes both pragmatist and process thought, James be-gins "The Moral Philosopher and the Moral Life" by baldly stat-ing his departure from established ethical theories: "The main purpose of this paper is to show that there is no such thing possible as an ethical philosophy dogmatically made up in advance."[21] Whitehead echoes James's sentiment when he argues in *Modes of Thought*, "There is no one behavior system belonging to the essen-tial character of the universe, as the universal moral ideal" (14). In sharp contrast to most modern ethical theories, then, James and Whitehead do not understand the task of moral philosophy to construct abstract moral laws. They agree that abstract principles have no place in moral philosophy for two interrelated reasons: (1) owing to our fallibility, it is not possible to know with absolute cer-tainty which state of affairs is to be preferred over another prior to a particular concrete situation; and (2) because of the dynamism of world process, every situation is, strictly speaking, ontologically unique. Let us examine each of these points.

Perhaps in the spirit of Socratic elenchus, it is standard proce-dure to test an ethical theory by posing various—often exaggerated —moral dilemmas. If an ethical theory is unable to neatly resolve a given dilemma, it is implied that it should be rejected whole cloth. Although testing the adequacy of proposed theories is itself a lauda-tory goal, from the fallibilist point of view, the motivation for this procedure often rests on the presupposition that moral inquiry leads to—or is in principle capable of—absolute certainty. Pragmatist and process philosophers, however, reject this notion of episte-mology, acknowledging that because absolute certainty is an un-realizable ideal, epistemological, and therefore moral, fallibility is inescapable. Thus, with James, we must acknowledge the limita-tions of moral philosophy imposed by the fallibility of human inquiry and not expect our moral theories to abstractly prescribe what ought or ought not to be done prior to a particular situation. As Aristotle recognized, "Our discussion will be adequate if it has as much clearness as the subject matter admits of; for precision is not to be sought for alike in all discussions, any more than in all the products of the crafts."[22] Unlike problems in mathematics, for example, every moral problem does not have a single indisputable answer existing prior to its solution that we need only divine and then codify in a moral law. Morality, like life, is inherently "messy."

James pushes this point even further when he argues that in fact "there can be no final truth in ethics any more than in physics."[23] Initially, this comparison may seem to imply the opposite of James's intention. Many in his audience at the Yale Philosophical Club must have regarded physics in particular and science in general as possessing absolutely certain truths. Given such a notion of physics, James's assertion of an isomorphism between physics and ethics would at best have seemed incongruous, and at worst scandalous.

The problem with this interpretation, James would contend, is that it embodies an attenuated notion of physics that is false. James's comparison is meant to promote the fact that moral inquiry is a species of inquiry in general and that all forms of inquiry are inherently fallible. Accordingly, the so-called laws of science are not infallible formulations exempt from development or revision; they are exceedingly probable formulations of observed regularities. As Whitehead notes, assuming the "unqualified stability of particular laws of nature and of particular moral codes is a primary illusion which has vitiated much philosophy" (MT, 13). Thus, although scientists may still use the language of "laws," few continue to perceive them as absolute, static formulations like Newton, for example.[24] If the last century's scientific discoveries have taught us anything, it should be that the "truths" of science are limited.[25]

In a sense, it is as if James and Whitehead are asking, "If we no longer believe physics contains 'final truths,' why should we find ethics to be any different?" Ethics, like every form of inquiry, is necessarily fallible. Of course, like Peirce, Dewey, and Whitehead, James recognizes that physics, like any other subject of investigation, no doubt possesses a great many truths. He is not denying that one account may be truer—more explanatorily adequate—than another; he denies that any of these "truths" could be called "final." In this context, I understand James's claim that "ethical science is just like physical science, and instead of being deducible all at once from abstract principles, must simply bide its time, and be ready to revise its conclusions from day to day." Put more succinctly, ethics, like physics, must "wait on facts."[26] Just as there is no final or absolute certainty in physics that allows us to make perfect predictions about future physical events, there is no final truth in ethics that allows us "dogmatically" to determine in advance the good in any particular situation. Like scientists who must wait and revise their conclusions on the basis of new evidence, to lead the moral life, we also must continually and resolutely revise our conclusions in light of the goods that we can at present see and resist the temptation to codify these conclusions in abstract moral laws. Whitehead states, "The codifications [of morality] carry us beyond our own direct immediate insights. They involve the usual judgments valid for the usual occasions in that epoch. They are useful, and indeed essential, for civilization. But we only weaken their influence by exaggerating their status" (MT, 14).[27]

In addition to the epistemological limitation placed on moral philosophy by our fallibility, there is a deeper, metaphysical justification for James's and Whitehead's rejection of moral philosophies dogmatically made up in advance. James hints at this view when he notes that, strictly speaking, every moral dilemma "is a universe without a precedent, and for which no adequate previous rule exists."[28] In the context of Whitehead's metaphysics of process, James's intuition regarding the metaphysical and moral uniqueness of every situation gains additional ontological teeth. For, as Whitehead argues in *Science and the Modern World*, strictly speaking, "nothing ever really recurs in exact detail. No two days are identical, no two winters. What has gone, has gone forever. Accordingly the practical philosophy of mankind has been to expect the broad recurrences, and to accept the details as emanating from the inscrutable womb of things beyond the ken of rationality. Men expected the sun to rise, but the wind bloweth where it listeth" (SMW, 5).[29] Strictly speaking, every situation is ontologically unique because every actual occasion brings together the diverse elements of its actual world in just this way, just here, and just now. Furthermore, because every situation is ontologically unique, it is also morally unique in the sense that the values obtainable in a situation are never strictly identical. Thus, in addition to the limits that our fallibility places on moral philosophy, given the ontological and moral uniqueness of every moral dilemma, we must be suspicious of any system that advances absolute moral codes or laws. In a processive cosmos, we must conceive of moral philosophy as a tentative and fallible formulation that "in the environment for which it is designed will promote the evolution of that environment towards its proper perfection" (AI, 292). Ethical theories, therefore, do not exist in an ahistorical vacuum. Any moral code that reaches beyond the environment for which it was designed, becomes, as Whitehead puts it, "a vacuous statement of abstract irrelevancies" (MT, 13). Once again, like science, morality must test its theories by actively seeking out and then incorporating new evidence.

Consequently, with George R. Lucas Jr. I find that that there can be no Archimedean ethical point; there is no "transcendental" privileged moral position outside of some cultural context rooted in some common life:

> When intuitionism, deontology, utilitarianism, and finally even emotivism are stripped of their Archimedean pretensions, we discover, as Hume apparently recognized, that there is no "transcendental" privileged moral position outside of some cultural context rooted in what Hume termed "the common life," or alternatively, in what MacIntyre identifies as narrative practices within the setting of a cultural tradition. Any attempt to get "outside of" or

"beyond" this situation is simply a fake—a covert smuggling of our particular cultural prejudices and dispositions into a theory of calculative rationality or "pure reason."[30]

Although human experience is the "inescapable context for whatever data we receive," the analysis of human experience discloses the status of values resident in the world.[31] In other words, to begin with human experience does not mean that we must end with human experience. The Whiteheadian metaphysics being advanced is concerned with elaborating the general structure of process as such; human experience is simply the exemplification of the general structure of process with which we are most familiar and to which we have the most access; the order of discovery does not dictate the order of being.

In abandoning the notion of a privileged Archimedean ethical point upon which we could leverage the world, we must recognize the situatedness of morality. "Morality is always the aim at that union of harmony, intensity, and vividness which involves the perfection of importance *for that occasion*" (MT, 13–14, emphasis added). In this way, we are affirming what may be called a "situated ethic": (1) it is situated in that what is morally appropriate will always be relative to the value and beauty present in and achievable through a given situation; and (2) it is situated in that it does not claim to be capable of extricating itself from the values of a given social context.

However, note that this does not amount to the affirmation of a gross relativism. As I will discuss in detail, what constitutes a moral or beautiful relation to one's world is not relative to one's own interests or even a culture's interests. Rather, what is moral will always be that action that achieves the maximum degree of harmony and intensity. Two things are relative: (1) the values that are potentially achievable, and (2) the moral agent's knowledge of those values. Again, morality must remain every bit as dynamic as reality itself.

With James, then, the ethics of creativity concludes that the honest embrace of the limits of moral inquiry forces us to admit that a moral philosophy in the "old-fashioned absolute sense of the term" is no longer possible.[32] Just as we have moved beyond the notion that nature's "laws" give us infallible access to natural processes, we must abandon dogmatic moral philosophies. In part, it is in this spirit—constructing a model of moral inquiry that appreciates our situatedness—that I present the ethics of creativity. Perhaps paradoxically, although James and Whitehead recognize the limits of moral philosophy, they do not abandon the possibility of a moral ideal as such. However, as we will see, it does drastically alter the status of such an ideal. Having recognized the limits of moral inquiry, let us turn to the ideal of the ethics of creativity.

The Ideal of a Genuine Ethical Universe

The Moral Philosopher in a Processive Cosmos

In "The Moral Philosopher and the Moral Life," James advances the bold idea that the ideal or aim of the moral life "is to find an account of the moral relations that obtain among things, which will weave them into the unity of a stable system, and make of the world what one may call a genuine universe from the ethical point of view."[33] Part 2 of this book is an attempt to formulate just such an account. At present, I am interested in investigating what James's ideal of a genuine ethical universe would look like through the lens of Whitehead's panexperientialism, a form of which James himself embraced at the end of his career.[34]

To achieve a genuine ethical universe by finding an account that weaves the moral relations between things into a unified, stable system, we must first determine which relations in an organic, processive cosmos are truly "moral relations." In other words, we must determine what the scope of direct moral concern would be in a processive cosmos and what impact this would have on our moral ideal. Once again, James locates the heart of the issue. Contrary to many conceptions of the good, the bad, and obligation, James contends that moral relations cannot "swing *in vacuo*." Rather, goodness, badness, and obligation must be concretely *"realized somewhere in order really to exist.*"[35] Good and bad must be felt by a particular individual in order to be real. To be more precise, it is only in being felt that good and bad are made real. In an important sense, James is advancing what may be called the moral correlate of Whitehead's ontological principle. Just as the ontological principle insists that "actual entities are the only *reasons*; so that to search for a *reason* is to search for one or more actual entities" (PR, 24), James's moral principle similarly insists that good and bad, better and worse, "must be *realized* in order to be real. If one ideal judgment be objectively better than another, that betterness must be made flesh by being lodged concretely in someone's perception. It cannot float in the atmosphere, for it is not a sort of meteorological phenomenon, like the aurora borealis or the zodiacal light."[36] This insight reveals the metaphysical basis of James's rejection of traditional moral theories. For given the moral principle that something is good or bad only if a particular individual feels it to be so, abstract moral laws are simply unintelligible. If abstract pronouncements regarding good and bad are to be real, they must be realized or felt as being good or bad by a particular individual, for example, God. However, in being the concrete demands of an individual, they may no longer be seen as abstract laws. Thus, James writes, "we have learned what the words 'good,' 'bad,' and 'obligation' severally mean. They mean no absolute natures, independent of personal support. They are objects of feeling and desire, which have no foothold or anchorage in Being, apart from the existence of actually living minds."[37] Taken in the context of Whitehead's philosophy of organism, how does this conclusion affect the scope of our direct moral concern?

Although Whitehead does not go as far as James's unguarded claim that "the whole universe . . . is everywhere alive and conscious,"[38] he does insist that there is nothing apart from the experience of subjects; nothing is a mere fact entirely devoid of feeling. Insofar as we repudiate the notion of vacuous actuality, everything —from the subatomic entity to the sequoia and from the snail to the human—is a unique subject of experience and center of value, everything has a good for it, everything we do fosters or frustrates the ends of another. Existence as such, no matter how small, weak, or insignificant, has value in and for itself, for others, and for the whole. Therefore, as a unique center of intrinsic value, no individual may be excluded from the scope of our direct moral concern. For if every individual is a unique subject of experience with intrinsic value, then everything to which a moral agent relates is at least a moral patient. That is, from the point of view of a moral agent, everything is an object of direct moral concern. Every relation into which we (human beings) enter, whether it be with another human being or with a pile of dung, is a moral relation; there are no "things" that are incapable of "moral relations."[39] Consequently, the scope of our direct moral concern may exclude nothing from its reach.

Inviolability and Moral Paralysis

Before examining the radical impact that this conclusion has for constructing an ethical theory, let us briefly examine two opposing objections that present themselves almost immediately if one affirms the intrinsic value of all of reality and the subsequent inclusion of every individual in the scope of our direct moral concern. It may be objected that either (1) Whitehead makes all values both equal and absolute, thereby putting the moral agent in a position of moral paralysis; or (2) he endangers the inviolability of humanity by making value a matter of degree.

According to the first objection, in affirming that everything in the universe has intrinsic value, Whitehead extends the scope of direct moral concern so as to include everything that exists. Everything from the most trivial occasion to God has intrinsic value.

However, an objector may note that in so doing Whitehead puts the moral agent, at best, in the position of having to choose arbitrarily between equally valuable but conflicting occasions or, at worst, in a position of moral paralysis, unable to choose one out of the sea of often mutually exclusive values. For if everything has intrinsic value and has it equally, then one must either make an arbitrary choice or do nothing at all.[40] One could object that if each option is presumably unsatisfactory, it is necessary to limit both intrinsic value and our moral concern to human beings or, perhaps, to sentient beings.

I contend that this objection is a result of an inability to extricate oneself from the metaphysical presuppositions of modern ethical theories. By rejecting these presuppositions, one also avoids their axiological implications. According to the model of individuality being advanced, all actual occasions are equal in *having* value, but we must also recognize that there are different grades of experience and, therefore, different grades of value and beauty. For the philosophy of organism, then, actuality is coextensive with value, but actuality itself is differentiated by degrees of complexity of organization—that is, by different degrees of beauty. In chapter 6, I will examine the effect of this conclusion on the practical employment of the ideal of the ethics of creativity. For now, it is sufficient simply to note that while everything is equal in having value, everything does not have value equally.[41]

This conclusion leads directly to the second objection, namely, that Whitehead's notion of a multidimensional continuum of beauty and value cannot support our intuition regarding the inviolability of human beings. Unlike the first, this objection does not arise from a misunderstanding. We simply do not share the objector's commitment to inviolability and the conception of absolute value upon which it rests. In other words, the axiology being advanced denies that anything has absolute value. I suggest that the very notion of absolute value is itself faulty and rests not only on what Hartshorne calls classical theism, but on an implicit Kantian con-

ception of autonomy. For Whitehead, autonomy cannot be metaphysically interpreted as substantial independence; in our processive
cosmos, there is no absolute independence. As an end in itself, every
individual has intrinsic value. But it does not follow from this that
any individual is inviolable.[42]

The Obligations of Beauty

To include every individual in our scope of direct moral concern,
which follows from affirming the intrinsic value of every individual, dramatically transforms our system of obligations. If the very
fact of being an individual introduces "the element of value, of
being valuable, of having value, of being an end in itself, of being
something which is for its own sake" (SMW, 136), then every individual lays an obligation on us (moral agents) to take it into account.[43] With James, then, the ethics of creativity advances the view
that claim and obligation are coextensive.[44] If we are to achieve a
genuine ethical universe, we must consider every individual as
laying an obligation on us (moral agents) that must be included in
the "stable system" of "moral relations" that we seek. No longer
can we regard nonhuman entities as objects of only indirect duties
or, even less, as objects strictly serving our own self-interest. No
matter how weak that individual may be, its demands ought, "for
its own sole sake," to be satisfied.[45] Obligation, then, is not a function of convenience, utility, or self-interest. Through the lens of
the axiology of process thought, the moral ideal of a genuine ethical universe entails that the air, the soil, the flower, and the animal
all make claims and obligations on us that must be considered for
their own sake. This conclusion begins to make it clear why Whitehead claimed that "the destruction of a man, or of an insect, or of
a tree, or of the Parthenon, may be moral or immoral" (MT, 14–15).
Contrary to most Western ethical theories, then, the ethics of creativity insists that every individual represents an obligation that
must be considered in its own right. To be more precise, if we examine the moral ideal of a genuine ethical universe through the

lens of Whitehead's axiology, aesthetics, and metaphysics, we arrive at five interrelated obligations:

1. the obligation always to act in such a way as to bring about the greatest possible universe of beauty, value, and importance that in each situation is possible (beauty);

2. the obligation to maximize the intensity and harmony of one's own experience (self-respect);

3. the obligation to maximize the harmony and intensity of experience of everything within one's sphere of influence (love);

4. the obligation to avoid the destruction (or maiming) of any actual occasion, nexus, or society, unless not doing so threatens the achievement of the greatest harmony and intensity that in each situation is possible (peace);[46]

5. the obligation to strive continually to expand the depth and breadth of one's aesthetic horizons (education).

These obligations will be explored in the sections to follow. However, first let us discuss briefly what each one entails. Because subsequent obligations are in some sense contained within the first formulation, the first obligation captures most fully the heart of the ethics of creativity. For the obligation to maximize beauty is not only the aim of morality, it is the ideal and aim of process itself. Thus, this obligation, the obligation of beauty, follows directly from the interpretation of actuality as a teleological process oriented toward the achievement of beauty, value, and importance for the self, the other, and for the whole.[47] Given such a worldview, we have an obligation always to act so as to bring about the greatest universe of beauty, value, and importance that in each situation is possible.

The second and third obligations concern the first two legs of the axiological triad of self, other, and whole. The second obligation affirms an individual's self-value. In rendering its perspective on the world determinate, each individual is an achievement of value experience in and for itself. Although ethical theory is normally concerned with moral agents' relations with others, the second obligation recognizes that all individuals should have respect for the achievement of value that they themselves represent. We (moral agents) have the obligation to respect our own self-value. That is, we are obliged to maximize the harmony and intensity or, equivalently, the beauty of our own experience. Accordingly, the second formulation may be called the obligation of self-respect.

However, as I have argued throughout this work, because Whitehead's notion of individuality essentially involves others, value of self cannot be separated from the intrinsic value of others. Accordingly, the third obligation recognizes that, as unique achievements of value experience, we are obliged to maximize the harmony and intensity of experience of every individual that we influence, no matter how small, weak, or seemingly insignificant. We have an obligation not to "deface the value experience which is the very essence of the universe" (MT, 111) by treating anything, whether it be another person, an insect, a tree, or the Parthenon, as having purely instrumental value. The appropriate attitude toward all of reality is one of respect and awe. In fact, according to the third obligation, not only do we have the negative duty to avoid violently defacing achieved forms of beauty and value, we have the positive obligation to seek to maximize the harmony and intensity of the experience of others. Because of its focus on the value of the other, I refer to this formulation as the obligation of love.[48]

Properly understood, the obligations of love and self-respect may be seen as the two poles on which the obligation of beauty turns. For if we are to truly act in such a way as to bring about the greatest possible universe of beauty, value, and importance that in each situation is possible, we must affirm not only our own value, but also the value of every individual we influence. Although the practical tragedy of cross-purposes is ultimately unavoidable, the good of the one and the many are not conceptually opposed. As an ethics of creativity, the system being advanced repudiates the view that we must sacrifice either the good of the individual or of the whole. Truly beautiful experience involves a harmony of the diverse parts of experience to achieve a complex and unified whole that is both beyond its parts and yet not destructive of them; moreover, by participating in such a unity, the value experience of each part becomes more intense.[49]

The possible tension between the one and the many or the obligations of self-respect and love is aptly captured in the notion of marriage. If a marriage is to be healthy, both individuals must at once respect, appreciate, and protect their own value and the value of their partner. If either of these poles is lacking, the relationship will degenerate and retard the experience of both. For instance, if one member fails to meet the obligation of self-respect, caring only about the welfare of the other, then the relationship will become imbalanced and the experience of both will suffer. At its extreme, such relationships lead to cycles of physical and emotional abuse that can scar entire families for generations. Unfortunately, in many cultures today, the overabundance of self-value is more often the case. Too often people are concerned only with their own narrow self-interest. Marriages involving such individuals are most often predicated on procuring status and convenience, not mutual respect and love. Thus, a marriage will be "healthy" only if each partner meets both the obligation of self-respect and the obligation of love. Such a marriage is beautiful in achieving a unity that enhances the intensity of the experience of both members while not destroying their individuality.

The fourth obligation provides practical guidance in how to conduct ourselves toward others, especially in instances of moral conflict. It has two parts. The first follows from the obligation of love. Because every individual is a unique locus of value, we should not, either through action (violence) or inaction (anesthesia), destroy or otherwise maim the value experience of others. Unfortunately, given the present structure of our cosmos, conflict is inevitable; ends are mutually exclusive. In James's words, "The actually possible world is vastly narrower than all that is demanded; and there is always a *pinch* between the ideal and the actual which can only be got through by leaving part of the ideal behind."[50] Thus, although we aim at satisfying the demands of everyone within our sphere of influence, inevitably we are forced to choose between competing goods. This is why the latter part of this obligation is crucial: ultimately, that course of action is to be preferred that maximizes the beauty possible in the situation as a whole. This seemingly innocuous affirmation is one of the more novel, and likely most controversial, claims of the ethics of creativity, for it demonstrates the full extent of its commitment to the claim that something is only as good as it is beautiful. As it essentially entails a "trust in the efficacy of beauty" (AI, 285), I call this formulation the obligation of peace.

Like the others, the fifth obligation of the ethics of creativity is an extension of an aspect of the obligation of beauty: we must continually strive to expand the depth and breadth of our aesthetic horizons. In this way, the fifth obligation demands the rejection of anesthesia or embracing lower forms of beauty when greater forms are possible. In an important sense, this obligation is a necessary condition for successfully following the other four. For if we are to continually affirm the greatest degree of beauty possible in any given situation, we must first recognize the forms of beauty that exist and are possible. Thus, to act morally, we must in good faith seek to attain the greatest depth and breadth of experience—that is, we must acquire the correct habits of character. Accordingly, this is the obligation of education.

6

Beyond the Ideal

Thus morality does not indicate what you are to do in mythological abstractions. It does concern the general ideal which should be the justification for any particular objective. The destruction of a man, or of an insect, or of a tree, or of the Parthenon, may be moral or immoral. . . . Whether we destroy or whether we preserve, our action is moral if we have thereby safeguarded the importance of experience so far as it depends on that concrete instance in the world's history.

Alfred North Whitehead, *Modes of Thought*

IF A MORAL PHILOSOPHY is to be of any practical use, it must move beyond "mythological abstractions" and concretely demonstrate how a "general ideal" can help moral agents make meaningful moral decisions. Although there is no Archimedean ethical point from which we can leverage our moral dilemmas, nevertheless, it is possible to construct a moral decision-making process consistent with the organic conception of reality being defended. If the aim of morality is understood to be the maximization of importance, and if importance is equivalent to beauty, then morality may be also understood as aiming at the maximization of beauty. Put differently, because everything in our processive cosmos aims at the achievement of beauty, the conditions of a beautiful experience are necessarily the conditions of a moral experience. Accordingly, as in Aristotle's use of the golden mean, we can devise an ethical system that in every situation aims at the most beautiful whole by negotiating the mean between simplicity and complexity on the one hand, and diversity and unity on the other. It is in this sense that I understand Hartshorne's claim that we must "lean ethics upon aesthetics."[1]

Leaning upon Aesthetics

The five obligations outlined in chapter 5 enable us to discern a three-step process of moral decision making. The first step in such a process should be education (the fifth obligation), or the attempt to understand and appreciate the beauty and value of the individuals involved in a given situation. For our ability to act in accordance with the moral ideal described above is directly proportionate to the adequacy of our aesthetic judgment. Clearly, if we do not know what values are affected and can be achieved by our actions, we cannot avoid the evils of anesthesia and violence. Anesthesia, we recall, is the frustration of greater possibilities by the interposition of lesser achievements, while violence is the active destruction of existing forms of value and beauty. Thus aesthetic education must be our first concern, so that we may understand the values affected by and achievable through our actions.

One of the greatest impediments to developing an ethical system that extends value beyond our own narrow and shortsighted concerns is, as Leopold recognized, "the fact that our education and economic system is headed away from, rather than toward, an intense consciousness of land."[2] The orientation of our education and economic systems toward the egoistic pursuit of ever greater material acquisition is as problematic for the ethics of creativity as it is for Leopold's land ethic. As currently structured, our education and economic systems often encourage even well-intentioned people to seek only what is perceived to be in their own narrow self-interest. To act morally, we must first train ourselves to recognize and appreciate the beauty that surrounds and pervades our experience. I agree with Gregory Moses in arguing that character transformation is an essential component of an ethical system grounded in a process metaphysics. In his words, "Process ecological ethics can't be just applying principles or balancing value. It has to do as well with character transformation, with what kinds of individuals and communities and nations we are, with ingrained changes in the way we operate. Everything is more or less creative taking into account etc., but everything depends on how and how depends on the who, the character, the style of the how, which is to say, with ecological virtue."[3] The success of the ethics of creativity largely depends upon instilling the virtues of intellect and character necessary to recognize what values are at stake in any given situation.[4] If we are to relate to the world so as to maximize the intensity and harmony of experience achievable in every situation, we must first expand the depth and breadth of our aesthetic horizons.

The first step in any moral decision, therefore, must be to educate ourselves as fully as possible regarding the values affected by and achievable through our actions. In an interrelated and interconnected cosmos, this is no small task. The morality of our actions requires that we conceive of the impact of our actions in the widest possible context. As Whitehead says, the morality of one's outlook is "inseparably conjoined" with the generality of one's outlook (PR, 15). "Moral education," he writes in *Aims of Education*, "is impossible apart from the habitual vision of greatness. The sense of greatness is the ground work of morals" (77). Our first priority, therefore, must always be to strive to perceive and pursue more than our own narrow self-interest in order to develop the "habitual vision of greatness" needed to understand and affirm the maximum beauty possible in each situation.

Of course, strictly speaking, we can never fully complete this first step. The vicissitudes of life require us to act, even when we are unprepared to do so. Therefore, although the moral person may aim at the ideal of a genuine ethical universe in which the moral relations among things are woven into the unity of a stable system, in James's words, "which particular universe this is he cannot know for certain in advance; he only knows that if he makes a bad mistake the cries of the wounded will soon inform him of the fact."[5] Once again, we must recognize the situatedness and fallibility of moral inquiry. With some fear and trembling we must begin by resolutely seeking to improve the scope and depth of our aesthetic understanding so as to always affirm the most beautiful whole that we can see. Yet, as Aristotle recognized, what is important is not mere knowledge of what it is to be virtuous, but actually acting virtuously. By focusing on the two dimensions of beauty—harmony and intensity—and the obligations that flow from them, it is possible to discern two further steps in the moral decision-making process.

The second step corresponds to the vertical dimension or the dimension of harmony, which concerns the mean between unity and diversity. If there is too great or too little diversity, the experience will be either too chaotic or so orderly as to be monotonous. Accordingly, in the second step the aim is to act so as to include the demands of others as far as possible. This step bears a strong relation to the obligations of peace and love. For to be as inclusive and respectful of the beauty and value of others as possible, we must not destroy or otherwise maim others unless not to do so threatens the achievement of the most beautiful whole possible. Thus, the second step involves relating to others so as to meet their demands as far as possible without sacrificing the unity of experience. James eloquently captures what is at stake in this second step of the process:

> Since victory and defeat there must be, the victory to be philo-sophically prayed for is that of the more inclusive side,—of the side which even in the hour of triumph will to some degree do justice to the ideals in which the vanquished party's interests lay. The course of history is nothing but the story of men's struggles from generation to generation to find the more and more inclu-sive order. *Invent some manner* of realizing your own ideals which will also satisfy the alien demands,—that and that only is the path of peace![6]

James's prescience is tragically seen in the events of September 11, 2001. Given a world in which individuals are willing to sacrifice their lives for their ideals, we must abandon the destructive and divisive attitude of "us against them," wherein others are either "with us or against us." Rather, the answer to be "philosophically prayed for" and practically sought is one that tears down false di-chotomies and attempts to achieve not only one's own ideals but also "alien demands." One's bias must always and everywhere be toward inclusiveness. The burden of justification, therefore, rests with those who would use violence to destroy achieved forms of beauty and value. This applies as much to human conflicts, such as the so-called war on terror currently being waged by the United States, as it does to our (human beings') relations with the extra-human world. Too often, for instance, decision makers hastily con-clude that economic prosperity and environmental protection are mutually exclusive. The second step in moral decision making, then, requires us to use the moral imagination formed by our aes-thetic education to think how we can "invent some manner" of realizing our own interests as well as the interests of others. As James notes, "That and that only is the path of peace!"

The third step in moral decision making corresponds to the horizontal dimension of beauty or the dimension of intensity, which concerns the mean between complexity and simplicity. If there is too great or too little complexity, then the experience will either be too profound to grasp or too trivial to be bothered with. This step is the most difficult to explain and the most important, for the complexity or the degree of organization of an experience gives it its depth. Thus, for an experience to be truly beautiful and moral, it must not only be as inclusive as possible, it must also be sufficiently complex in its organization as to introduce new contrast; harmony without intensity is trivial or superficial. For instance, the beauty created by a child who skillfully draws a picture using every crayon in its possession is merely "pretty" compared to the complex beauty of a painting by Monet. While the child's drawing may bring a significant degree of diversity into unity, it lacks sufficient complexity or integration to achieve effective contrasts.[7] Recall that the major form of beauty involves not merely the lack of mutual inhibition involved in harmony, but also the achievement of intensity through the introduction of new contrasts. These new contrasts are not only mutually compatible but also mutually enhancing.[8] Accordingly, this final step requires that we strive not only to include the greatest variety possible, but also to seek the most intense whole possible. It is intensity that gives experience its depth. As James beautifully puts it, we must "vote always for the richer universe, for the good which seems most organizable, most fit to enter to complex combinations, most apt to be a member of a more inclusive whole."[9] The idea of organizability, or the whole that is "most fit to enter to complex combinations," captures the aim of the third step in moral decision making.

Therefore, ethics must lean upon aesthetics in that, as with every process, its aim is to achieve the most beauty possible. That is, the morality of one's action is determined by the extent to which it recognizes and affirms the most inclusive and organizable whole possible in any given situation. With this decision-making process as our context, let us now examine how we ought to behave toward each type of individual.

The Moral Ideal and Our Ethical Comportment toward Others

Compound and Aggregate Entities

I begin by reiterating my rejection of the notion of absolute onto-logical divisions between different kinds of individuals. In our processive cosmos, difference is very real, but it is ultimately a function of the degree of an individual's organization. Abstracting from the particulars of any given situation, how ought we, as moral agents, to comport ourselves toward the types of individuals at the most basic levels of reality? First, because the fundamental entities or actual occasions out of which all individuals are com-posed perish no sooner than they are completed, it is not possible to affect them directly. After all, as Whitehead once remarked, "You can't catch a moment by the scruff of the neck—*it's gone*, you know."[10] However, our actions do affect societies and nexūs of ac-tual occasions. Thus, our analysis should begin with the most basic types of individuals that our actions can potentially affect, namely, compound and aggregate entities.

The term "compound entity" refers to a nonsystematic society of actual occasions constituted by strong internal relations, for example, an electron or a molecule of water. In contrast to most traditional worldviews, which often banish the "material" or "phys-ical" world to the vacuous realm of mere fact, the position defended here insists that even a subatomic event is intrinsically valuable for itself, for others, and for the whole. Thus, even compound indi-viduals that last only a fraction of a second are unique achieve-ments of beauty and value and are, therefore, objects of direct moral concern. Though compound entities are kalogenic individ-uals deserving of our respect, we must recognize that, because the occasions which comprise them are so dominated by the influx of the past, their degree of novelty is exceedingly low and, con-sequently, the depth of beauty achievable by such individuals is comparatively trivial.[11] Furthermore, regarding our ethical comportment toward such individuals, there is little we can do about their steady vibratory achievements of definite actuality.

The same is generally true of aggregate entities, such as boulders. For aggregate entities are largely products of our (human) interests and are therefore more appropriately analyzed at the molecular or compound level of existence. That is, the intrinsic value of a boulder does not significantly exceed the intrinsic value of the compound entities of which it is composed.

For many, the claim that compound entities have intrinsic value and are objects of direct moral concern is the height of absurdity. They note that there is no reciprocity between, for instance, rocks and myself. However, this point is irrelevant. The question is not whether the events that make up the "physical universe" are moral agents, for they are not. The appropriate question is whether or not they are moral patients; that is, must we (as moral agents) consider them as objects of direct moral concern?[12] As unique achievements of beauty and value, even compound and aggregate entities are objects of direct moral concern. However, the nature of this concern lies primarily in the instrumental value of such aggregates to other types (such as systematic and organic) individuals. For instance, if one decides not to grind up a particularly beautiful boulder for gravel, this is primarily for the sake of present and future appreciators of that beauty, not for the boulder's sake. For since, properly speaking, aggregate entities such as boulders are largely a function of human space-time scales, interests, and purposes, it is inappropriate to say that we respect a boulder for its own sake. Indeed, as Ferré reminds us, *qua* boulder, "it has no 'sake of its own,' but is a paradigm case of a nexus that looms large in importance for many valuers of many sorts, from earthworms to honeymooners, but is nothing for itself since 'it' is largely a construct."[13]

Given this assessment, how should we (as moral agents) comport ourselves toward the compound and aggregate individuals that make up much of the so-called physical universe? How should we orient our relations toward such individuals so as to fulfill our obligation to maximize the harmony and intensity of experience? Given our current understanding, we will have satisfied our obligations of beauty, love, and peace toward the "physical universe" if we always (1) respect and appreciate the beauty and value of such individuals and (2) orient our relations toward such individuals so as to achieve the greatest possible degree of beauty, value, and importance. In an important sense, this aligns the ethics of creativity with at least the spirit of Leopold's land ethic, according to which "a thing is right when it tends to preserve the integrity, stability, and beauty of the biotic community. It is wrong when it tends otherwise."[14] We may no longer treat the "land" as merely instrumentally valuable property to be disposed of however one sees fit. Leopold writes, "Conservation is getting nowhere because it is incompatible with our Abrahamic concept of land. We abuse land because we regard it as a mere commodity belonging to us. When we see land as a community to which we belong we may begin to use it with love and respect. There is no other way for land to survive the impact of mechanized man, nor for us to reap from it the esthetic harvest it is capable, under science, of contributing to culture."[15]

While there are significant points of disagreement between the land ethic and the ethics of creativity, both agree that the land is not a commodity; it is a community of which we are a part.[16] Social crises such as overpopulation, starvation, malnutrition, and environmental crises such as global climate change, deforestation, desertification, and species extinction, all make a moral philosophy that calls on us to respect and love the land "an evolutionary possibility and an ecological necessity."[17] In addition to suggesting a radical reorientation toward appreciating the value and beauty of compound and aggregate entities, this conclusion also suggests a shift in how we ought to behave toward the macroscopic wholes in which these individuals are situated, such as ecosystems and species.

Systematic and Temporal Formal Entities (Species)

Chapter 3 outlined the very important difference between a systematic entity, such as an ecosystem, and a temporal formal entity, such as a species. In a certain sense, species are a kind of entity because they can support properties of their own. For instance, only species, not their members, are able to evolve, and while individuals may be endangered, only species can become extinct.[18] However, there is an important difference between species and other types of entities: although they refer to real historical processes, species are constituted by their internal relations to what is possible. As Ferré explains, "The species is not an individual thing but it is real: it goes beyond the simpler formal entities, it is a complex formal entity but also a historical process. At some point in time it evolves from pure potentiality into second-order actuality through the successful replication at the individual level of a specific vital form."[19] This has an important implication for their axiological status and, consequently, for our behavior toward them.

As a "second-order actuality," the ontological principle and the fallacy of misplaced concreteness bar us from referring to species as individuals with intrinsic value.[20] Species are not individuals with a good of their own that can be helped or hurt by our actions. Only the individuals that instantiate them have interests, goals, or value. Understood in this context, the Endangered Species Act was not enacted for the sake of the species, *qua* species, but for current and future members of such species and the systems on which they depend. Yet, as Ferré reminds us,

> When we seek to protect an endangered species, it is not simply the current individuals of that vital form we value; it is the long, improbable, and unrepeatable historical process we honor, too; and, more particularly, it is the indefinitely large possibility of more actual individuals manifesting that species' form, and what this will mean both for these future individuals themselves and for

the interlocking network of internal relations with other species processes that every actual species-process mutually influences.[21]

Thus, although a species, as a formal entity, is unique in that it does not have intrinsic value, it may still have a very great instrumental value to the community. If human culture continues on its present course and allows ten to one hundred species to go extinct every day,[22] not only do we lose the beauty achieved by the individuals that perish, but, by weakening the harmony of the whole, we diminish the depth of intensity possible for every individual within that system. This is a concrete example of the importance of harmony for effective beauty. By undermining diversity, species extinction trivializes and cheapens the beauty of the whole and of every individual within it.

Perhaps there is no clearer demonstration of the moral gravity of Whitehead's rejection of the doctrine of independence of existence than in the consideration of the moral significance of systematic entities. Systematic entities, we recall, are distinguished from aggregate entities by the strong internal relations between their parts that allow the parts to perform a single function. That is, given its strong internal relations, a systematic entity is able to function as a weak whole, and, as a whole, its ends may be frustrated or satisfied. In a sense, systematic entities are "as concrete as species are abstract."[23] Thus, with the emergence of systematic entities, we reach a new level of organization that brings with it a new level of moral obligation.

Since the ends of a systematic entity may be frustrated or satisfied, the obligation of love requires that we comport ourselves toward each systematic entity in such a way that not only respects and protects its beauty and value, but also maximizes the intensity and harmony of its experience. Moreover, in keeping with the obligation of peace, we must never destroy or maim the beauty and value achieved by a systematic entity unless not doing so would threaten the achievement of the greatest beauty possible in that situation; that is, we must not destroy or maim a system unless our action is justified.

Again, our bias must be toward inclusivity; the burden of proof is on those who seek to do violence. Even though our (human) experience of beauty and value may be more intense and complex, to meet our obligation to always affirm the greatest depth of beauty possible, it may be necessary to sacrifice the interests of human beings or other organic individuals for the vital needs of the great ecological systems in which we are situated and on which we depend. In other words, the most beautiful whole may sometimes require the sacrifice of more complex and intensely beautiful individuals for the sake of a less complex system. For instance, scores of ecosystems today are threatened by the proliferation of non-native, invasive species of plants and animals. While these creatures play a supporting role in their native niches, in foreign systems they spread unchecked by natural predators and, as a result, may lead to the destabilization or destruction of the entire system's native inhabitants. In such a case, even though an individual plant or animal has a greater depth of beauty and value open to it than an ecosystem, it may be morally appropriate to remove and perhaps (if no other option were open and if doing so would achieve the greatest degree of harmony and intensity) to destroy the non-native plant or animal. However, before this claim can be fully understood we must analyze the beauty and value of the "organic entities" that populate these systems and the nature of our obligations toward them.

Organic Entities

As with all distinctions of kind in the philosophy of organism, the difference between a systematic entity and an organic entity is ultimately a matter of degree. Specifically, with organic individuals, the level of organization and coordination rises to such a degree that the organism as a whole manifests significant spontaneity or "life."[24] Before examining the moral implications of this greater degree of organization, let us look more closely at the two major types of organic individuals: plants and animals.

In the language of Whitehead's metaphysics, a plant is a complex, structured society or a society that is comprised of many subordinate societies (cells), each of which is its own complex society. Accordingly, a plant is a vast network of societies that work as a whole to form a macroscopic individual with "objective interests" of its own. Its ends may be frustrated or satisfied. Unlike an aggregate entity such as a stone, a blade of grass has ends that may be frustrated or satisfied; for instance, it may have greater or lesser access to the sun or nutrient-rich soil. In *The Liberation of Life*, John Cobb Jr. and Charles Birch provide this analysis of the difference between a cell and stone: "A cell, unlike a stone, has an inherent unity and cellular events are constituted by a new level of internal relations with their environment. This means that a cell has experience of its world in some dim way analogous to our own, although we doubt that its experience is conscious."[25] However, following Whitehead, most process philosophers, including Cobb and Birch, argue that because plants lack a central nervous system, they are more of a "democracy" than a "monarchy" of societies.[26] That is, whereas the society of cells that make up an animal seem to be guided by a dominant personal society, the society of cells that comprises a plant seem to be more democratically organized, with each being equal to the others.

In a certain sense, this characterization seems to be appropriate, for plants do not appear to manifest the centrally coordinated actions seen in animals. In this general sense, Whitehead's reference to "democratic" and "monarchic" societies is appropriate. Yet I suspect that many process philosophers have come dangerously close to ontologizing Whitehead's political metaphor. We should not fall prey to the very ontological errors that Whitehead's system was designed to overcome. If anything, contemporary research has revealed that some plants are far more complex than we first realized. As Ferré observes, "Some plants are capable of defending themselves as a whole, receiving stimuli when attacked and responding with toxins or other defenses in appropriate ways. . . . Plants may turn out to have more tightly organized internal relations than traditional botany has suggested."[27] For instance, Ferré cites a study that documents how the tomato plant "uses an electric signal to alert its defense system against grazing caterpillars. Attack on one leaf results in chemical antidigestants being produced in others, slowing the grazing process, thereby longer exposing the caterpillars to predators of their own."[28] If we are to honestly meet our obligation of education, we must be willing to admit that some plants may be sufficiently complex to support a form of personal society that provides some degree of central coordination. If this is true, the difference between plants and animals may not be quite as neat as the distinction between "democratic" and "monarchic" societies implies. Thus I agree with Ferré, who writes, "From a metaphysical point of view, the distinction between them [plants and animals] is far less interesting than the great similarities that unite them as innovative, responsive, creative systems."[29] If plants are indeed more complex than previously recognized, then the intensity of experience open to them is greater than previously realized and we must modify our behavior toward them accordingly. Yet before examining how we (as moral agents) ought to comport ourselves toward plants, let us examine the other major type of organic entity, namely, animals.

Like plants, animals are complex, structured societies. While the degree of coordination achievable by plants may be in question, it is clear that, given the degree of coordination between their parts, animals have not only a complex body, which is itself a society involving vast arrays of subordinate societies and nexus, they also have a "soul" or a regnant, personally ordered subsociety that makes centrally coordinated decisions possible through consciousness. In the words of Cobb and Birch:

In animal life, in distinction from plant life, a new level of experience arises. At some point in the evolution of the central nervous system, conscious feeling, as distinct from non-conscious feeling entered into the world. This is a qualitatively different experience which presumably increases progressively with the development of the nervous system. With the increased complexity of the nervous system and the development of the brain we have every reason to suppose there is increased capacity for richness of experience.[30]

In allowing the organism to abstract from its massive causal background and attend to a narrow foreground of experience, consciousness introduces an unprecedented degree of novelty of functioning.[31] Accordingly, while some may question whether there is a "subjective good" for a blade of grass as a whole, all but the most hardened reductionist materialist would deny this of a complex animal such as a horse. As conscious individuals, animals are particularly high-order creators of beauty, and the depth of our respect and appreciation should recognize this. But what about the difference between human and nonhuman animals?

As with the others, this distinction ultimately reflects the degree of coordination and organization possessed by the subordinate societies and nexus of which each is composed. Like other animals, a human is a complex, structured society that encompasses both an animal body as well as a regnant, personally ordered society. However, in the case of healthy adult human beings, this personally ordered society makes not only consciousness possible, the degree of coordination is so great that self-consciousness emerges. Thus, because human animals are "complex enough to be conscious and free enough to be responsible,"[32] they are moral agents.

Yet, as we saw in chapter 3, whether healthy human adults are the only moral agents remains an empirical question. Whether or not, for instance, chimpanzees or dolphins are moral agents ultimately concerns whether they are complex enough to be conscious and free enough to be responsible. A growing number of scholars suggest that there are indeed other animals that rise to this level of complexity. For instance, Juan Carlos Gómez argues that "apes are intentional agents (subjects) endowed with brain mechanisms specialized in perceiving and treating others as intentional agents." He concludes that while it is essential to avoid the error of "humanizing," apes nevertheless do "act and feel as persons in the most essential sense of the word, which I take to be the ability to recognize others and themselves as individual subjects capable of feeling and behaving intersubjectively."[33] When research such as this is combined with studies focusing on the achievements of particular individuals such as Alex the parrot, Kanzi the Bonobo, and Washoe the Chimpanzee,[34] we may suspect that there are indeed nonhuman moral agents. If this conclusion is correct, we must, among other things, stop conceiving of nonhuman animals as mere property.[35]

It is, furthermore, possible that there are individuals in other corners of our vast universe who surpass human animals in the intensity of their experience. As Ferré writes, "If experience extends beyond the human species, at least to the higher animals and—as required for coherence—is found pervasively in nature, then the human scale of values represents just one small segment on a spectrum. At the upper end, intense, complex human realizations of experiential elements—what I call Mozartian moments—are at or near the top of the known scale, though, for all we know, even now there may be entities capable of still more remarkable experiences somewhere in the universe, and such entities may perhaps evolve here on earth in time."[36] By recognizing that difference is a matter of degree rather than kind, this position has the benefit of avoiding what Peter Singer famously labeled "speciesism."[37]

This analysis is an attempt to meet our obligation of education by understanding and appreciating the beauty and value achieved by organic entities. Accordingly, let us now proceed to the second and third steps of moral decision making and seek to determine how human beings ought to conduct ourselves toward plants and other animals so as to affirm the greatest universe of beauty, value, and importance that we can see. In *Process and Reality*, Whitehead

notes that this task is made particularly difficult by the relation between an organic individual and its environment. Although every
individual depends upon interplay with its environment, in the case
of organic individuals, Whitehead believes, this interplay takes the
form of "robbery." Simply put, the very act of existence requires
that organic individuals consume others in order to sustain themselves. However, unlike many ethical theories, this conclusion highlights a moral conflict. "It is at this point that with life morals
become acute. The robber requires justification" (PR, 105). This
statement wonderfully captures the revolutionary nature of the
ethics of creativity. Whereas in most traditional ethical systems the
consumption of food would not even be a moral issue unless it involved the consumption of another human being, for the ethics of
creativity, in that every individual is a unique achievement of beauty
and value, the robber requires justification. The question, then, is
what sort of justification is available to someone advocating the
ethics of creativity in such a situation? How are we to decide between our own intrinsic value as human beings and the intrinsic
value of the organisms that we destroy in order to sustain ourselves?
These questions will test the adequacy and applicability of the ideal
of the ethics of creativity.

The Robbery of Life and the Ethics of Food

Let us first ask this question: What kind of relationship between
human beings and plants and other nonhuman animals would
assure the most inclusive, complex, and unified whole? When, if
ever, are we justified in robbing from others to sustain ourselves?
Limiting our attention to the organic entities involved, there are
four courses of action possible: (1) human beings should eat neither plants nor other animals;[38] (2) they should eat both plants and
animals; (3) they should eat only animals; or (4) they should eat
only plants. Let us consider each option as it relates to the obligations of beauty, self-respect, love, peace, and education.

The first option—that is, human beings should eat neither plants nor other animals—essentially affirms that the most beautiful whole is one in which human beings starved so that plants and nonhuman animals could thrive unmolested by humanity. However, a world lacking the deep beauty and value of human beings could not be the most harmonious and intense world that is possible. This option would violate the obligations of beauty, self-respect, and peace. The extinction of humanity would be a glaring instance of the evil of anesthesia or the substitution of lower forms of experience for greater. Note, however, that rampant population growth is at least partly responsible for the diminished quality of life for both human and nonhuman animals and for the degradation of the environment. Thus, the ethics of creativity finds that achieving the most beautiful whole would require a gradual decrease in the human population.[39] Nevertheless, given the current lack of viable alternatives, it is currently necessary for human beings to eat either animals or plants (or both) to sustain themselves.

If it is morally inappropriate to sacrifice humans for the sake of plants and nonhuman animals (option 1), what is our appropriate moral relation toward plants and nonhuman animals? The key to the answer is found in the obligation of peace, whereby we must avoid destroying or diminishing the beauty and value achieved by others, unless such action is necessary to achieve the most intense and harmonious (that is, beautiful) whole possible. Therefore, the appropriate relationship toward plants and nonhuman animals depends on whether eating them is necessary in order to achieve the most beautiful whole. In the context of option 2, we must ask, "Is it necessary for human beings to eat both animals and plants in order to flourish?" The fact that for millennia hundreds of millions of people worldwide have lived long and fruitful lives without eating animals is indisputable evidence that human beings do not have to eat both plants and animals (option 2).[40] In addition to the number of vegetarians in the world today, much evidence suggests that a plant-based diet is healthier than a diet including animal flesh. For more than a decade the American Dietetic Association has endorsed vegetarian diets as "healthful and nutritionally adequate."[41] However, it is not necessary to examine such evidence in detail. The burden of proof is on the shoulders of those who maintain that human beings cannot be healthy without consuming both animals and plants. Thus, we are left with two options, a carnivorous diet (option 3) or a vegetarian diet (option 4). Which would achieve the most inclusive, complex, and organizable whole possible?

I contend that, because of their complex organization, animals are capable of an intensity of value and beauty greater than that of even the most complex plants, the most inclusive, diverse, and complex whole—that is, the most beautiful whole—could not be one in which human beings consumed only animals (option 3). First, since the destruction of the deep intrinsic value of nonhuman animals is not necessary for human beings to flourish, this option violates the obligation to always act so as to bring about the greatest possible universe of beauty, value, and importance that is possible in each situation. Considering that over 100 million cows, pigs, and sheep and over 5 billion chickens are raised and slaughtered annually in the United States alone, this is no small matter.[42] Not only is the affirmation of this less complex whole an instance of anesthesia, but also the unnecessary destruction of these beautiful individuals is a paradigmatic example of violence.

Second, there are also substantial arguments from efficiency against raising nonhuman animals for consumption. Although over twenty years ago Frances Moore Lappé in *Diet for a Small Planet* refuted the myth that hunger is caused by scarcity, many still tenaciously hold that the consumption of animals is necessary for human survival. Yet as she notes in her 2002 sequel, *Hope's Edge*, coauthored with her daughter Anna Lappé, "For every human being on the planet, the world produces two pounds of grain per day—roughly 3,000 calories, and that's without even counting the beans, potatoes, nuts, fruits, and vegetables we eat, too. This is clearly enough for all of us to thrive; yet nearly one in six of us still goes hungry."[43] The United Nations World Food Program corroborates this assessment:

> There is enough food in the world today for every man, woman and child to have the nourishment necessary for healthy and productive lives. And yet, more than 800 million people on earth today suffer from chronic malnutrition. . . . The hunger statistics for children are the most horrifying. An estimated 183 million children below the age of five are underweight and at high risk of dying within a year. Each day, malnutrition is a significant factor in the deaths of 18,000 of these children, one child every five seconds.[44]

Accordingly, the problem is not in the quantity of food available, it is in how we use it. "Worldwide, we're feeding more and more of this grain, now almost *half* to livestock, but animals return to us in meat only a tiny fraction of the nutrients we feed them. To get just one calorie of food energy from a steak, we burn 54 irreplaceable fossil-fuel calories, so producing one pound of steak—providing less than 1,000 calories—uses up 45,000 fossil fuel calories."[45] Thus the question is not "Why hunger?" but "Why hunger in a world of plenty?" This provides a second considerable argument against an animal-flesh based diet (option 3). To continue the grossly inefficient raising and consumption of animals is a tragic instance of frustrating greater possibilities by the interposition of lesser achievements; it is as tragic as it is ugly.

Thus, in general—that is, abstracting from the particularities of any given situation—because it is not necessary for human beings to consume animals in order to flourish, the obligation to always act so as to maximize the harmony and intensity of our experience requires us to adopt a plant-based diet (option 4). That is, for most people in our contemporary society, a vegetarian diet is morally required. This conclusion follows directly from the obligation of peace, which requires that we avoid the destruction or maiming of any individual, unless not doing so threatens the achievement of the greatest harmony and intensity that in each situation is possible. To continue the unnecessary and wasteful consumption of animals is both the destruction of achieved values (violence) and the substitution of lesser values for greater ones (anesthesia); it is an example of ugliness. However, we must qualify this conclusion in several ways.

First, although robbery of the life of plants may, under certain conditions, be justified, this does not mean that plants have purely instrumental value that we may use with impunity, or that a plant's destruction is not tragic. The loss of any form of beauty is tragic. Accordingly, our obligation to respect and protect their beauty and value does not change just because it may (currently) be morally appropriate for us to destroy plant life in order to sustain our own. Thus, in our agricultural practices we must devise some way of meeting our obligation to maximize the harmony and intensity of the experiences of plant cells and of whole plants (to whatever extent whole plants are capable of experience). Accordingly, we must move away from farming methods, for instance, that cause soil erosion or desertification, pollute the air and the water, or destroy habitat, and move toward a system that respects and protects the beauty of the land and the biotic community.

Second, many take issue with the claim that a vegetarian life style may be a moral obligation by noting that other animals do not limit themselves to consuming only vegetation. Here the discussion of tragedy, ugliness, and discord in chapter 4 is helpful. The destruction of one nonhuman animal by another, while a tragic loss of a beautiful individual, is not wholly evil. For instance, in the United States, before major predators such as wolves were reintroduced into some wilderness areas, authorities often found it necessary to reduce the population of grazing animals so that they would not overburden an ecosystem. For, if left unchecked, the decimation of an ecosystem's plant life would not only disrupt the balance of the system as a whole and the multitudes of individuals that depend on it, but also ultimately lead to the death of the grazing animals themselves. Although reintroducing predators means the painful, violent death of other animals, it does not diminish the overall beauty achieved. On the contrary, encouraging the stability and vitality of the ecosystem enriches the experience of the system as well as every individual within it. Accordingly, unlike many other positions, the ethics of creativity affirms the importance of predation to the healthy functioning of natural systems, while arguing for moral vegetarianism.

While such an assessment may seem unfeeling toward the violent death of an individual, it is in fact life-affirming. An objection such as this is often based on the assumption that pain and pleasure are equivalent to good and evil. J. Baird Callicott argues to the contrary that, from the perspective of ecological biology, "pain and pleasure seem to have nothing at all to do with good and evil."[46] Pain is not a *prima facie* evil; it is a critical form of information. "In animals, it informs the central nervous system of stress, irritation, or trauma in outlying regions of the organism."[47] Accordingly, while the pain suffered by an individual is often relevant to a moral agent's moral decision making, its presence or absence does not cleanly point to the moral character of an event. Our aim, therefore, is not to eliminate all pain. Rather, like the aim of every process, it is always to affirm the most beautiful whole possible. The ethics of creativity is able to justify the moral obligation to avoid the unnecessary consumption of animals without the objection that it is inconsistent with the predation that occurs elsewhere in nature. As Whitehead notes, life is robbery. The question is: is that robbery justified? In the case of predation, the violent death of an individual may be both tragic and justified. Again we are reminded that, as James put it, "the actually possible world is vastly narrower than all that is demanded; and there is always a *pinch* between the ideal and the actual."[48]

Another problem with pointing to predation in nature as an argument against the obligation of vegetarianism is that it fails to recognize the distinction between a moral agent and a moral patient. Though extremely complex and beautiful, most nonhuman animals are not complex enough to be both free and responsible, while most healthy adult human animals are. In other words, most nonhuman animals do not possess sufficient freedom to choose not to prey on other forms of life for survival. Most human beings have no such excuse.[49]

Finally, it is important to note that the ethics of creativity does not advocate an absolute prohibition of the consumption of animals or promote the view that animals, human or nonhuman, have absolute value. The ethics of creativity is a situated ethic; it does not trade in the currency of absolutes. Although it may be appropriate to rob from other forms of life, it is not always appropriate to do so. Accordingly, if a human being were in an environment abundant with animal life and where plant life was unavailable, say, in arctic tundra, the destruction of an animal for survival could be morally appropriate. Similarly, if the plants or animals involved were endangered, or if at some point it becomes feasible for humans to flourish without eating either plants or animals, then the morally appropriate action would be significantly altered. Thus, in the ethics of creativity, morality does not simply give preference to more complex individuals. Ultimately, the only justification open to any action is that it maximizes the beauty, value, and importance that is possible in each situation.

7

The Promise of a
Kalocentric Worldview

In beauty may I walk.
All day long may I walk.
Through the returning seasons may I walk.
. . . .
On the trail marked with pollen may I walk.
With grasshoppers about my feet may I walk.
With dew about my feet may I walk.
With beauty may I walk.
With beauty before me, may I walk.
With beauty behind me, may I walk.
With beauty above me, may I walk.
With beauty below me, may I walk.
With beauty all around me, may I walk.
In old age wandering on a trail of beauty,
lively, may I walk.
In old age wandering on a trail of beauty,
living again, may I walk.
It is finished in beauty.
It is finished in beauty.

Navajo, *Night Chant*

HAVING PRESENTED THE ETHICS of creativity, I am now in a position
to bring it into conversation with established moral and environmental philosophies. To put this in the form of a question, "What
is the proper classification of the ethics of creativity?" Depending

upon what features one focuses on, there could be many different answers to this question. For instance, because it places a high value on education and the character of the moral agent, is it perhaps a form of virtue ethics? However, in calling for the maximization of beauty, value, and importance, perhaps it is closer to a form of utilitarianism? Or, since it affirms the irreplaceable uniqueness of every individual, maybe it is closer to a form of deontology? Or again, in demanding respect for every form of life, perhaps it should be classified with Schweitzer's ethic of reverence for life? However, because it also recognizes the beauty and value of the ecological communities in which each individual is nested and on which all depend, perhaps it is closer to Leopold's land ethic? Finally, in that it affirms the intrinsic value of everything in the universe, maybe it should be classified with deep ecology? Such comparisons help to situate the ethics of creativity vis-à-vis established moral and environmental philosophies, extending our previous analyses. Here I cannot provide an exhaustive comparison. Rather, I am interested in providing a basic sense of how the ethics of creativity both relates to and seeks to transform the presuppositions of many established moral and environmental philosophies. Although it bears important familial relationships to established moral and environmental theories, an ethical theory grounded in Whitehead's aesthetico-metaphysics of process cannot be neatly categorized under existing ethical paradigms. Attempts to force it within established theories would inevitably result in misunderstandings and confusions. In the end, while the ethics of creativity undoubtedly draws from established moral and environmental philosophies, it must stand or fall on its own merits.

Engaging Moral Traditions: Virtue Ethics, Utilitarianism, and Deontology

A processive view of reality has as much, if not more, to do with axiology as with ontology. At the very heart of the philosophy of organism is the conviction that to exist is to have value for oneself, for others, and for the whole. Hence, the first step toward moral decision making must be to educate oneself, to understand, appreciate, and respect the beauty and value of others. This suggests a strong connection to the tradition of virtue ethics. Indeed, the ethic being advanced is viable insofar as it inspires moral agents to embrace the virtues of intellect and character necessary to achieve what Whitehead called the "habitual vision of greatness"—the vision needed to understand, appreciate, and respect the beauty and value achievable in each situation. However, this comparison can be taken too far. While virtue is a condition necessary for moral action, the central aim of the ethics of creativity is to bring about the greatest possible universe of beauty, value, and importance in each situation. That is, although morality depends upon the virtue of the moral agent, it also seeks to maximize the beauty, value, and importance of every individual. In a sense, then, along with an element of virtue ethics, a Whiteheadian moral philosophy such as the ethics of creativity also includes elements of consequentialist utilitarianism.

If utilitarianism means adhering to some version of the greatest happiness principle or the principle of utility, then the ethics of creativity is not utilitarian. As Hartshorne notes, abstract laws such as these violate the fallacy of misplaced concreteness; for "the greatest happiness of the greatest number is not itself an actual happiness to anyone, and so is not a value in a clearly intelligible sense."[1] To make this general claim more specific, I will contrast my project with the work of a prominent utilitarian, Peter Singer.

First, although the ethics of creativity parallels Singer's ideas in repudiating anthropocentric speciesism and, in general, calling for human beings to adopt a plant-based diet, the justifications for these conclusions differ in important respects. For instance, while both find that inflicting unnecessary suffering on sentient individuals ought to be avoided, Singer holds that it is ultimately the pain that is caused that makes eating animals immoral.[2] However, according to the ethics of creativity, it is the failure to affirm the most beautiful whole possible in that situation that makes it immoral, not the infliction of pain *per se*. I agree with J. Baird Callicott who argues that "the doctrine that life is the happier the freer it is from pain and that the happiest life conceivable is one in which there is continuous pleasure uninterrupted by pain is biologically preposterous. . . . The idea that pain is evil and ought to be minimized or eliminated is as primitive a notion as that of a tyrant who puts to death messengers bearing bad news on the supposition that thus his well-being and security is improved."[3] Not only is pain not intrinsically evil; it is in fact biologically necessary to inform an individual of what it ought to avoid. Hence the first way in which my project differs from utilitarianism is that it seeks to achieve the most harmonious and intensely beautiful whole possible, not merely to maximize pleasure and minimize pain for the greatest number.

Singer's sentient-centered perspective highlights a more fundamental difference between his version of utilitarianism and the ethics of creativity: whereas even the most fleeting individual has moral standing according to the ethics of creativity, Singer's utilitarianism limits moral standing to those individuals with the capacity for suffering and enjoyment. Accordingly, Singer argues, "If a being is not capable of suffering, or experiencing enjoyment or happiness, there is nothing to be taken into account."[4] By making moral standing completely dependent upon whether an individual is sentient, Singer relegates nonsentient entities such as plants and ecosystems to the status of second-class moral citizens. In stark contrast to utilitarianism's myopic axiological commitments, the ethics of creativity affirms that *every* individual is an intrinsically valuable and intensely beautiful object of direct moral concern.

Despite these considerable differences, in *Environmental Ethics and Process Thought*, Clare Palmer argues that a Whiteheadian moral philosophy is essentially a form of totalizing consequentialist utilitarianism.[5] She concludes that a Whiteheadian ethic leads to (1) the unjust sacrifice of entities (if such a sacrifice promotes increased total richness of experience), and (2) the possibility of replaceability even for "high-grade" organisms (provided that total richness of experience remains constant or increases by the substitution).[6] Because both of these objections follow from her characterization of Whitehead's system as a totalizing utilitarianism, I will address both branches of her argument by attacking their common root, utilitarianism.

According to Palmer, process thought is essentially utilitarian because "the ultimate aim of ethical behaviour is to produce the greatest possible value for the consequent nature of God."[7] If all ethical behavior and all value are to be understood only in terms of how they contribute to God, then morality becomes the maximization of a certain form of experience (value, beauty, importance) for God. Thus, as with utilitarianism, one ought always to choose that course of action that maximizes utility, happiness, and value for the relevant entity, which, in our processive cosmos, is God. Given this interpretation, Palmer concludes, "Value is contributory; God sums the value generated by actual occasions and within Himself; the system must therefore be consequentialist and totalizing."[8]

Admittedly, Palmer's interpretation of Whitehead's metaphysics is not completely without representation in process scholarship. In fact, her interpretation, referred to as "contributionism," has a very prominent position in process theology. As Hartshorne characterizes it, the contributionist doctrine states that "the ultimate value of human life, or anything else, consists *entirely* in the contribution it makes to the divine life. Whatever importance we, and those we can help or harm, have is without residue measured by and consists in the delight God takes in our existence."[9] Given such an interpretation of process thought, it begins to become clear why Palmer makes the argument she does. If the value of an entity consists entirely in its contribution to the divine life, if whatever importance it has is without residue both measured by and consists in the delight God takes in its existence, then Whitehead would seem to be subject to some degree of totalization. Hence Palmer's objection may be seen as the inverse of the problem of subjectivism. Whereas subjectivism implies that Whitehead is unable to affirm the intrinsic value of others and the whole, as Palmer interprets it, contributionism implies that Whitehead cannot affirm anything but the intrinsic value of the whole.

First, while one might respond to this argument from within the contributionist framework,[10] one could simply avoid this aspect of the debate by recognizing that whatever value an entity has is not entirely measured by, nor does it consist in its contribution to God. Every individual has value for the whole, but, as I have sought to demonstrate, every individual also has value for itself and for others. This interpretation responds to Palmer's position in two ways. First, for Whitehead, each part of the axiological triad of self, other, and whole equally characterizes actuality. "These three divisions are on a level. No one in any sense precedes the other. There is the whole fact containing within itself my fact and the other facts. Also the dim meaning of fact—or actuality—is intrinsic importance for itself, for the others, and for the whole" (MT, 116–17). As an ethics of *creativity*, the philosophy being advanced refuses to admit that the good of the one and the many are opposed. As the aim of every process, beauty is the achievement of a harmonious balance that brings diverse individuals into a unity that is at once beyond them and yet not destructive of them; in achieving this whole, it increases the intensity of experience of the parts (MT, 62).

Second, Palmer fails to sufficiently recognize that every individual is, strictly speaking, a unique achievement of beauty and value. For Whitehead, nothing ever "recurs in exact detail. No two days are identical, no two winters." (SMW, 5). Accordingly, although there is a strong consequentialist element in aiming at the maximization of beauty, value, and importance, in affirming the irreplaceable uniqueness of each individual, the ethics of creativity also involves what Dombrowski calls the "neglected deontological dimension of process ethics."[11]

The deontological dimension does not mean the model of autonomy that grounds most deontological systems. Rather, the deontological dimension of Whitehead's system refers to the fact that, to some degree, every individual sets ends for itself in deciding what it will become and is therefore intrinsically valuable. However, in that every individual is essentially related to every other, Whitehead fundamentally repudiates the possibility of autonomy. Dombrowski defends this point in his response to Palmer's arguments:

> Palmer emphasizes the point that in process ethics nothing is lost in replaceability if total value stays the same or increases. I deny this claim. Something significant *is* lost if animals are replaced *both* in terms of the cessation of unique value intensities/unique internal cumulativeness of individual animals *and* in terms of value contrasts among animals and other creatures that are contributed to God. To kill and then replace one dog or cow or chicken with another still involves tragedy both for the animal killed and for those who might care for it; and these tragic contributions to the divine life are nothing short of perverse if they are unnecessary. In effect, there are deontological dimensions to process ethics along with consequentialist ones, with Palmer noting only the latter.[12]

Every individual is a unique subject of experience that is an intrinsically valuable end in itself. However, unlike Kant's axiology, for instance, the recognition that every individual is an end-in-itself does not bring with it the notions of autonomy or "absolute value." Every individual is a unique achievement of beauty and value, but its depth of beauty and value varies according to the harmony and intensity of its experience. Thus, not only are rational human beings ends-in-themselves, but, as unique subjects of experience, every individual, from a subatomic event to God, is an intrinsically valuable end-in-itself. More specifically, the intrinsic value of individuals must be understood not merely in terms of the value they have for themselves (intrinsic value), but also in terms of their value for each other (instrumental value), and their value to the whole (religious value). Given such an axiology, I am unable to fully agree with those, such as Tom Regan, who use a deontological approach to defend the absolute rights of nonhuman animals.

While there are certain similarities between my project and Regan's, they are fundamentally different; as with Singer, this difference ultimately lies in the locus of intrinsic value and the scope of direct moral concern. The ethics of creativity rejects deontology's binary conception of axiology whereby an individual's value can be absolute. This is not only axiologically problematic, it is metaphysically inaccurate. Intrinsic value is not all or nothing, and it is not limited to those individuals that are determined to be a "subject-of-a-life." Every individual, no matter how small and seemingly insignificant, is an intrinsically valuable achievement of beauty that deserves our respect, appreciation, and protection. However, nothing has value absolutely, not human beings, not animals, perhaps not even God. Given these axiological commitments, we should avoid the language of rights when discussing less complex individuals such as plants. While the discussion of rights is clearly valuable in many contexts, attempts to extend such notions too far distort the multidimensional axiological structure of our world wherein every individual has value for itself, for others, and for the whole.[13] This rich metaphysical and axiological basis not only allows the ethics of creativity to appreciate the intrinsic value of even the most simple individual, but also the obligations of beauty—particularly the obligation of peace—provide a means by which to arbitrate between mutually exclusive ends.

Therefore, although the ethics of creativity is similar to and contains elements of virtue ethics, utilitarianism, and deontology, it is not reducible to any of them. Is it perhaps more appropriate to compare this project to more biocentric environmental philosophies such as Schweitzer's ethic of life, Leopold's land ethic, or Naess's deep ecology?

Anthropocentrism, Biocentrism, Kalocentrism

With Albert Schweitzer, I recognize that every creature has intrinsic value and must be respected. "Ethics thus consists in this, that I experience the necessity of practicing the same reverence for life toward all will-to-live, as toward my own. Therein I have already the needed fundamental principle of morality. It is good to maintain and cherish life; it is evil to destroy and check life."[14] Like Schweitzer's reverence for life, the obligation of love requires that we strive to respect, appreciate, and protect each individual for its own sake. In a sense, this is the "deontological element" to which Dombrowski refers. However, there are several potential difficulties with embracing Schweitzer's approach. The first concerns the use of "life" as the criterion for moral inclusion. If by "life," Schweitzer refers to what biologists call "organic beings," for example, individual plants and animals, then it conflicts with the ethics of creativity, which excludes nothing from the scope of direct moral concern. However, if Schweitzer were to agree with Whitehead that life essentially refers to novelty and that the possibility of novelty may be greater or lesser but is never zero, then "there is no absolute gap between 'living' and 'non-living'" individuals; that is, everything is, to some degree, alive.[15] Schweitzer may have intended this broader understanding of "life." Consider the following passage: "To him [the ethical person] life as such is sacred. He shatters no ice crystal that sparkles in the sun, tears no leaf from its tree, breaks off no flower, and is careful not to crush any insect as he walks."[16] While insects, leaves, and flowers are clearly living, this is less likely to be true of ice crystals. Perhaps, then, Schweitzer could agree to Whitehead's expanded use of "life."

However, even if Schweitzer were to adopt Whitehead's conception of life, there is a more basic tension between their respective axiologies. Schweitzer seems to be unwilling to make distinctions in grades of value, arguing instead that the ethical person "does not ask how far this or that life deserves sympathy as valuable in it-self, nor how far it is capable of feeling. To him life as such is sa-cred."[17] The difficulty here is that such a position gives the moral agent no way of arbitrating between mutually exclusive ends. In fact, in making every living being sacred, Schweitzer eliminates any objective basis for choosing one living being over another. Accordingly, in instances where individuals' interests are truly mutually exclusive, we are either forced to arbitrarily sacrifice one individual for the sake of the other, or, recognizing the sacred na-ture of all life, we are simply morally paralyzed.[18] In the end, then, the similarities between the ethics of creativity and Schweitzer's reverence for life are more familial than substantive.

In affirming the beauty and value not only of individual organ-isms but also of communities and systems of individuals, perhaps the ethics of creativity is closer to a form of Aldo Leopold's land ethic?[19] For with Leopold it recognizes that no individual exists in isolation; each individual exists only in and through its relation-ships to others and to the "biotic whole."[20] Accordingly, we must not only protect and respect macroscopic individuals such as ani-mals and plants, but also systems such as the land and aggregates such as mountains. Interestingly, in "The Historical Foundations of American Environmental Attitudes," Eugene Hargrove suggests that Leopold may have been inspired by Whitehead's work:

> Most interesting of all is the similarity of some of Whitehead's comments and those of environmentalist Aldo Leopold. There are long passages in the last chapter of *Science and the Modern World*, for instance, which could easily have served as the source of some of Leopold's ideas, and which suggest that Leopold's no-tion of community could be derived from Whitehead's theory of organism without much difficulty. In one place especially White-head speaks of "associations of different species which mutually cooperate," and he refers to the forest environment as "the tri-umph of the organization of mutually dependent species." A few lines further on he adds that "every organism requires an envi-

ronment of friends, partly to shield it from violent changes, and partly to supply it with its wants."[21]

It is a small step, Hargrove tells us, "from Whitehead's 'environment of friends' to Leopold's 'biotic community.'"[22] Both Leopold and Whitehead share a commitment to appreciating the interdependent communities of which we are a part and on which we depend. Furthermore, there is more than a passing similarity between Whitehead's view that "the real world is good when it is beautiful" (AI, 268) and Leopold's claim that "a thing is right when it tends to preserve the integrity, stability, and beauty of the biotic community. It is wrong when it tends otherwise."[23] The land ethic and the ethics of creativity share a deep and abiding commitment to the moral force of beauty. In the end, however, since Leopold's "sketches" are more suggestive than systematic, it is difficult to determine how far to take such comparisons.[24]

In *Deep Ecology*, George Sessions and Bill Devall argue that the "central intuition" that fundamentally distinguishes a "deep" ecology from a "shallow" one is "the idea that we can make no firm ontological divide in the field of existence: That there is no bifurcation in reality between the human and the non-human realms . . . ; to the extent that we perceive boundaries, we fall short of deep ecological consciousness."[25] Contrary to the dominant trend in contemporary moral philosophy in general and environmental philosophy in particular, deep ecology begins from an ontological claim: namely, that there are no absolute gaps in the fabric of reality. Reality is not a multitude of isolated individuals; it is a single, complex web of interrelations. From this most basic ontological insight, proponents of deep ecology defend "eight-points" or basic principles. For our purposes, the first three principles are most relevant: "1. The well-being and flourishing of human and nonhuman Life on Earth have value in themselves (synonyms: intrinsic value, inherent value). . . . 2. Richness and diversity of life forms contribute to the realization of these values and are also values in themselves. 3. Humans have no right to reduce this richness and diversity except to satisfy *vital* needs."[26] As I will discuss shortly, Whitehead's philosophy of organism agrees completely with the first two points and would give a qualified assent to the third. Where process philosophy and Devall and Session's version of deep ecology part company is not over any of the eight-points *per se*, but over the doctrine of "biocentric equality" or what I call "ecological equality." Following Arne Naess,[27] the founder of deep ecology, Devall and Sessions present the doctrine of ecological equality as follows: "All things in the biosphere have an equal right to live and blossom and to reach their own individual forms of unfolding and self-realization within the larger self-realization. This basic intuition is that all organisms and entities in the ecosphere . . . are equal in intrinsic worth."[28] Accordingly, this interpretation of deep ecology entails not merely that every individual has value, but that every individual has value equally. I contend that this further conclusion is not only factually mistaken, but in fact ethically dangerous. Let us examine the latter charge first.

One of the chief tests of any moral philosophy is its ability to help moral agents make meaningful moral decisions in the face of competing or mutually exclusive claims. In these all too frequent situations, the problematic nature of ecological egalitarianism becomes most apparent. Insisting that every individual is truly equal in intrinsic worth leaves the moral agent with two equally undesirable options: either the arbitrary choice of one course of action over another, without any basis for this decision, or, recognizing the equality of the competing values, moral paralysis. Let us examine this argument in the context of a hypothetical moral conflict.

For example, if I suspect that the mosquito that is about to bite my infant daughter's arm may be carrying the potentially deadly malaria virus, what justification could I give for taking one course of action over another? According to Sessions and Devall's interpretation of deep ecology, both the mosquito and the infant have an *"equal* right to live and blossom." Therefore, how can I justify sacrificing the life of one individual over the other? Because, according to Sessions and Devall's reading of deep ecology, the mosquito has just as much value as my daughter, I am either morally paralyzed, unable to justify my choice, or I must arbitrarily choose between them. The problem stems not from the fundamental principles of deep ecology, but from the argument that ecological equality necessarily follows from these principles.

As John Cobb Jr. argues in "Deep Ecology and Process Thought," the doctrine of ecological egalitarianism does not necessarily follow from the "eight-points" of deep ecology. I agree with Cobb that "it is puzzling to a Whiteheadian how the fact that the diversity of life forms contribute to the value of the whole and has value in itself can be understood to require ecological egalitarianism."[29] To emphasize his point, Cobb notes that Naess himself seems to make distinctions in degrees of value in his justification for living in the mountains of Norway.

> To a Whiteheadian it appears likely that some judgment of relative value is in fact implicit in Naess's practice and attitude. If he really believes that each plant has an *equal* right to live as he, then killing thousands in order that he may enjoy living in that area seems immoral. Further, if living in the Norwegian mountains required him to cause suffering to thousands of rabbits or deer, one wonders whether he would adopt just the same attitude.[30]

With Cobb, I contend that deep ecologists should abandon the doctrine of ecological egalitarianism in favor of Whitehead's rich metaphysics of process and its multidimensional continuum of beauty and value.[31] Whitehead's axiology and aesthetics are a continuum in the sense that there are no absolute gaps. Beauty and value may be more or less, but never zero. But it is not a flat continuum. It is complex and multidimensional. Strictly speaking, the kinds and types of beauty are as numerous as the modes of togetherness. Thus, the differences between organisms that we experience are very real; there are different kinds of being, beauty, and value. However, these kinds are not grounded in a monolithic, static hierarchy of being or beauty. Differences of kind are real but not ontologically ultimate.[32] That is, an occasion is more complex and organized the closer it comes to achieving the golden mean of beauty. In this way, Whitehead's multidimensional continuum of beauty and value provides a firm ontological grounding for our moral decisions, while it does not directly constitute them.

Yet given such a view, some deep ecologists would likely ask: "Doesn't this 'multidimensional continuum of value and beauty' ultimately amount to the same illicit use of an ontological hierarchy found in more traditional systems?" For millennia, people have erroneously appealed to the great chain of being to justify atrocities such as the annihilating and enslaving of "inferior cultures" and the wanton destruction of the environment. These invidious uses of hierarchy have rightly been ridiculed and criticized. Insofar as Whitehead affirms a multidimensional continuum of value and beauty that affirms that one individual may have a greater depth of beauty and value than another, doesn't process thought run the same risk of using hierarchical schemes for illicit purposes?

The difficulty of answering this question is compounded by the fact that many process scholars do appeal to what I call an individual's "onto-aesthetic status" to justify its moral significance. For instance, in *Hartshorne and the Metaphysics of Animal Rights*, Dombrowski argues that if a conflict arises between the vital needs of a higher-order individual and a lower-order individual, then the needs of the higher-order individual are to be given preference *because it is a higher-order individual*: "A process approach would condemn the destruction (or maiming) of any society of actual occasions, unless such a society clearly threatened the intensity or satisfaction of a higher-order society."[33] To return to the previous example, many process philosophers seem to argue that if one must choose between the vital needs of an infant and the vital needs of a mosquito, the moral action would be to give preference to the needs of the infant *because* it is more beautiful and valuable.

Thus, the justification for giving preference to the vital needs of the infant over the mosquito depends solely on the onto-aesthetic status of the individuals involved.

Arguments such as these lead deep ecologists to argue that although Whitehead's metaphysics of process is laudable, it is ultimately not a suitable basis for a truly "deep" ecology. Echoing John Rodman, Sessions claims that process philosophy is actually just a thinly disguised form of "moral extensionism." As its name suggests, moral extensionism designates those positions that extend direct duties to nonhuman natural entities because these entities have intrinsic value. Accordingly, the problem with extensionist positions is that they only *appear* to break with anthropocentrism. "'Subhumans' may now be accorded rights," Rodman argues, "but we should not be surprised if their interests are normally overridden by the weightier interests of humans, for the choice of the quality to define the extended base class of those entitled to moral consideration has weighted the scales in that way."[34] Thus, Rodman and Sessions believe that process philosophy does not take its rejection of anthropocentrism far enough. I agree that using an individual's onto-aesthetic status to determine its moral significance is potentially dangerous and unjustified. However, I am not convinced that this is what Whitehead's system entails.

Although an individual's onto-aesthetic status plays a significant role in determining its moral significance, the former does not constitute the latter. Rather, Whitehead writes in *Modes of Thought*, our obligation is not simply to give preference to the interests (vital or otherwise) of higher-order individuals, but always to act so as to maximize the beauty, importance, and value possible in each situation: "The generic aim of process is the attainment of importance, in that species and to that extent which *in that instance* is possible" (MT, 12, emphasis added). "Morality is always the aim at that union of harmony, intensity, and vividness which involves the perfection of importance *for that occasion*" (MT, 14, emphasis added). Further, "our action is moral if we have thereby safeguarded the importance of experience so far as it depends *on that concrete instance* in the world's history" (MT, 15, emphasis added). Accordingly, the only justification for putting the interests of one individual over another is that doing so achieves the most beauty possible in the situation taken as a whole. That is, although an individual's onto-aesthetic status plays a significant role in determining its moral significance in a given situation, the former is not strictly constitutive of the latter.

Given this analysis, we should analyze the moral conflict between the infant and the mosquito in this way: first, with deep ecologists, we must affirm that both infants and mosquitoes are intrinsically valuable and beautiful individuals deserving of our respect and appreciation. Yet, with other process philosophers, I recognize that, compared to the beauty and value of a complex being such as a human infant, the beauty and value of a single mosquito is comparatively superficial. However, according to the model being advanced, this conclusion is not sufficient to justify preferring the needs of the infant over those of the mosquito. The aim is not merely to give preference to the more complex individual; the aim in our moral decision making is to determine what would achieve the most harmonious and intense whole with regard to the individuals involved. Though the beauty and value of a human child greatly surpasses that of a mosquito, the ultimate justification for killing the mosquito is that protecting the child would achieve the most beautiful whole possible in that situation. To choose the mosquito over the infant would be to affirm the less beautiful of two options. Thus, the destruction of the mosquito would be tragic but morally justifiable.

Yet, depending upon the situation, it may be morally appropriate to sacrifice the vital needs of the higher-order individual. Although the depth of beauty sometimes experienced by human beings—and this is not invariable[35]—is of a very high grade, this does not mean that human needs (even vital needs) and interests should always be given preference. Although an individual's onto-aesthetic status is a determining factor, it does not strictly constitute its moral significance. Our obligation is always to affirm the most beautiful whole that we can see. Whether this puts human needs and interests over those of others depends solely on what would achieve the most inclusive, complex, and unified whole for all involved.

I will illustrate this point with another instance of moral conflict, say, that between a blade of grass and a hungry horse.[36] Compared to the beauty and value of a complex animal such as a horse, the beauty and value of a single blade of grass is comparatively superficial. Thus, most process philosophers would argue that if one must choose between the vital needs of a horse and the vital needs of a blade of grass, the moral action would be to give preference to the horse because it is more beautiful and valuable. Thus, the justification for giving preference to the vital needs of the horse over the blade of grass depends solely on the onto-aesthetic status of the individuals involved. How would the present project differ from this judgment?

With other process philosophers, I recognize that, although both horses and grasses are intrinsically valuable and beautiful individuals deserving of our respect and appreciation, because of the greater complexity of horses, the potential depth of their beauty and value is greater. However, unlike the interpretation above, this conclusion alone is not sufficient to justify putting the needs of the horse over that of the grass. For the ethics of creativity, the second and third steps in moral decision making are to determine what would achieve the most harmonious and intense whole regarding the individuals involved in this particular situation. In most cases, to achieve the most beautiful whole it would be necessary and morally appropriate to sacrifice the life of the blade of grass for the life of the horse. "But," Ferré points out, "if the choice were to be between the individual animal, or even a herd, and the health of grasses generally in an ecosystem, the weight of the good might well swing from considerations of intrinsic satisfaction for the few (the horses) toward the instrumental good for the many (the grasses)."[37] Thus, depending upon the situation, it may be morally appropriate to sacrifice the vital needs of the higher-order individual, the horse, to achieve the most beauty in the situation taken as a whole.[38]

In general, then, the chief difference that separates the ethics of creativity from both deep ecology and more traditional process philosophies lies in the ultimate aim of and justification for our actions. The position being defended insists that while an individual's onto-aesthetic status plays an important role in our decision making, this status does not by itself constitute an individual's moral significance.[39] Whether we ought to satisfy the needs of one individual at the expense of another depends not merely on which is more complex. An action is morally appropriate only if it would achieve the most beauty possible in the situation taken as a whole. In this respect, it is the ethics of creativity that truly leads to a "deep ecological consciousness." For contrary to deep ecology's "third point," which allows for the sacrifice of nonhuman individuals whenever their interests conflict with the "vital needs" of humans, the ethics of creativity insists that our obligation is not simply to give preference to the interests (vital or otherwise) of higher-order individuals, but always to act in such a way that we maximize the beauty, importance, and value possible in each situation.[40] Our primary obligation, therefore, is always to affirm the most beautiful whole that we can see. Whether this puts human needs and interests over those of others depends solely upon what would achieve the most inclusive, complex, and unified whole for all involved.

Ultimately, the ethics of creativity is neither biocentric nor anthropocentric. It is kalocentric.[41] Although it may be seen to share aspects of more traditional moral and environmental philosophies, in the end, a Whiteheadian moral philosophy is every bit as unique, speculative, fallible, and dynamic as the metaphysics on which it is based.

Notes

Quotations from Alfred North Whitehead's works are cited in the text and notes with the following abbreviations:

AI   *Adventures of Ideas*. New York: Free Press, 1933.

AE   *The Aims of Education and Other Essays*. New York: Free Press, 1929.

FR   *The Function of Reason*. Princeton: Princeton University Press, 1920.

IM   "Immortality." In *The Philosophy of Alfred North Whitehead*, ed. Paul Arthur Schilpp, 682–700. 2d ed. LaSalle: Open Court, 1951.

MT   *Modes of Thought*. New York: Free Press, 1938.

PR   *Process and Reality*. Corrected edition. Ed. David Ray Griffin and Donald W. Sherburne. New York: Free Press, 1978.

RM   *Religion in the Making*. Ed. Judith A. Jones. New York: Fordham University Press, 1996.

SMW   *Science and the Modern World*. New York: Free Press, 1925.

Introduction

1. Utilitarianism is an exception in extending moral standing to all sentient creatures. For instance, Mill calls for the extension of moral standing "to the whole sentient creation" (John Stuart Mill, *Utilitarianism*, ed. Mary Warnock [New York: Meridian Books, 1962], 263). Of course, utilitarianism does not extend its sphere of concern to the relations beyond animals to animate entities such as plants or insects, much less inanimate entities such as rocks.

2. As I argue in chapter 7, this approach has the potential to serve as a bridge between the often acrimonious relationship between animal welfare advocates and environmental philosophers.

3. This is not to say that Whitehead's work has been unimportant in environmental philosophy. In fact, according to Eugene Hargrove, long-time editor of *Environmental Ethics*, the first philosophical dissertation written on environmental ethics, "The Rights of Nonhuman Beings: A Whiteheadian Study," was written by a Whiteheadian, Susan Armstrong (1976). For a copy of her dissertation and reference to Hargrove's statement, see Armstrong's Web site at Humboldt State University, http://www.humboldt.edu/~phil/armstrong/armstrong.html.

Chapter 1: From Mechanism to Organism

1. By "scope of direct moral concern," I mean those entities that must be included in their own right as objects of direct duties in one's moral deliberations. These define the scope or extension of one's moral concern. As we will see, the scope of direct moral concern is coextensive with the scope of intrinsic value.

2. According to Whitehead, this has the effect of making Descartes' system incoherent. "Incoherence is the arbitrary disconnection of first principles. In modern philosophy Descartes' two kinds of substance, corporeal and mental, illustrate incoherence. There is, in Descartes' philosophy, no reason why there should not be a one-substance world, only corporeal, or a one-substance world only mental" (PR, 6).

3. For further defense of this interpretation, see Tom Regan, *The Case for Animal Rights* (Berkeley: University of California, 1983), 3–6. For an opposing interpretation of Descartes, see John Cottingham, "'A Brute to the Brutes?': Descartes' Treatment of Animals," *Philosophy* 53 (1978): 551–59; Peter Harrison, "Descartes on Animals," *Philosophical Quarterly* 42 (1992): 219–27; or Cecilia Wee, "Cartesian Environmental Ethics," *Environmental Ethics* 23 (2001): 275–86.

4. René Descartes, *Discourse on Method*, in *The Philosophical Writings of Descartes*, vol. 1, trans. John Cottingham, Robert Stoothoff, and Dugald Murdoch (Cambridge: Cambridge University Press, 1985), 59.

5. Thanks to Michael Miller for bringing these passages in Descartes' letters to my attention. The following description is paraphrased from Miller's forthcoming essay, "The Meaning of Descartes' Animal Agnosticism."

6. René Descartes, *The Philosophical Writings of Descartes*, vol. 3, trans. Anthony Kenny et al. (Cambridge: Cambridge University Press, 1991), 81–82.

7. Ibid., 317.

8. Leonora Cohen Rosenfield, *From Beast-Machine to Man-Machine: Animal Soul in French Letters from Descartes to La Mettrie* (New York: Octagon Books, 1968), 54.

9. René Descartes, *Principles of Philosophy*, in *The Philosophical Writings of Descartes*, vol. 2, trans. John Cottingham, Robert Stoothoff, and Dugald Murdoch (Cambridge: Cambridge University Press, 1985), 210.

10. Immanuel Kant, *Groundwork of the Metaphysics of Morals*, trans. H. J. Paton (New York: Harper Torchbooks, 1964), 428–65, author's emphases.

11. Immanuel Kant, "Duties towards Animals and Spirits," in *Lectures on Ethics*, trans. Louis Infield (New York: Harper and Row, 1963), 239.

12. St. Thomas Aquinas also argues for an indirect duties view toward nonhumans but, not surprisingly, on more consequentialist grounds. In book 3, chap. 112, of the *Summa Contra Gentiles*, for instance, he argues that

"if any statements are found in Sacred Scripture prohibiting the commission of an act of cruelty against brute animals . . . this is said either to turn the mind of man away from cruelty which might be used on other men, lest a person through practicing cruelty on brutes might go on to do the same to men; or because an injurious act committed on animals may lead to a temporal loss for some man" (*Summa Contra Gentiles*, in *Human Life and the Natural World*, trans. Vernon J. Bourke, ed. Owen Goldin and Patricia Kilroe [New York: Broadview, 1997], 95).

13. Kant wrote this about experiments such as those carried out by the Cartesians: "Vivisectionists who use living animals for their experiments, certainly act cruelly, although their aim is praiseworthy, and they can justify their cruelty, since animals must be regarded as man's instruments" ("Duties towards Animals and Spirits," 239). Note that Kant does not claim that acting cruelly toward animals is to be avoided for an animal's sake. Again, we have no direct duties toward animals whatever. According to Kant's logic, the animal's suffering is of no direct concern. The mutilation of a live animal is no worse, morally speaking, than the smashing of a tractor. Tractors and animals are simply "instruments" or "means." See Christina Hoff, "Kant's Invidious Humanism," *Environmental Ethics* 5 (1983): 63–70.

14. David Hume, *A Treatise of Human Nature*, ed. Ernest C. Mossner (New York: Penguin, 1969), 523, author's emphases.

15. In making value relative, materialism renders unintelligible, among other things, the notions of intercultural criticism and social progress. For if value is purely relative, then there is no standard independent of one's own culture against which such criticism or progress can be measured. See James Rachels, "The Challenge of Cultural Relativism," in *Elements of Moral Philosophy*, 4th ed. (New York: McGraw-Hill, 2003), 16–31.

16. Hume, 521, author's emphases.

17. There are many sides to this debate. For some, the abortion debate is not merely over the status of the fetus, but equally over the status of the pregnant woman. Even if one grants that the fetus is a human being with intrinsic value, this does not straightforwardly resolve its relationship to the mother, who is also a human being with intrinsic value. See Judith Jarvis Thomson, "A Defense of Abortion," *Philosophy and Public Affairs* 1 (1971): 47–66.

18. In the strictest sense, moral relations, for the axiological dualist, are limited to those obtaining between rational beings because only rational beings "count," morally speaking. If moral relations include those beings to which we have indirect duties, our dealings with nonhumans would be moral relations and every action by a human agent would be a moral action. However, note that even this dilution of the sense of morality would not change the status of nonhumans. For the ethical dualist, nonhumans can never have more than instrumental or "conditional" value and cannot

therefore be objects of direct moral concern. Again, the scope of direct moral concern and the scope of intrinsic value are coextensive.

19. Peter Singer, *Animal Liberation*, 3d ed. (New York: Avon Books, 2002).

20. Ibid., 54.

21. See C. Ray Greek and Jean Single Greek, *Sacred Cows and Golden Geese: The Human Cost of Experiments on Animals* (New York: Continuum, 2000).

22. Peirce contrasts *synechism* with other metaphysical systems in the following passage: "The word *synechism* is the English form of the Greek συνεχισμός, from συνεχής, continuous. For two centuries we have been affixing *-ist* and *-ism* to words, in order to note sects which exalt the importance of those elements which the stem-words signify. Thus, *materialism* is the doctrine that matter is everything, *idealism* the doctrine that ideas are everything, *dualism* the philosophy which splits everything in two. In like manner, I have proposed to make *synechism* mean the tendency to regard everything as continuous" (Charles Sanders Peirce, "Immortality in the Light of Synechism," in *The Essential Peirce: Selected Philosophical Writings*, vol. 2, ed. Edition Project [Indianapolis: Indiana University Press, 1998], 1).

23. Charles Sanders Peirce, "The Law of Mind," in *The Essential Peirce*, vol. 1, ed. Nathan Houser and Christopher Kloesel (Indianapolis: Indiana University Press, 1992), 312. Peirce's theory of *synechism* is all the more amazing when we recall the period in which he was writing. Unlike Dewey, Peirce did not have the evidential support provided by the work of scientists such as Einstein, Heisenberg, and Bell, and thus was out on a speculative limb unsupported by the Newtonian science of his day. Peirce's perceptivity and vision are truly a testament to his genius.

24. Charles Sanders Peirce, "Man's Glassy Essence," in *The Essential Peirce*, vol. 1, 349.

25. William James writes, "A concept means a *that-and-no-other*. Conceptually, time excludes space; motion and rest exclude each other; approach excludes contact; presence excludes absence; unity excludes plurality; independence excludes relativity; 'mine' excludes 'yours'; this connexion excludes that connexion—and so on indefinitely; whereas in the real concrete sensible flux of life experiences compenetrate each other so that it is not easy to know just what is excluded and what not" (*Pluralistic Universe*, in *William James: Writings, 1902–1910* [New York: Library of America, 1987], 746).

26. Ibid., 728.

27. Ibid., 748.

28. Ibid.

29. Ibid., 725.

30. Ibid., 697.

31. John Dewey, "Time and Individuality," in *John Dewey, The Later Works*, vol. 14, ed. JoAnn Boydston (Carbondale: Southern Illinois University Press, 1991), 107.

32. Ibid., 103.

33. I refer to Dewey's interpretation of Heisenberg, and others like it, as the "ontological interpretation." According to this interpretation, indeterminacy is an ontological aspect of nature. Reality is not *completely* determined (though it certainly is restricted by a great many things, such as the particular metric of our universe). Thus, reality itself is ontologically indeterminate in that, at its root, there is a certain "window" that is not rendered determinate by purely external forces. In contrast is what I call the "epistemological interpretation" of Heisenberg, according to which the uncertainty of the position and velocity of a particular particle is due only to our own failing, technological or otherwise. The implication is, of course, that reality is not itself indeterminate. Rather, given sufficient time and resources, nature would be revealed as completely determinate and therefore completely certain. Accordingly, the epistemological interpretation is only a modified version of Laplace and is subject to the same criticisms. Dewey is clearly asserting the ontological indeterminacy of existence and is therefore closer to what I have labeled the ontological interpretation.

34. Dewey, "Time and Individuality," 107.

35. Ibid.

36. Ibid., 104, emphasis added. Cf. "Experience thus reaches down into nature; it has depth" (John Dewey, *Experience and Nature*, 2d ed. [La Salle, Ill.: Open Court, 1929], 4).

37. Dewey, "Time and Individuality," 108.

38. Dewey, *Experience and Nature*, 207–8.

39. Ibid., 351.

40. Ibid., 352.

41. I do not claim that there is something intrinsically wrong with pragmatism. I am enlisting its help to overturn the implicit hegemony of modern metaphysics and, more important, modern axiology. Thus, while some pragmatists would doubtless eschew such metaphysical speculations, I contend that, as long as it is undertaken within a fallibilistic framework, it is irresponsible not to do so. Though I cannot develop the claim here, in many ways, Whitehead's metaphysics and the pragmatists' epistemology are complementary. Whereas the pragmatists devote much time to developing a new model for epistemology and psychology, Whitehead devoted his career to developing a speculative metaphysics. While Whitehead focuses on the microscopic, the pragmatists focus on the macroscopic. This similarity is no coincidence. Whitehead was deeply affected by the work of James, whom he once referred to as an "adorable genius" (SMW, 2).

42. These are the four criteria by which Whitehead expects his system to

be judged (PR, 3–7). See also Frederick Ferré's discussion of these criteria in *Being and Value: Toward a Constructive Postmodern Metaphysics* (Albany: State University of New York Press, 1996), esp. 1–18.

43. Paul A. Schilpp, "Whitehead's Moral Philosophy," in *The Philosophy of Alfred North Whitehead*, ed. Paul Arthur Schilpp, 2d ed. (LaSalle, Ill.: Open Court, 1951), 664.

44. In Whitehead's words, "Philosophy is at once general and concrete, critical and appreciative of direct intuition. It is not—or, at least, should not be—a ferocious debate between irritable professors. It is a survey of possibilities and their comparison with actualities. In philosophy, the fact, the theory, the alternatives, and the ideal, are weighed together. Its gifts are insight and foresight, and a sense of the world of life, in short, that sense of importance which nerves all civilized effort" (AI, 98).

45. Whitehead writes, "Morality of outlook is inseparably conjoined with generality of outlook" (PR, 15).

46. See also PR, 137.

47. Etymologically, the term "substance" is from the Latin *sub* (under) and *stare* (to stand) and is a translation of the Greek term *hypostasis* from *hypo* (under) and *hitasthai* (to stand). W. L. Reese, *The Dictionary of Philosophy and Religion* (Highlands, N.J.: Humanities Press, 1980), 555–56.

48. Aristotle, *Categories*, 2a12.

49. William James, *Principles of Psychology*, vol. 1 (New York: Dover, 1890), 488.

50. See also, "The simple notion of an enduring substance sustaining persistent qualities, either essentially or accidentally, expresses a useful abstract for many purposes in life. But whenever we try to use it as a fundamental statement of the nature of things, it proves itself mistaken. It arose from a mistake and has never succeeded in any of its applications. But it has had one success: it has entrenched itself in language, in Aristotelian logic, and in metaphysics. For its employment in language and in logic, there is—as stated above—a sound pragmatic defence. But in metaphysics the concept is sheer error" (PR, 79). Also, "This error [of a vacuous substratum] is the result of high-grade intellectuality. The instinctive interpretations which govern human life and animal life presuppose a contemporary world throbbing with energetic values" (AI, 219).

51. See SMW, 51–53, 58.

52. See PR, 79.

53. According to Whitehead, "The term 'actual occasion' is used synonymously with 'actual entity'; but chiefly when its character of extensiveness has some direct relevance to the discussion, either extensiveness in the form of temporal extensiveness, that is to say 'duration,' or extensiveness in the form of spatial extension, or in the more complete signification of spatio-temporal extensiveness" (PR, 77). See also PR, 211. There is, however, one

notable exception to the equivalence of these terms: "In the subsequent discussion, 'actual entity' will be taken to mean a conditioned actual entity of the temporal world, unless God is expressly included in the discussion. The term 'actual occasion' will always exclude God from its scope" (PR, 88). I prefer "actual occasion" (often simply "occasion") over "actual entity" because "entity" connotes properties such as "static," "enduring," and "independent," properties that Whitehead explicitly rejects, whereas "occasion" emphasizes "temporality," "relation," and "dynamism."

54. The ontological principle states that all reasons must make an appeal to an actual entity. "The ontological principle asserts the relativity of decision; whereby every decision expresses the relation of the actual thing, *for which* a decision is made, to an actual thing *by which* that decision is made. But 'decision' cannot be construed as a causal adjunct of an actual entity. It constitutes the very meaning of actuality. An actual entity arises from decisions *for* it, and by its very existence provides decisions *for* other actual entities which supersede it. . . . 'Actuality' is the decision amid 'potentiality.' It represents stubborn fact which cannot be evaded. The real internal constitution of an actual entity progressively constitutes a decision conditioning the creativity which transcends that actuality" (PR, 43). See also PR, 19, 24, 32, 40, 41, 46, 244, 256.

55. See James, *A Pluralistic Universe*, 733–34.

56. Cf. "The objects are the factors in experience which function so as to express that that occasion originates by including a transcendent universe of other things. Thus it belongs to the essence of each occasion of experience that it is concerned with an otherness transcending itself. The occasion is one among others, and including the others which it is among" (AI, 180).

57. Cf. "The first phase is the phase of pure reception of the actual world in its guise of objective datum for aesthetic synthesis. In this phase there is the mere reception of the actual world as a multiplicity of private centers of feeling, implicated in a nexus of mutual presupposition. The feelings are felt as belonging to the external centres, and are not absorbed into the private immediacy" (PR, 212).

58. See, "The initial situation includes a factor of activity which is the reason for the origination of that occasion of experience. This factor of activity is what I have called 'Creativity.' The initial situation with its creativity can be termed the initial phase of the new occasion. It can equally well be termed the 'actual world' relative to that occasion. It has a certain unity of its own, expressive of its capacity for providing the objects requisite for a new occasion, and also expressive of its conjoint activity whereby it is essentially the primary phase of a new occasion. It can thus be termed a 'real potentiality.' The 'potentiality' refers to the passive capacity, the term 'real' refers to the creative activity, where the Platonic definition of 'real' in the *Sophist* is referred to" (AI, 179).

59. See SMW, 158–72, esp. 167.

60. Cf. "The analysis of concrescence, here adopted, conceives that there is an origination of conceptual feeling, admitting or rejecting whatever is apt for feeling by reason of its germaneness to the basic data. The graduation of eternal objects in respect to this germaneness is the 'objective lure' for feeling; the concrescent process admits a selection from this 'objective lure' into subjective efficiency" (PR, 87).

61. The principle of process is Whitehead's ninth category of explanation: "That *how* an actual entity *becomes* constitutes *what* that actual entity is; so that the two descriptions of an actual entity are not independent. Its 'being' is constituted by its 'becoming.' This is the 'principle of process'" (PR, 23). See also PR, 150, 222, 255.

62. To be more precise, "Each occasion exhibits its measure of creative emphasis in proportion to its measure of subjective intensity" (PR, 47). The exaggeration of the *causa sui* nature of actual entities by Whitehead scholars has led many critics to accuse Whitehead of making homuncular entities out of his actual entities. This problem is of the classical interpretation's own making. Whitehead is quite clear that entities' "freedom" is often exceedingly narrow. "But there is no such fact as absolute freedom; every actual entity possesses only such freedom as is inherent in the primary phase 'given' by its standpoint of relativity to its actual universe. Freedom, givenness, potentiality, are notions which presuppose each other and limit each other" (PR, 133). Freedom is never zero, but for the vast majority of entities it is closer to this limit than not.

63. See, "There are two species of process, macroscopic process, and microscopic process. The macroscopic process is the transition from attained actuality to actuality in attainment; while microscopic process is the conversion of conditions which are merely real into determinant actuality. . . . The former process is efficient; the latter process is teleological" (PR, 214).

64. Although scholars such as Ivor Leclerc, William Christian, Lewis S. Ford, Donald Sherburne, Joseph Bracken, and Jorge Nobo have extensively analyzed various elements of Whitehead's metaphysics of process, none of them devotes more than an occasional line or paragraph to the importance of axiology to Whitehead's system. For instance, even though Leclerc devotes a number of pages to Whitehead's repudiation of vacuous actuality, he fails to significantly examine the axiological foundation of this repudiation. See Ivor Leclerc, *Whitehead's Metaphysics* (Highlands, N.J.: Humanities Press, 1958), 125–30. This omission may be owing to process scholars thinking that their analyses of other key terms covers value *in cursu*. An exception is Frederick Ferré's trilogy *Being and Value: Toward a Constructive Postmodern Metaphysics* (Albany: State University of New York Press, 1996); *Knowing and Value: Toward a Constructive Postmodern Epistemology* (Albany: State University of New York Press, 1998); and *Living and Value:*

Toward a Constructive Postmodern Ethics (Albany: State University of New York Press, 2001).

65. See, "A logical requirement of any value system is that it should clarify the idea of no value, or the value zero. I hold that, as value diminishes, its limit of zero is not in a form of existence without value, but in total nonexistence. The zero of feeling, or of intrinsic value, and of actuality are one and the same" (Charles Hartshorne, "The Rights of the Subhuman World," *Environmental Ethics* 1 [1979]: 54).

66. See, "The term panexperientialism, I should add, is my own, not Whitehead's or Hartshorne's" (David Ray Griffin, *Reenchantment Without Supernaturalism* [Ithaca: Cornell University Press, 2000], 97). In a note, Griffin adds, "I first used the term panexperientialism in print, to my knowledge, in Cobb and Griffin 1977, 98."

67. Cf. "Each occasion has its physical inheritance and its mental reaction which drives it on to its self-completion. The world is not merely physical, nor is it merely mental. Nor is it merely *one* with many subordinate phases. Nor is it merely a complete fact in its essence static with the illusion of change. Wherever a vicious dualism appears, it is by reason of mistaking an abstraction for a concrete final fact" (AI, 190).

68. Whitehead himself points to this political metaphor: "We find ourselves in a buzzing world, amid a democracy of fellow creatures" (PR, 50). Jones refers to this principle as the ethical correlate of Whitehead's ontological principle.

Chapter 2: An Ecstatic Axiology

1. David L. Schindler, "Whitehead's Inability to Affirm a Universe of Value," *Process Studies* 13 (1983): 117–31.

2. My main concern is not with Schindler's own analysis, but the argument he presents against Whitehead's system and its ability to affirm a true universe of value.

3. Chapter 5 addresses the claim that a Whiteheadian moral philosophy is a form of moral interest theory.

4. Schindler, 118. Schindler asks, "If the value of actuality lies in actuality's character as subject . . ., what warrants my assigning value to others, the data, that is, the *objects* in relation to which I (or any actual entity) constitute myself as subject?" (ibid., 121).

5. Ibid., 121.

6. Ibid., 128.

7. Ivor Leclerc, *Whitehead's Metaphysics* (New Jersey: Humanities Press, 1958). William Christian, *An Interpretation of Whitehead's Metaphysics* (New Haven: Yale University Press, 1959).

8. Ivor Leclerc, "Being and Becoming in Whitehead's Philosophy," in

Explorations in Whitehead's Philosophy, ed. Lewis S. Ford and George L. Kline (New York: Fordham University Press, 1983), 56.

9. Leclerc, *Whitehead's Metaphysics*, 101, 108.

10. Christian, *Whitehead's Metaphysics*, 37, emphasis added.

11. Ibid., 321.

12. Lewis S. Ford uses this concise phrase in *Transforming Process Theism* (Albany: State University of New York Press, 2000), 10.

13. As Leclerc puts it, "Their own subjective immediacy is then over, and they have 'perished' as actual. That is, they no longer exist in the full sense" (*Whitehead's Metaphysics*, 135). This would seem to make a superject into a vacuous actuality. Of course, in a sense, this is simply another formulation of the problem of subjectivism.

14. George L. Kline, "Form, Concrescence, and Concretum," in *Explorations in Whitehead's Philosophy*, ed. Lewis S. Ford and George L. Kline (New York: Fordham University Press, 1983), 104.

15. Ibid.

16. Ibid., 132. See Judith A. Jones's detailed analysis of the problems with Kline's affirmation of a sharp ontological distinction between concrescence and concretum in *Intensity: An Essay in Whiteheadian Ontology* (Nashville: Vanderbilt University Press, 1998), esp. 86–87.

17. Kline, 132.

18. Ibid., 119.

19. John Goheen, "Whitehead's Theory of Value," in *The Philosophy of Alfred North Whitehead*, ed. Paul Arthur Schilpp, 2d ed. (LaSalle, Ill.: Open Court, 1951), 449.

20. As we will see in part 2, this interpretation of Whitehead's axiology has led some commentators to conclude that any ethics based on Whitehead's metaphysics could never be more than a moral interest theory. I contend that the classical interpretation's overemphasis on the subject lends itself to the interpretation of Whitehead's ethics as a subjectivistic moral interest theory or, even worse, as a moral solipsism. We need to establish another interpretation of Whitehead's metaphysics before elaborating an ethical theory. See chapter 5.

21. See Ford, *Transforming*, 10.

22. Ibid., 247–48.

23. Ford provides surprisingly little justification for rejecting the past as the locus of creativity and the justification may beg the question. For instance, he asserts, "As long as the future is thought to contain nothing actual, everything that an occasion needs must be derived from the past. Under that restriction it makes sense to derive creativity from the past, even though every individual past actuality has no creativity. (If it has any creativity, it would still be on the way to becoming past. There is no real pastness unless its creativity has perished.) If the future is actual, and particularly if the fu-

ture is creativity itself, it can be the source of creativity. If creativity cannot simply well up in the present, nor come from the creativity-less past, it must come from the future" (ibid., 12–13). See also, "How can the past be potential? It can neither transfer creativity (as can the future) nor actualize it (as can the present), for the past lacks all creativity. Nor is there anything the past can do, for it is absolutely immutable, absolutely inert. But the past can be taken up into other modes of actuality by being actively appropriated by them by means of prehension" (Lewis S. Ford, "The Modes of Actuality," *Modern Schoolman* 67 [1990]: 282). The problem is that Ford is simply asserting that the past cannot be the source of creativity based on his own definition of the past, which makes it devoid of creativity. Interestingly, Ford even explicitly denies Whitehead's own claims that the past is the source of creativity: "To be sure, Whitehead seems to suggest in *Adventures of Ideas* that creativity can come from the past" (Ford, *Transforming*, 12). Again, Ford simply seems unwilling to even entertain the possibility that the past could be the source of creativity because he has defined it in such a way that it is devoid of creativity. This only begs the question at hand.

24. Ford, *Transforming*, 11.

25. Ibid., 248. Ford adds, "Since the temporal difference between past and present does not introduce the incoherence the principle of ontological primacy was designed to guard against, I propose we adopt a more restricted principle: Only one species of actualities primarily exists in any particular temporal mode. In the present mode only concrescences primarily exist. In the past mode only concrete determinants primarily exist. Actuality signifies whatever has ontological primacy in a given temporal mode" (ibid.).

26. Schindler, 121, author's emphasis.

27. Ford, *Transforming*, 10.

28. Ford, "Modes of Actuality," 279; *Transforming*, 12.

29. Ford, "Modes of Actuality," 278–79.

30. Lewis S. Ford, "Nancy Frankenberry's Conception of the Power of the Past," *American Journal of Theology and Philosophy* 14 (1993): 294.

31. Ford, "Modes of Actuality," 282.

32. Ford, *Emergence*, 87.

33. Ford, "Modes of Actuality," 278–79.

34. Because their axiological implications are the same, unless otherwise noted, future references to the classical interpretation should be taken to include Ford's temporal interpretation.

35. For instance, as Jorge Luis Nobo argues, "an entity is actual when it has, *or has had*, significance for itself" (*Whitehead's Metaphysics of Extension and Solidarity* [Albany: State University of New York Press, 1986], 294, author's emphasis). According to this interpretation, an actual occasion *qua* superject is just as actual as an actual occasion *qua* subject.

36. As Nobo notes, by "at once" Whitehead does not mean that an actual

occasion is simultaneously a subject and a superject. An entity cannot be both a process of development and a completed product of development at the same time. One must, in some sense, follow the other. "In other words, an actual entity first exists as subject, and then as superject. Both modes of existence cannot belong to it at once. Nevertheless, *in regard to its complete history*, an actual entity is both process *and* product, both becoming *and* being, both subject *and* superject" (ibid., 16, author's emphases). Schindler contends that the only way to affirm the intrinsic value of the objective world is to affirm that an actual occasion is literally both a subject and a superject. However, to follow the trajectory of Schindler's argument and affirm that an entity must be simultaneously subject and superject, then passage would become illusory. Only in the complete satisfaction of an actual entity, in the perishing of its subjectivity, is a single quantum of time achieved. By collapsing the superject into the subject, Schindler succeeds only in affirming a universal temporal monism, a present undifferentiated by a past or future. The origin of Schindler's mistake is in his omission of Whitehead's epochal theory of time, according to which "the genetic passage from phase to phase is not in physical time" (PR, 283). For Whitehead, the process of concrescence *results* in time but is not *in* time. "There is a becoming of continuity, but no continuity of becoming" (PR, 35). Therefore, if one were to grant Schindler's thesis and collapse the superject into the subject, Whitehead's philosophy would result in a monism that would make change impossible and render any reference to *individual* intrinsic value meaningless.

37. As Nancy Frankenberry notes, one benefit of this emphasis on the activity of past occasions is that it diminishes and downplays the miraculousness of the *causa sui* element of concrescence, which element has been the target of numerous criticisms of Whitehead's metaphysics. "Without a proper appreciation of the power of the past as immanent in the initial conformal phase of concrescence, the *causa sui* character of the concrescence is apt to be exaggerated, and the notion of emergence will seem to be *ex nihilo*" ("The Power of the Past," *Process Studies* 13 [1983]: 135).

38. Ibid., 137.

39. Neither Frankenberry nor Kraus denies that subjectivity perishes in the achievement of satisfaction, which is necessary to have any real achievement. They do deny that the perishing of subjectivity implies that the superject is dead, lifeless, or passive.

40. Elizabeth M. Kraus, "Existence as Transaction: A Whiteheadian Study of Causality," *International Philosophical Quarterly* 25 (1985): 360.

41. Frankenberry, "Power of the Past," 140, emphasis added.

42. Nobo, *Extension and Solidarity*, 32, author's emphases. Nobo observes that, in missing the full importance of this and other key metaphysical principles, the "major received interpretations endanger significant areas of the *applicability* of Whitehead's organic metaphysics" (ibid., 8). Schindler's the-

sis seems to be a case in point. If I am correct in my assessment of the classical interpretation, it has indeed endangered any possibility of creating a meaningful ethical system based on Whitehead's metaphysics.

43. Ibid., 79, author's emphases.

44. W. Norris Clarke, a contemporary neo-Thomist whose work I challenge in chapter 3, argues for a similar view of causality, which he also describes in ecstatic terms. "It involves an *efficacious, productive power* in the cause such that the cause makes the effect to be, in whole or in part. It is the positive overflow of one being into another, 'the ecstasy of one being in another,' as Etienne Gilson has put it, rooted in the radical fecundity of the act of existence as inner act and energy of every real being, in virtue of which, given the opportunity, it naturally flows over and communicates being to others according to its capacities" (*The One and the Many: A Contemporary Thomistic Metaphysics* [Notre Dame: Notre Dame University Press, 2001], 187). See also, "Thus efficient causality is the immanence of the cause at work in the effect, as long as the effect is still being actually produced—a presence not by identity of essence but by a continuum of power as the cause powers over and communicates being in some way to the effect, 'the ecstasy of the cause in the effect,' as Gilson aptly puts it" (ibid., 190).

45. Jones writes, "I have elected to term this capacity for intrusion that appears to be the very mark of what Whitehead means by actuality the 'ecstatic existence' of an individual subject. Past and future aspects of the intensive actuality procured by concrescence are to be conceived of apiece with the subject of concrescence considered as an atomic fact. An actuality is intensively deep in the rich ontological sense of being ecstatically located in (a) whatever contributes to it so as to be provocative of it as an occasion and (b) whatever includes it as an element in its (the future actuality's) satisfaction" (*Intensity*, 71).

46. Ibid., 89.

47. Ibid., xii, author's emphasis.

48. Ibid., 9.

49. Ibid., 89.

50. Ibid.

51. Ibid., 97.

52. Ibid., 94.

53. Ibid., 103.

54. Ibid., 95.

55. In Jones's words, "Past and future aspects of the intensive actuality procured by concrescence are to be conceived as existentially of a piece with the subject of concrescence considered as an atomic fact" (ibid., 71).

56. Ibid., 29.

57. Following deep ecologists, I do not make a distinction between "intrinsic value" and "inherent value." See Bill Devall and George Sessions,

Deep Ecology: Living As If Nature Mattered (Salt Lake City: Gibbs Smith, 1985), esp. 70.

58. John O'Neill, "The Varieties of Intrinsic Value," *Monist* 75 (1992): 119–37.

59. Ibid., 119.

60. Ibid., 120.

61. Holmes Rolston III, "Are Values in Nature Subjective or Objective?" *Environmental Ethics* 4 (1982): 138.

62. Holmes Rolston III, *Environmental Ethics: Duties to and Values in the Natural World* (Philadelphia: Temple University Press, 1988), 110.

63. Although I ultimately disagree with him, here I agree with J. Baird Callicott's claim that Rolston "does not take up arms against the Cartesian object-subject duality—the very castle keep of the subjectivity of values—in respect to which the Humean fact-value dichotomy is but a footnote. This dualism remains an unchallenged substrate of his treatise ("Rolston on Intrinsic Value: A Deconstruction," *Environmental Ethics* 14 [1992]: 137). "As long as he grants that there are independent ('freestanding') objects and correspondingly independent subjects, and primary qualities and secondary qualities—and these basic, essentially conservative presuppositions are never mooted in his book—all the argument in the world to the effect that goodness is more objective than greenness is going to look like a magic show, brought off with smoke and mirrors" (ibid., 138). To the extent that Rolston retains a sharp distinction between subjects and objects, his position is incompatible with the philosophy of organism.

64. As Daniel A. Dombrowski notes, "Mary Midgley has done an excellent job of showing that there is no major problem in arguing from facts to values; the difficulty arises in getting both the facts and the values right. That is, *good* is problematic not because it is evaluative but because it is such a general term. I agree with Midgley that the naturalistic fallacy is a stuffed dragon and that philosophers (including, to a certain extent, Regan) should stop marching around with its head on their spears" (*Babies and Beasts: The Argument from Marginal Cases* [Chicago: University of Illinois Press, 1997], 181).

65. Jones, *Intensity*, 3, author's emphasis.

66. Although Schindler quotes this passage at length, what he concludes from it indicates that he does fully appreciate its significance. First, Schindler understands Whitehead's statement to support his conclusion that "actuality is subjective experience which in turn is value experience" (120). However, such an interpretation misses Whitehead's point. In stating that everything has value for others and for the whole, Whitehead is emphasizing the relativity of existence, the inherent relatedness of being. In so doing, Whitehead is also affirming the *intrinsic* "worth" of the other and of the whole. It is this, contrary to Schindler's interpretation, which "characterizes the meaning of

actuality" (109). Moreover, by equating actuality with subjectivity to the exclusion of superjectivity, Schindler once again implicitly introduces a division between the subject and superject. However, Whitehead is quite explicit in his statement that actuality has *two* sides and that either aspect "is a factor of the other."

67. This conclusion will become important in part 2 when we look at Clare Palmer's objection that process theology's doctrine of contributionism leads to a form of totalizing utilitarianism. To anticipate, although I find that Hartshorne and Cobb's doctrine of contributionism is correct that the value of an entity derives from the "contribution" it makes to God's experience, at times it seems that they so emphasize this aspect of value that they are in danger of reducing the other two to the third alone. To the extent that they do this, they could be subject to Palmer's criticisms. See chapter 7. Chapter 4 presents a more complete discussion of God and an individual's value for the whole.

68. See Whitehead: "In our own relatively high grade of human existence, this doctrine of feelings and their subject is best illustrated by our notion of moral responsibility" (PR, 222).

69. Ferré, *Living and Value*, 140.

Chapter 3: An Organic Model of Individuality

1. See, "An actual occasion has no . . . history. It never changes it only becomes and perishes. Its perishing is its assumption of a new metaphysical function in the creative advance of the universe" (AI, 204).

2. The importance of the latter has often been missed due to commentators' overemphasis on the former. It is, as I have argued, the vacuousness of existence that Whitehead was primarily critical of, not merely its bifurcation. I am indebted to Jones for emphasizing this important point.

3. Ferré, *Living and Value*, 134. See also, "There is no absolute line between living and nonliving entities; some entities, like cut flowers, can be 'partially living,' but on a scale, living entities become more and more capable of significant novelty. As growing complexity allows the mental pole to wax in importance, capacities increase for innovating, adapting to changing environments, finding and filling ecological niches, guiding locomotion, sensing, and responding intelligently to the environment" (ibid., 116).

4. This further emphasizes the importance of the ecstatic interpretation defended in chapter 2. According to the classical interpretation the past is wholly inactive and consequently cannot be said to "impose" itself on anything.

5. Societies are to be understood in terms of "layers of social order" where "the defining characteristics [are] becoming wider and more general as we widen the background" (PR, 90).

6. See PR, 103. Joseph A. Bracken writes, "While the generic concept of structured society, for example, should in principle apply to human communities as well as physical organisms, it is apparent that the functioning of a community cannot simply be likened to the functioning of a physical organism without grave danger of collectivism or totalitarianism within the body politic. The soul, as we have already seen in chapter 3, exercises agency for the entire physical organism; but there is no subsociety within the body politic corresponding to the soul" (*Society and Spirit: A Trinitarian Cosmology* [London: Associated University Presses, 1991], 114).

7. See, "A structured society as a whole provides a favorable environment for the subordinate societies which it harbours within itself. Also the whole society must be set in a wider environment permissive of its continuance. Some of the component groups of occasions in a structured society can be termed 'subordinate societies.' . . . For example, we speak of a molecule within a living cell, because its general molecular features are independent of the environment of the cell. Thus a molecule is a subordinate society in the structured society we call the 'living cell'" (PR, 99).

8. According to Whitehead, another characteristic of a living society is that it requires food (PR, 105). I analyze this in chapter 6.

9. With Ferré, I am not convinced that the division between animals and plants is appropriately drawn by this distinction. See chapter 6.

10. Dewey, "Time and Individuality," 108.

11. See, "The animal grade includes at least one central actuality, supported by the intricacy of bodily functioning. Purposes transcending (however faintly) the mere aim at survival are exhibited" (MT, 27–28).

12. I am indebted to Daniel A. Dombrowski for making the importance of this crucial distinction clear.

13. See Jones's *Intensity* for a detailed analysis of what she calls the "structural conditions" of intensity (esp. 23–39).

14. I say "potentially." Ferré does not provide an explicit definition that gives both the necessary and sufficient conditions required to consider something an entity. Note that Ferré's use of the term "entity" should not be confused with the technical term "actual entity." As Ferré uses it, "actual entity" is a subclass of "entity."

15. Ferré, *Being and Value*, 329.
16. Ibid., 326.
17. Ibid., 336.
18. Ibid., 327.
19. Ibid., 336–37.
20. Ibid., 327.
21. Ibid., 337.
22. Ibid., 329, author's emphasis.
23. Ibid., 337.

24. Ibid.

25. Ibid., 330.

26. Ibid., 337.

27. Ibid., 331, author's emphases. Ferré uses the term "creativity" as a concept that embodies all preceding terms. He is not referring to Whitehead's category of the ultimate.

28. Hartshorne, "Subhuman World," 52, author's emphasis. See chapter 1.

29. Ferré, *Being and Value*, 334, author's emphasis.

30. Ibid., 338.

31. Ibid., 335.

32. See ibid., 338.

33. Strictly speaking, there is no such thing as mere appearance. For Whitehead, the distinction between appearance and reality is functional, rather than a contrast between different types of things. "Unfortunately the superior dominance in consciousness of the contrast 'Appearance and Reality' has led metaphysicians from the Greeks onwards to make their start from the more superficial characteristic. This error has warped modern philosophy to a greater extent than ancient or medieval philosophy. The warping has taken the form of a consistent reliance upon sensationalist perception as the basis of all experiential activity. It has had the effect of decisively separating 'mind' from 'nature,' a modern separation which found its first exemplification in Cartesian dualism" (AI, 210).

34. See, "The Grouping of Occasions is the outcome of some common function performed by those occasions in the percipient experience. The grouped occasions then acquire a unity; they become, for the experience of the percipient, one thing which is complex by reason of its divisibility into many occasions, or into many subordinate groups of occasions. The subordinate groups are then complex unities, each belonging to the *same metaphysical category of existence as the total group*" (ibid., 201, emphasis added).

35. W. Norris Clarke also objects to Whitehead's conception of God and its relation to creativity, but this does not directly concern my investigation. See "God and the Community of Existents: Whitehead and St. Thomas," *International Philosophical Quarterly* 158 (2000): 265–88.

36. Clarke, *The One and the Many*, 102.

37. Ibid., 125. Resources in Whitehead's work and process literature generally address this interpretation.

38. Clarke, "God and Community," 268.

39. Ibid.

40. See James W. Felt, "Whitehead's Misconception of 'Substance' in Aristotle," *Process Studies* 14 (1985): 224–36.

41. Clarke, *The One and the Many*, 32, author's emphases.

42. Ibid.

43. Ibid., 33.

44. Ibid., 129.

45. See, "In a word, *self-identity and immutability* are not at all identical or interchangeable concepts. The self-identity of a real being is not a static, immutable 'thing' but more like an abiding force that actively assimilates and integrates all of the less-than-substantial changes which it undergoes: a unity-identity-whole that maintains itself within certain flexible limits; when these are breached, the identity collapses" (Clarke, "God and Community" 272, author's emphases).

46. Clarke, *The One and the Many*, 128.

47. Ibid., 129. See also, "It would be hard to conceive a more dynamic notion of substance than this, one furthest from the static, inert one of Locke which prevailed later. Furthermore, this substance, as abiding center and source of activity, is actively involved immanent in each of its multiple and successive acts; yet, at the same time, it transcends them all" (Clarke, "God and Community," 270).

48. Clarke, "God and Community," 276.

49. Clarke, *The One and the Many*, 102.

50. Clarke, "God and Community," 271.

51. Ferré, *Being and Value*, 337.

52. Clarke, *The One and the Many*, 136.

53. Strictly speaking, even the most ephemeral spark of activity in a distant galaxy has some effect on what we do here and now. However, if degrees of relevance are taken into consideration, many relations are, practically speaking, accidental. Furthermore, this does not, I contend, jeopardize freedom. Although every actual occasion is internally related to the occasions that preceded it, in the end, a nascent occasion still has some degree of freedom to "decide" whether and how to include the past. See the analysis of the ecstatic interpretation in chapter 2.

54. Clarke, "God and Community," 269.

55. See Bernard Lonergan, *Insight: A Study of Human Understanding* (Toronto: Toronto University Press, 1992), esp. 418, 562; Clarke, *The One and the Many*, 18–19.

56. Clarke, *The One and the Many*, 135, author's emphasis. See also, "*What is a system?* It is a set of relations forming a new unified order, or 'togetherness,' being-together (*mit-sein* in German), which has its own set of properties as a system and influences its members accordingly" (ibid., 136).

57. Ibid., 136.

58. Ibid., 136–37.

59. In "God and the Community of Existents," Clarke seems to flirt with a position surprisingly similar to the one being advanced. Rather than simply affirming something as having sufficient unity to be a substance or not a substance, Clarke advances the idea that an essential form can have a

greater or lesser degree of control over its parts. "The ontological unity of living beings is not just a static state, either given univocally or not, but an active achievement, an ongoing act of cohering achieved by the energy and power of the central form. And there seems to be a spectrum of degrees of control of the form over its parts: certain basic ones are firmly under the control of the form; others, for various reasons, show a little more resistance to orders from above. . . . The unity of real material beings turns out to be complex, changing in intensity—in a word, messy—and needs a flexible theory of degrees of unity to do justice to it" ("God and Community," 272). However, this does not help him with the ontological status of systems. For Clarke is considering the degree of control exercised by an essential form, again from above, as it were, rather than the degree of coordination of the parts that brings about a form of a particular type. Thus, even with this model he still is only talking about degrees of control by the substance, rather than allowing for a level of explanation more basic than the macroscopic level of the essential form.

60. Clarke, *The One and the Many*, 125.

61. Ibid. See also Clarke, "God and Community," 270ff., and *The One and the Many*, 128.

62. Clarke, *The One and the Many*, 125.

63. Human beings who, either because of physical or psychical defect or injury, do not have central control over their bodies may, at one extreme, not be persons, or, at the other extreme, be multiple people. Note that according to this definition some nonhuman animals are, technically speaking, persons. See Gary L. Francione, "Animals—Property or Persons?" in *Animal Rights: Current Debates and New Directions*, ed. Cass R. Sunstein and Martha C. Nussbaum (Oxford: Oxford University Press, 2004).

64. Aristotle, *Nicomachean Ethics* 1098a20.

65. On the traditional notion of substantial form and its relation to ethical theory, see Terrence L. Nicols, "Aquinas' Concept of Substantial Form and Modern Science," *International Philosophical Quarterly* 36 (1996): 303–18.

66. Clarke, *The One and the Many*, 102.

67. Recall the qualifications discussed in the previous section when interpreting the use of the language of "kind" in an organic model of individuality.

68. Bracken, *Society and Spirit*, 56.

69. Ibid., 47, 51. Though I am sympathetic with Bracken's argument that there must be some form of collective agency at the macroscopic level and that societies are a true form of ontological existence, I am unconvinced by Bracken's further claim that societies are equiprimordial with actual occasions or can be rectified with the ontological principle (ibid., 51). Nevertheless, in his more cautious statements, Bracken's interpretation marshals

previously ignored resources within Whitehead's work to demonstrate that a metaphysics of process can account for the unity, self-identity, and agency of macroscopic individuals.

70. Ibid., 47. See also, "As I see it, this is a quite satisfactory description of the way in which a Whiteheadian society exercises a collective agency via the common element of form resident in each of its constituent actual occasions. That is, the form does not exist apart from the occasions, which are thus linked with one another according to a specific structural pattern. It comes into being with a given generation of occasions and ceases to be as they pass out of existence. At the same time, as the all-pervasive form of a given society here and now, it provides the necessary context or environment for the emergence of the next generation of occasions" (ibid., 54–55).

71. Ibid., 45.

72. Clarke, *The One and the Many*, 102.

73. Bracken, *Society and Spirit*, 111.

74. See, "For even though it functions as the principle of order and stability for successive generations of actual occasions, the form or structure of a Whiteheadian society is derived from the interrelated activities of its constituent occasions. Unlike the Aristotelian substantial form, therefore, it does not actively impose its antecedent unity on constituent parts or members" (ibid., 54). Also, "That is, the 'common element of form' is not imposed from without on the constituent occasions and/or member societies; instead, at each level of existence and activity, it arises out of the dynamic interrelatedness of the occasions active at that level" (ibid., 51).

Chapter 4: Process as Kalogenic

1. Ferré writes, "Actuality is inherently *kalogenic* (from the Greek *kalós*, 'beauty,' added to the familiar 'birth or coming to be' stem, *genesis*)" (*Being and Value*, 340).

2. Ibid., 358.

3. This conclusion may seem inappropriate, for metaphysics deals with the most abstract and general features of reality, while aesthetics deals with *aesthesis*, or feeling and beauty. However, these differences fade if we recall that "the whole universe consists of elements disclosed in the analysis of the experiences of subjects" (PR, 166). Whitehead's metaphysics must be an aesthetics, in the sense that it deals with the most abstract and general features of the experience of subjects, which subjects aim at the achievement of beauty.

4. Few scholars have examined Whitehead's aesthetics, with the notable exception of Donald W. Sherburne, *A Whiteheadian Aesthetic* (New Haven: Yale University Press, 1961). However, Sherburne would not agree with my characterization of aesthetics as primarily concerning beauty. He argues, "It is true, of course, that many philosophers have wanted to restrict

aesthetics to the single task of defining beauty. . . . One might, by using 'aesthetics' in this narrow sense, conclude that in defining beauty Whitehead has worked out the implications for aesthetics of his metaphysical speculation. It is my contention that in the broader, today more generally accepted, sense of the term Whitehead has not himself worked out the implications for aesthetics of his metaphysical system" (6, n. 3). My analysis is limited to the so-called narrow sense of aesthetics in that it focuses predominantly on defining and exploring the importance of beauty. Of course, since the achievement of beauty is the aim of every process, such an analysis should not be characterized as narrow.

5. Jones, 12.

6. Charles Hartshorne, "The Aesthetic Matrix of Value," in *Creative Synthesis and Philosophic Method* (La Salle, Ill.: Open Court, 1970), 305. According to Hartshorne, this diagram was created by himself, Max Dessoir, a German writer on aesthetics, and Kay Davis, an artist and former student at Emory University. See also Charles Hartshorne, "The Kinds and Levels of Asthetic Value, in *The Zero Fallacy and Other Essays in Neoclassical Philosophy*, ed. Mohammad Valady (La Salle, Ill.: Open Court, 1997), 205.

7. Hartshorne, "Aesthetic Matrix," 204.

8. Charles Hartshorne, "The Aesthetics of Birdsong," *Journal of Aesthetics and Art Criticism* 26 (1968): 311.

9. Hartshorne, "Aesthetic Matrix," 204.

10. See also, "There are many actualities, each with its own experience, enjoying individually, and yet requiring each other. Any description of the unity will require the many actualities; and any description of the many will require the notion of the unity from which importance and purpose is derived. By reason of the essential individuality of the many things, there are conflicts of finite realizations. Thus the summation of the many into the one, and the derivation of importance from the one into the many, involves the notion of disorder, of conflict, of frustration" (MT, 51).

11. Whitehead explicitly links discord and novelty: "In considering the life-history of occasions, forming the historic route of an enduring physical object, there are three possibilities as to the subjective aims which dominate the internal concrescence of the separate occasions. Either (i), the satisfactions of the antecedent occasions may be uniform with each other, and each internally *without discord or incitement to novelty*. . . . Such pure conformation involves the exclusion of all the contraries involved in the lure, with their various grades of proximity and remoteness. . . . Or (ii), there is a zest for the enhancement of some dominant element of feeling, received from the data, enhanced by decision admitting nonconformation of conceptual feeling to other elements in the data, and culminating in a satisfaction transmitting enhancement of the dominant element by reason of novel contrasts and inhibitions. Such a life-history involves growth dominated by a single

final end. . . . Or (iii), there is a zest for the elimination of all dominant elements of feeling, received from the data. In such a case, the route soon loses its historic individuality. It is in a state of decay" (PR, 187–88, emphasis added). Thus, in an importance sense, significantly novel experience depends upon discord. See also Hartshorne, "Aesthetic Matrix," 204.

12. Jones, 179. See also, "The right chaos, and the right vagueness, are jointly required for any effective harmony. They produce the massive simplicity which has been expressed by the term 'narrowness.' Thus chaos is not to be identified with evil" (PR, 112).

13. A better example of this type of complexity may be the human brain, the most complex unity known. Its complexity is beyond our grasp, at least at present.

14. Hartshorne writes, "There are cases of unified variety where the degree of intensity and level of complexity in the kinds and instances of variety is so low that the resulting beauty is rather trivial. We often use the word *pretty* for such a case. At the other extreme, where the complexity and intensity are great, we are likely to use the adjective *sublime* rather than *beautiful*. Where the variety is insufficiently unified, we may, if the intensity and complexity are not too great, experience the situation as *ridiculous, funny*; while, if intensity and complexity are great, the lack of unity or harmony may be felt as *tragic*. Thus, all the aesthetic values are accommodated" (Hartshorne, "Subhuman World," 55). See also Hartshorne, "Aesthetics of Birdsong" and "Aesthetic Matrix."

15. Hartshorne, "Aesthetics of Birdsong," 311.

16. Hartshorne, "Aesthetic Matrix," 306.

17. Ibid.

18. Ferré, *Being and Value*, 374.

19. Ferré characterizes it thus: "The continuum is complex, made up both of intrinsic and instrumental value. What may be relatively low-grade intrinsic value, such as grass, may be of extremely high instrumental (ecological) value in the interdependent community of things. And what may be of low instrumental value, such as the appreciation of a magnificent sunrise, may be of high intrinsic value. . . . Neither the temptations of ecofascism nor the arrogance of anthropocentrism can be warranted on this theory of reality" (ibid., 374).

20. Whitehead's repudiation of any ontological dualism makes it significantly easier for him to explain the ontological evolution of the universe. As he argues in his late essay "Immortality," "According to this account of the World of Activity there is no need to postulate two essentially different types of Active Entities, namely, the purely material entities and the entities alive with various modes of experiencing. The latter type is sufficient to account for the characteristics of that World, when we allow for the variety of recessiveness and dominance among the basic factors of experience, namely

consciousness, memory, and anticipation. This conclusion has the advantage of indicating the possibility of the emergence of Life from the lifeless material of this planet—namely, by the gradual emergence of memory and anticipation" (IM, 695).

21. Studies of chimpanzees suggest that Whitehead's limitation of culture to human animals may be unjustified. See, for instance, A. Whiten et al., "Cultures in Chimpanzees," in *The Animal Ethics Reader*, ed. Susan J. Armstrong and Richard G. Botzler (New York: Routledge, 2003), 125–33. However, the overall point of this passage remains: even if humans are capable of more complex functions, morally speaking, they may be worth less than other, less complex beings.

22. See AI, 255ff.

23. Unless otherwise indicated, the term "individual" applies equally either to the concrescence of a microscopic actual occasion or to the collective agency of the macroscopic individuals such as we experience. Of course, at the level of concrescence, an actual occasion does not consciously choose and is not morally responsible for the amount of beauty it embodies. However, it is still possible to say that an actual occasion did not achieve the depth of beauty it could have, owing to inhibiting factors in its experience. See chapter 3.

24. Ferré, *Living and Value*, 216.

25. See, "The other meaning of inhibition—the meaning which derogates from perfection—involves the true active presence of both component feelings. In this case there is a third feeling of mutual destructiveness, so that one or other—or both—of the component feelings fails to attain the strength properly belonging to the prehension of the datum from which it arises" (AI, 256).

26. See also, "The common character of all evil is that its realization in fact involves that there is some concurrent realization of a purpose toward elimination. The purpose is to secure the avoidance of evil. The fact of the instability of evil is the moral order of the world" (RM, 95).

27. As Ferré notes, "Without healthy conservatism, without a major effort to perpetuate a stable status quo, neither biological species nor human cultures could establish themselves, nor could they perpetuate themselves against pervasive disintegration in a universe of constant perishing" (*Living and Value*, 220).

28. Augustine, *Confessions*, trans. Henry Chadwick (Oxford: Oxford University Press, 1991), VII. xii (18).

29. Although Augustine did not make the distinction, he could have formulated this in a similar manner. Something can be evil in that it fails to achieve a good that it should have or it can be evil in destroying something it should not have.

30. Of course, Augustine would not have used the term "positive." Nev-

ertheless, even for Augustine, although evil is ontologically a privation, in its destructiveness it is morally positive in that it has a real impact.

31. See Augustine, *Free Choice of the Will*, trans. Thomas Williams (Indianapolis: Hackett, 1993), esp. book 2.

32. In this way Whitehead avoids violating the ontological principle. For as an actual entity, God is the individual or reason responsible for the universal striving for beauty.

33. See also, "The power of God is the worship He inspires. That religion is strong which in its ritual and its modes of thought evokes an apprehension of the commanding vision" (SMW, 192).

34. In this sense, it resembles the experience of the Christian mystic or the Buddhist monk. "Thus Peace is self-control at its widest,—at the width where the 'self' has been lost, and interest has been transferred to coördinations wider than personality" (AI, 285).

35. William James, "The Moral Philosopher and the Moral Life," in *The Will to Believe and Other Essays in Popular Philosophy* (New York: Dover, 1956), 214, 212.

36. See also, "The actual world, the world of experiencing, and of thinking, and of physical activity, is a community of many diverse entities; and these entities contribute to, or derogate from, the common value of the total community. At the same time, these actualities are, for themselves, their own value, individual and separable. They add to the common stock and yet they suffer alone. The world is a scene of solitariness and community" (RM, 88).

37. James, "Moral Philosopher," 209.

Chapter 5: A Whiteheadian Aesthetics of Morals

1. Although Whitehead did not dedicate any one work to the ethical implications of his metaphysics of process, he was deeply concerned with the good.

2. Hartshorne, "Beyond Enlightened Self-Interest," 214.

3. Schilpp, 571.

4. According to Schilpp, "It would seem that the founding of real morality upon the quicksand of largely emotional reactions provides a treacherously thin foundation for morals. It would hardly seem possible that Mr. Whitehead could be satisfied with such a flimsy and all too shifty foundation" (ibid., 611). This comment demonstrates that Schilpp interprets Whitehead's use of "feeling" in an overly superficial sense. Schilpp himself admits that he does not spend any significant amount of time examining the nature of the "emotional reactions" that constitute the internal relatedness of entities (ibid., 587, n. 97). It is a lack of appreciation for the complexity and depth of Whitehead's use of such language that leads to erroneous conclusions such as Schilpp's.

5. Although Schilpp recognizes that Whitehead wants to give importance a broader meaning, he is convinced that, insofar as it is basically a value judgment grounded in a largely subjective emotive process, importance is ultimately equivalent to interest. It is perplexing that Schilpp simultaneously recognizes that Whitehead wants to extend the notion of importance beyond mere interest, yet he concludes that Whitehead's philosophy should be classified as a moral interest theory. This derives from his dependence on the classical interpretation of Whitehead's metaphysics. See ibid., 568, 572, 589.

6. Ibid., 572.

7. Ibid., 614–15.

8. Ibid., 615.

9. Ibid.

10. Lynne Belaief, *Toward a Whiteheadian Ethics* (Lanham, Md.: University Press of America, 1984). Although this is one of the few book-length attempts to develop a Whiteheadian moral philosophy, I will not directly engage her work other than indicating my disagreement with her interpretation regarding the relation of beauty and ethics. In constructing her position in terms of classical moral philosophy's concepts, Belaief imports many of the views that Whitehead's system was designed to avoid. On Belaief's early work on this project, see Richard S. Davis, "Whitehead's Moral Philosophy," *Process Studies* 3 (1973): 75–90.

11. Belaeif, *Whiteheadian Ethics*, 53. Belaief reiterates this claim almost verbatim in "Whitehead and Private-Interest Theories," *Ethics* 76 (1996): 279.

12. Whitehead writes, "Of course the word *importance*, as in common use, has been reduced to suggest a silly little pomposity which is the extreme trivialization of its meaning here. This is a permanent difficulty of philosophic discussion; namely, that words must be stretched beyond their common meanings in the marketplace" (MT, 12).

13. Kline, 119.

14. Jones, 180.

15. Of course, this statement does *not* include eternal objects: "The only thing in Whitehead's scheme that is bereft of inherent activity is an eternal object" (ibid., 89). See also chapter 2.

16. If there is a difference, it is merely a matter of emphasis. Whereas the term *value* seems to suggest that which is achieved in process, *importance* seems to emphasize the end toward which process strives.

17. Schilpp, 615.

18. James, "Moral Philosopher," 184–85.

19. Ibid., 207–8.

20. See James, *Pluralistic Universe*, 697.

21. James, "Moral Philosopher," 184.

22. *Nicomachean Ethics* 1094b12–14. Aristotle continues, "We must be content, then, in speaking of such subjects and with such premises to indi-

cate the truth roughly and in outline, and in speaking about things which are only for the most part true and with premises of the same kind to reach conclusions which are no better. In the same spirit, therefore, should each of our statements be received; for it is the mark of an educated man to look for precision in each class of things just so far as the nature of the subject admits: it is evidently equally foolish to accept probable reasoning from a mathematician and to demand from a rhetorician demonstrative proofs" (*Nicomachean Ethics* 1094b20–27).

23. James, "Moral Philosopher," 184.

24. In *Modes of Thought*, Whitehead was insistent that the "laws" of nature should not be seen in a necessitarian light: "Life on this planet depends on the order observed throughout the spatio-temporal stellar system, as disclosed in our experience. These special forms of order exhibit no final necessity whatsoever. The laws of nature are forms of activity which happen to prevail within the vast epoch of activity which we dimly discern" (MT, 87). "Thus the laws of nature are merely all-pervading patterns of behaviour, of which the shift and discontinuance lie beyond our ken" (MT, 143). "None of these laws of nature gives the slightest evidence of necessity. They are the modes of procedure which within the scale of our observations do in fact prevail. . . . They exist as average, regulative conditions because the majority of actualities are swaying each other to modes of interconnection exemplifying those laws" (MT, 155).

25. Most contemporary scientists have begun to abandon their positivism and reductionism, recognizing that revision and development are unending. Though many seek the grail of a so-called unified theory, in their more lucid moments, scientists acknowledge that they seek greater and greater adequacy of formulation, not a final, once-and-for-all theory that leaves nothing left to investigate. See Dewey's attack of Laplace in chapter 1.

26. James, "Moral Philosopher," 208. See also, "His books [the moral philosopher's] upon ethics, therefore, so far as they truly touch the moral life, must more and more ally themselves with a literature which is confessedly tentative and suggestive rather than dogmatic,—I mean with novels and dramas of the deeper sort, with sermons, with books on statecraft and philanthropy and social and economical reform. Treated in this way ethical treatises may be voluminous and luminous as well; but they never can be *final*, except in their abstractness and vaguest features; and they must more and more abandon the old-fashioned, clear-cut, and would-be 'scientific' form" (ibid., 210).

27. See also, "Moral codes have suffered from the exaggerated claims made for them. The dogmatic fallacy has here done its worst. Each such code has been put out by a God on a mountain top, or by a Saint in a cave, or by a divine Despot on a throne, or, at the lowest, by ancestors with a wisdom beyond later question. In any case, each code is capable of improvement;

and unfortunately in details they fail to agree either with each other or with our existing moral institutions. The result is that the world is shocked, or amused, by the sight of saintly old people hindering in the name of morality the removal of obvious brutalities from a legal system" (AI, 290).

28. James, "Moral Philosopher," 209.

29. See also, "No two actual entities originate from an identical universe; though the difference between the two universes only consists in some actual entities, included in one and not in the other, and in the subordinate entities, included in one and not in the other, and in the subordinate entities which each actual entity introduces into the world" (PR, 22–23).

30. George R. Lucas Jr., "Agency after Virtue," *International Philosophical Quarterly* 28 (1988): 300.

31. Ferré, *Being and Value*, 353.

32. James, "Moral Philosopher," 208.

33. Ibid., 184–85. This ideal and the meaning it takes on in light of a process metaphysics is the inspiration for the title of part 2.

34. See chapter 1. Although he moves toward panexperientialism in *A Pluralistic Universe*, in 1891 James clearly intended to limit his conclusions to conscious or "sentient" beings.

35. James, "Moral Philosopher," 190.

36. Ibid., 193, author's emphasis.

37. Ibid., 197.

38. James, *Pluralistic Universe*, 697.

39. Although it is true that aggregate entities, such as a pile of dung, are largely, though not entirely, a function of our interests, we still have obligations to respect and appreciate them, even if it is primarily the compound entities out of which they are made that we are really respecting. See chapter 6.

40. I argue in chapter 7 that deep ecology is guilty of affirming an axiology that leads either to moral paralysis or to arbitrary decisions.

41. I am indebted to Jones for this formulation.

42. See chapter 7 on the nature of rights within the ethics of creativity.

43. However, as I will discuss, this is not what Kant might call an absolute obligation.

44. See, "But the moment we take a steady look at the question, we see not only that without a claim actually made by some concrete person there can be no obligation, but that there is some obligation wherever there is a claim. Claim and obligation are, in fact, coextensive terms; they cover each other exactly" (James, "Moral Philosopher," 194, author's emphasis). This passage confirms that James intended his statements in "The Moral Philosopher and the Moral Life" to be limited to humans. However, James later abandoned this dualistic framework for a form of panexperientialism in *A Pluralistic Universe*. Viewed through the lens of this later position, every individual must be seen as making a "claim."

45. Ibid., 195.

46. This is adapted from an argument in Daniel A. Dombrowski, *Hartshorne and the Metaphysics of Animal Rights* (Albany: State University of New York Press, 1988), 46. However, my version of this obligation differs in an important respect. See chapter 6.

47. It is in this context that I understand Whitehead's claim that "There are experiences of ideals—of ideals entertained, of ideals aimed at, of ideals achieved, of ideals defaced. . . . We are essentially measuring ourselves in respect to what we are not. A solipsist experience cannot succeed or fail, for it would be all that exists. There would be no standard of comparison. Human experience explicitly relates itself to an external standard. The universe is thus understood as including a source of ideals" (MT, 103).

48. "Love" is open to numerous interpretations. Here it is closer to the notion of *agape* than *eros*. For whereas *eros* implies an asymmetrical relationship between the lover and the beloved, *agape* requires a symmetrical relationship. See Charles Sanders Peirce, "Evolutionary Love," in *The Essential Peirce*, vol. 1, ed. Nathan Houser and Christopher Kloesel (Indianapolis: Indiana University Press, 1992), 352–71.

49. Cf. "The whole displays its component parts, each with its own value enhanced; and the parts lead up to a whole, which is beyond themselves, and yet not destructive of themselves" (MT, 62).

50. James, "Moral Philosopher," 202.

Chapter 6: Beyond the Ideal

1. Charles Hartshorne, "Beyond Enlightened Self-Interest: A Metaphysics of Ethics," *Ethics* 84 (1974): 214. See also chapter 4.

2. Leopold, 261.

3. Gregory James Moses, "Process Ecological Ethics," Center for Process Studies, vol. 23, no. 2, http://www.ctr4process.org./MembersOnly/Member-Papers/vol23no2.htm (accessed February 2, 2001).

4. My references to Aristotle are not meant to imply that the form of virtue ethics contained in the ethics of creativity is limited to the Western tradition's understanding of virtue. See Nicholas F. Gier, "Whitehead, Confucius, and the Aesthetics of Virtue," *Asian Philosophy* 14 (2004): 171–90.

5. James, "Moral Philosopher," 210.

6. Ibid., 205, author's emphasis.

7. Hartshorne's comparison of a bird song and a symphony also illustrates the same point. (See chapter 4.)

8. Cf. "The whole displays its component parts, each with its own value enhanced; and the parts lead up to a whole, which is beyond themselves, and yet not destructive of themselves" (MT, 62).

9. James, "Moral Philosopher," 210.

10. Ernest William Hocking, "Whitehead as I Knew Him," in *Alfred North Whitehead: Essays on His Philosophy*, ed. George L. Kline (Englewood Cliffs, N.J.: Prentice Hall, 1963), 8. See chapters 1 and 2.

11. In terms of Hartshorne's Aesthetic Circle, the diameter of the inner of circle is particularly small (see chapter 4).

12. See the discussion of concrescence in chapter 1.

13. Frederick Ferré, letter to the author, 25 June 2004.

14. Leopold, 262.

15. Ibid., xix.

16. See chapter 7 on the similarities and differences between the ethics of creativity and Leopold's land ethic.

17. Leopold, 239.

18. Ferré, *Being and Value*, 329.

19. Ibid., 330.

20. Ibid., 329.

21. Ibid., 330.

22. James P. Sterba, "Introduction," in *Earth Ethics: Environmental Ethics, Animal Rights, and Practical Applications*, ed. James P. Sterba, 2d ed. (Englewood Cliffs, N.J.: Prentice Hall, 2000), 1.

23. Ferré, *Living and Value*, 138.

24. Strictly speaking, nothing is entirely devoid of life or the novel response toward the past (see chapters 1 and 3). The question is not *whether* something is living, but to what *degree* it is living. Thus, it is not entirely appropriate to refer to atomic events as the "physical universe," as if they were without novelty.

25. John Cobb Jr. and Charles Birch, *The Liberation of Life: From the Cell to the Community* (Cambridge: Cambridge University Press, 1981), 152–53.

26. See *Modes of Thought*, "In the case of vegetables, we find bodily organization which decisively lack any one centre of experience with a higher complexity either of expressions received or of inborn data. A vegetable is a democracy; an animal is dominated by one, or more centres of experience. But such domination is limited, very strictly limited. The expressions of the central leader are relevant to that leader's reception of data from the body. Thus an animal body exhibits the limited domination of at least one of its component activities of expression. If the dominant activity be severed from the rest of the body, the whole coördination collapses, and the animal dies. Whereas in the case of the vegetable, the democracy can be subdivided into minor democracies which easily survive without much apparent loss of functional expression" (MT, 24).

27. Ferré, *Being and Value*, 332–33. Although he does not say so explicitly, "traditional botany" seems to designate those views formed prior to the emergence of ecology.

28. Ibid.

29. Ibid., 332.

30. Cobb and Birch, 153.

31. See Jones's discussion of the "structural conditions of order" and their relation to the foreground and background elements of experience (*Intensity*, 36f.).

32. Ferré, *Living and Value*, 140.

33. Juan Carlos Gómez, "Are Apes Persons? The Case for Primate Intersubjectivity," in *The Animal Ethics Reader*, ed. Susan J. Armstrong and Richard G. Botzler (New York: Routledge, 2003), 142–43; see also Gary L. Francione, "Animals—Property or Persons?" in *Animal Rights: Current Debates and New Directions*, ed. Cass R. Sunstein and Martha C. Nussbaum (Oxford: Oxford University Press, 2004), 108–42.

34. Irene Maxine Pepperberg, *The Alex Studies: Cognitive and Communicative Abilities of Grey Parrots* (Cambridge: Harvard University Press, 1999); Sue Savage-Rumbaugh and Roger Lewin, *Kanzi: The Ape at the Brink of the Human Mind* (London: Doubleday, 1994); Roger Fouts and Stephen Tukel Mills, *Next of Kin: My Conversations with Chimpanzees* (New York: Living Planet Books, 1997).

35. See Cass R. Sunstein and Martha C. Nussbaum, eds., *Animal Rights: Current Debates and New Directions* (Oxford: Oxford University Press, 2004).

36. Ferré, *Being and Value*, 355.

37. See Peter Singer, *Animal Liberation*, 3d ed. (New York: Avon Books, 2002), esp. chap. 1.

38. I occasionally refer simply to "human beings" rather than "human animals" or "animals" rather than "nonhuman animals." This is not meant to imply that humans are not animals.

39. See John B. Cobb Jr., "Palmer on Whitehead: A Critical Evaluation," *Process Studies* 33 (2004): 4–23, esp. 18f.

40. For instance, in the United States alone, "The U.S. 2000 census found that there are 209 million people 18 and older in the U.S. If we subtract 4 million institutionalized of all ages, based on 2.8 percent vegetarians, we calculate there are about 5.7 million adult vegetarians in the U.S." ("How Many Vegetarians Are There? A 2003 National Harris Interactive Survey Question Sponsored by the Vegetarian Resource Group," *Vegetarian Journal*, May–June 2003).

41. See Steve F. Sapontzis, ed., *Food for Thought: The Debate over Eating Meat* (New York: Prometheus, 2004), 36–69.

42. Singer, *Animal Liberation*, 95.

43. Frances Moore Lappé, *Diet for a Small Planet* (New York: Ballantine Books, 1991), 15.

44. "Fighting to Eradicate World Hunger," United Nations World Food Program, http://www.wfp.org/newsroom/downloads/2002/action2002-E-web.pdf (accessed October 14, 2004).

45. Frances Moore Lappé and Anna Lappé, *Hope's Edge: The Next Diet for a Small Planet* (New York: Putnam, 2002), 15. Although put in terms of fossil fuel calories, the authors' point is that we should not waste 44,000 calories of energy in any form. Evelyn Pluhar argues for a similar position, but in terms of the amount of land needed to sustain different eating habits. "A typical U.S. omnivore needs 3.5 acres of cropland per year to sustain himself or herself. An ovo-lacto vegetarian needs 1/2 an acre, while a vegan needs 1/6 of an acre. The land needed to feed one average omnivore would feed twenty-one vegans. There is an urgent need for more food as our population climbs upward from the 6 billion mark. Every five to ten days, hunger kills as many people as the atomic bomb dropped on Hiroshima. Although political factors certainly play a role in this tragedy, current food production is also inadequate" (Evelyn B. Pluhar, "The Right Not to Be Eaten," in *Food for Thought*, ed. Steve F. Sapontzis, 92–93). See also Peter Singer's discussion of the argument from efficiency in *Animal Liberation*, 164ff.

46. J. Baird Callicott, *In Defense of the Land Ethic: Essays in Environmental Philosophy* (Albany: State University of New York Press, 1989), 32.

47. Ibid.

48. James, "Moral Philosopher," 202.

49. I agree with Pluhar's position that, contra scholars such as Carruthers and Cohen, "Being able to *recognize* moral significance is sufficient but not obviously necessary for *having* moral significance" (Pluhar, 103). Pluhar notes that to make *recognition* of moral significance both sufficient and necessary for *having* moral significance would "disenfranchise legions of humans who cannot achieve moral agency. Nothing would rule out their being vivisected or served as appetizers along with the bacon bits and goose liver" (ibid.). See Dombrowski, *Babies and Beasts*.

Chapter 7: The Promise of a Kalocentric Worldview

Epigraph: John Bierhorst, ed., *Four Masterworks of American Indian Literature: Quezalcoatl, The Ritual of Condolence, Cuceb, The Night Chant* (New York: Farrar, Straus, and Giroux, 1974), 307–8. The selection is from the Navajo Nightway Ceremony, which fills nine days and eight nights and includes some four hundred songs.

1. Quoted in Thomas A. Nairn, "Hartshorne and Utilitarianism: A Response to Moskop," *Process Studies* 17 (1988): 171.

2. See Singer, 7ff. Defense of this claim does not commit one to a utilitarian framework; it is neutral as to any particular moral system. See James Rachels, "The Basic Argument for Vegetarianism," in *Food for Thought*, ed. Steve F. Sapontzis, 70–80.

3. Callicott, *Land Ethic*, 32–33.

4. Singer, 8.

5. Clare Palmer, *Environmental Ethics and Process Thinking* (Oxford: Clarendon Press, 1998). Though the title suggests that Palmer is interested in many of the diverse strains of thought that fall under the rubric of "process thinking," she is primarily concerned with process theology. She does not deal with process thinkers such as John Dewey or C. S. Peirce, nor examines the work on Whitehead's metaphysics by scholars such as William Christian, Ivor Leclerc, Jorge Nobo, or Judith A. Jones.

6. Palmer, *Process Thinking*, 213.

7. Ibid., 15. The "consequent nature" refers to that aspect of God which is in an ongoing, temporal relation with world process. See chapter 4.

8. Ibid., 213.

9. Hartshorne, "Subhuman World," 49–50, author's emphasis. John C. Moskop argues that Hartshorne's moral philosophy is "strikingly similar" to Mill's utilitarianism ("Mill and Hartshorne," *Process Studies* 10 [1980]: 18–33). Thomas A. Nairn defends Hartshorne's contributionism, but argues that a broader reading of his work demonstrates that it is not utilitarian ("Hartshorne and Utilitarianism: A Response to Moskop," *Process Studies* 17 [1988]: 170–80).

10. See Daniel A. Dombrowski, "The Replaceability Argument," *Process Studies* 30 (2001): 22–35; John B. Cobb Jr., "Palmer on Whitehead: A Critical Evaluation," *Process Studies* 33 (2004): 4–23; Timothy Menta, "Clare Palmer's *Environmental Ethics and Process Thinking*: A Hartshornean Response," *Process Studies* 33 (2004): 24–45; Clare Palmer, "Response to Cobb and Menta," *Process Studies* 33 (2004): 46–70.

11. Dombrowski, "Replaceability," 30. Palmer concedes this point: "If we accept Dombrowski's case (as I am inclined to) that a sufficiently personal thread of experience extends to all animals whether in the first or second tier, this conclusion certainly militates against any system where killing and replacing painlessly is morally acceptable" (Palmer, "Response to Cobb and Menta," 62).

12. Dombrowski, "Replaceability," 32. See also George R. Lucas, "Moral Order and the Constraints of Agency: Toward a New Metaphysics of Morals," in *New Essays in Metaphysics*, ed. Robert C. Neville, 117–39 (Albany: State University of New York Press, 1987); John W. Lango, "Does Whitehead's Metaphysics Contain an Ethics?" *Transactions of the Charles S. Peirce Society* 37 (2001): 515–36.

13. Although the status of rights is beyond my scope, the ethics of creativity would support a nonabsolutist version of rights that extends to all moral agents. See Evelyn Pluhar, who argues, "The rights argument pertains to any being who is capable of acting to achieve goals; that is, to any agent. As an agent, one has basic interests in and desires for life, health, and general well-being. Because one wants and needs these things, one also thinks

that others should at the very least not interfere with one's attempts to get them; that is, one holds that others must not interfere. This is tantamount to one's claiming the right to non-interference in these regards. . . . Thus, the argument goes, all agents should be accorded basic moral rights. Any agent who is mentally advanced enough to claim rights and then realize their universality perforce becomes a *moral* agent, however immorally he or she might go on to behave" (Evelyn B. Pluhar, "The Right Not to Be Eaten," in *Food for Thought: The Debate over Eating Meat*, ed. Steve F. Sapontzis [New York: Prometheus, 2004], 94).

14. Albert Schweitzer, "The Ethics of Reverence for Life," in *Animal Rights and Human Obligations*, ed. Tom Regan and Peter Singer, 2d ed. (Englewood Cliffs, N.J.: Prentice Hall, 1989), 32.

15. See, "It is obvious that a structured society may have more or less 'life,' and that there is no absolute gap between 'living' and 'non-living' societies. For certain purposes, whatever 'life' there is in a society may be important; and for other purposes, unimportant" (PR, 102).

16. Schweitzer, 33.

17. Ibid.

18. Schweitzer does propose that moral conflicts should be decided in terms of the necessity of sacrificing an individual. "Whenever I injure life of any kind I must be quite clear as to whether this is necessary or not. I ought never to pass the limits of the unavoidable, even in apparently insignificant cases" (ibid., 36). Because Schweitzer does not define what it means to call something "necessary," it is unclear how this is consistent with his claim that every living individual is equally sacred. Necessary for whom and why? If the will-to-live of the plant is as sacred as my own, necessity gives no justification for violence. This sort of dilemma is shared by any system that adopts an axiology unwilling to make distinctions in grades of value.

19. Many of the similarities between Whitehead's project and Leopold's were brought to my attention by Jay McDaniel, whose work I paraphrase here. See Jay McDaniel, "Land Ethics, Animal Rights, and Process Theology," *Process Studies* 17 (1988): 88–102.

20. Ibid., 94.

21. Eugene Hargrove, "The Historical Foundation of American Environmental Attitudes," *Environmental Ethics* 1 (1979): 239.

22. Ibid.

23. Leopold, 262.

24. For instance, the claim that the human being is simply a "plain member and citizen" of the biotic community is unclear (ibid., 240). If Leopold argues that human beings are not fundamentally separate from the natural world, I would agree. However, if this means that human beings and the biotic community are *equal* in intrinsic value and beauty, I do not. See

Susan Armstrong-Buck, "Whitehead's Metaphysical System as a Foundation for Environmental Ethics," *Environmental Ethics* 8 (1986): 241–57, esp.
253; Jay McDaniel, "Land Ethics, Animal Rights, and Process Theology,"
Process Studies 17 (1988): 88–102; and Dombrowski, *Animal Rights*, 47.

25. Warwick Fox, quoted in Devall and Sessions, *Deep Ecology*, 66.

26. Ibid. The eight-points of deep ecology are: "1. The well-being and
flourishing of human and nonhuman Life on Earth have value in themselves
(synonyms: intrinsic value, inherent value). These values are independent
of the usefulness of the nonhuman world for human purposes. 2. Richness
and diversity of life forms contribute to the realization of these values and
are also values in themselves. 3. Humans have no right to reduce this richness and diversity except to satisfy *vital* needs. 4. The flourishing of human
life and cultures is compatible with a substantial decrease of the human
population. The flourishing of nonhuman life requires such a decrease. 5.
Present human interference with the nonhuman world is excessive, and the
situation is rapidly worsening. 6. Policies must therefore be changed. These
policies affect basic economic, technological, and ideological structures. The
resulting state of affairs will be deeply different from the present. 7. The
ideological change is mainly that of appreciating *life quality* (dwelling in situations of inherent value) rather than adhering to an increasingly higher
standard of living. There will be a profound awareness of the difference between big and great. 8. Those who subscribe to the foregoing points have an
obligation directly or indirectly to try to implement the necessary changes"
(Devall and Sessions, 70).

27. See Arne Naess, "The Shallow and the Deep, Long-Range Ecology
Movements: A Summary," in *Deep Ecology for the 21st Century: Readings on
the Philosophy and Practice of the New Environmentalism*, ed. George Sessions
(Boston: Shambhala, 1995), 151–52.

28. Devall and Sessions, 67.

29. John B. Cobb Jr., "Deep Ecology and Process Thought," *Process Studies* 30 (2001): 114.

30. Ibid., 116.

31. On the notion of a multidimensional continuum, see Ferré, *Being
and Value*, 374.

32. John Dewey anticipates a further objection when he points out what
affirming a continuity of actuality does *not* entail: "This statement does not
mean that physical and human individuality are identical, nor that the
things which appear to us to be nonliving have the distinguishing characteristics of organisms. The difference between the inanimate and the animate is not so easily wiped out. But it does show that there is no fixed gap
between them" (Dewey, "Time and Individuality," 108).

33. Dombrowski, *Hartshorne and the Metaphysics of Animal Rights*, 46.
See also Armstrong-Buck, "Whitehead's Metaphysical System"; and John

Cobb and Charles Birch, *The Liberation of Life: From the Cell to the Community* (Cambridge: Cambridge University Press, 1981), esp. 158ff.

34. John Rodman, "Four Forms of Ecological Consciousness Reconsidered," in *Deep Ecology for the 21st Century*, ed. Sessions, 125.

35. William James's metaphor of consciousness as a series of flights and perches is illustrative here.

36. Ferré, *Living and Value*, 135.

37. Ibid.

38. My example of invasive plant species from chapter 6 also illustrates this point. Hartshorne suggests that it may be appropriate to sacrifice the vital needs of a higher-order individual for a lower-order individual: "To say that the human species is more important than other species suggests the question, how much more? Can we, even if only in the vaguest way, quantify the answer? One human person is 'of more value than many sparrows,' but is one person of more value than an entire species of bird? . . . I could perhaps seriously consider giving up the remainder of my life if it would definitely save a threatened species for millennia. But it would be merely silly to risk one's life for a single individual bird, whose life expectancy anyway is probably less than three years" (Hartshorne, "Subhuman World," 57). See also, "To risk a man's or woman's life for a subhuman individual is, I believe, unwarranted. But to do so to save an entire species, say of whale, ape, or elephant, would this be unwarranted? I'm not so sure" (Charles Hartshorne, "The Environmental Results of Technology," in *Philosophy and Environmental Crisis*, ed. William. T. Blackstone [Athens: University of Georgia Press, 1974], 72). However, as an abstract, temporal formal entity, a species cannot be the locus of intrinsic value and cannot be the object of direct duties.

39. It is in this context that I understand Whitehead's statement that "Without doubt the higher animals entertain notions, hopes, and fears. And yet they lack civilization by reason of the deficient generality of their mental functionings. . . . Civilization is more than all these; and in moral worth it can be less than all these" (MT, 3–4). See chapter 4.

40. When pushed to explain how deep ecology could apply in instances of moral conflict, Rodman refers to a "loose-cluster" of values such as, "diversity, complexity, integrity, harmony, stability, scarcity, etc.," as "criteria for evaluating alternative courses of permissible action in terms of *optimizing* the production of good effects, the better action being the one that *optimizes* the qualities taken as *interdependent*, mutually constraining cluster" (Rodman, 128, emphasis added). Yet this sort of reasoning is illicit if every individual is truly equal in value. Ironically, Rodham's approach is strikingly similar to my own. Yet, given its deep metaphysical basis, the present project has several advantages over Rodham's brief proposal. First, the "loose cluster" of criteria to which Rodman refers are, for the ethics of cre-

ativity, unified in the rich conception of beauty, which aims at the ideal balance between unity, diversity, simplicity, and complexity. In this way, rather than a mere afterthought, these criteria are systematically defined in terms of Whitehead's complex account of reality.

41. I am indebted to Frederick Ferré for making this distinction clear. See Ferré's *Being and Value* and *Living and Value*.

Bibliography

Aquinas, St. Thomas. *Summa Contra Gentiles*. In *Human Life and the Natural World*, Translated by Vernon J. Bourke, edited by Owen Goldin and Patricia Kilroe. New York: Broadview, 1997.

Aristotle. *The Complete Works of Aristotle*. Translated by Jonathan Barnes. Princeton: Princeton University Press, 1984.

Armstrong, Susan. "Nonhuman Experience: A Whiteheadian Analysis." *Process Studies* 18 (1989): 1–18.

———. "The Rights of Nonhuman Beings: A Whiteheadian Study." Ph.D. diss., Bryn Mawr College, 1976.

Armstrong-Buck, Susan. "Whitehead's Metaphysical System as a Foundation for Environmental Ethics." *Environmental Ethics* 8 (1986): 241–57.

Augustine. *Confessions*. Translated by Henry Chadwick. Oxford: Oxford University Press, 1991.

———. *On Free Choice of the Will*. Translated by Thomas Williams. Indianapolis: Hackett, 1993.

Austin, Richard Cartwright. "Beauty: A Foundation for Environmental Ethics." *Environmental Ethics* 7 (1985): 197–208.

Auxter, Thomas. "The Process of Morality." In *Hegel and Whitehead: Contemporary Perspectives on Systematic Philosophy*, edited by George R. Lucas Jr., 219–38. Albany: State University of New York Press, 1986.

Bates, Stanley. "G. E. Moore and Intrinsic Value." *Personalist* 54 (1977): 163–70.

Baumer, Michael R. "Whitehead and Aquinas on the Eternity of God." *Modern Schoolman* 62 (1984): 27–41.

Belaief, Lynne. *Toward a Whiteheadian Ethics*. Lanham, Md.: University Press of America, 1984.

———. "Whitehead and Private-Interest Theories." *Ethics* 76 (1996): 277–86.

———. "A Whiteheadian Account of Value and Identity." *Process Studies* 5 (1975): 31–46.

Bierhorst, John, ed. *Four Masterworks of American Indian Literature: Quezalcoatl, The Ritual of Condolence, Cuceb, The Night Chant*. New York: Farrar, Straus and Giroux, 1974.

Boyle, Deborah. "William James's Ethical Symphony." *Transactions of the Charles S. Peirce Society* 34 (1998): 977–1003.

Bracken, Joseph A. "Energy-Events and Fields." *Process Studies* 18 (1989): 153–65.

———. "Prehending God in and through the World." *Process Studies* 29 (2000): 4–15.

———. "Proposals for Overcoming the Atomism within Process-Relational Metaphysics." *Process Studies* 23 (1994): 10–24.

———. "Revising Process Metaphysics in Response to Ian Barbour's Critique." *Zygon* 33 (1998): 405–14.

———. *Society and Spirit: A Trinitarian Cosmology*. London: Associated University Presses, 1991.

———. "Substance—Society—Natural System: A Creative Rethinking of Whitehead's Cosmology." *International Philosophical Quarterly* 25 (1985): 3–13.

Brady, Emily. "Aesthetic Character and Aesthetic Integrity in Environmental Conservation." *Environmental Ethics* 24 (2002): 75–92.

Bube, Paul Custodio. "A Process Perspective of Justice." In *Ethics in John Cobb's Process Theology*, 131–44. Atlanta: Scholars Press, 1988.

Callicott, J. Baird. *In Defense of the Land Ethic: Essays in Environmental Philosophy*. Albany: State University of New York Press, 1989.

———. "Rolston on Intrinsic Value: A Deconstruction." *Environmental Ethics* 14 (1992): 129–43.

Carter, Curtis L. "Hegel and Whitehead on Aesthetic Symbols." In *Hegel and Whitehead: Contemporary Perspectives on Systematic Philosophy*, edited by George R. Lucas Jr., 239–56. Albany: State University of New York Press, 1986.

Cauthen, Kenneth. *Process Ethics: A Constructive System*. New York: Edwin Mellen Press, 1984.

Chaloupka, William. "John Dewey's Social Aesthetics as a Precedent for Environmental Thought." *Environmental Ethics* 9 (1987): 243–60.

Cheney, Jim. "Intrinsic Value in Environmental Ethics: Beyond Subjectivism and Objectivism." *Monist* 75 (1992): 227–35.

Christensen, Darrel E. *Hegelian/Whiteheadian Perspectives*. New York: University Press of America, 1989.

Christian, William A. *An Interpretation of Whitehead's Metaphysics*. New Haven: Yale University Press, 1959.

Clarke, Bowman L. "Process, Time, and God." *Process Studies* 13 (1983): 245–59.

Clarke, W. Norris. "God and the Community of Existents: Whitehead and St. Thomas." *International Philosophical Quarterly* 158 (2000): 265–88.

———. *The One and the Many: A Contemporary Thomistic Metaphysics*. Notre Dame: Notre Dame University Press, 2001.

Cobb, John B., Jr. "Deep Ecology and Process Thought." *Process Studies* 30 (2001): 112–31.

———. "Palmer on Whitehead: A Critical Evaluation." *Process Studies* 33 (2004): 4–23.

———. "Toward Clarity in Aesthetics." *Philosophy and Phenomenological Research* 18 (1957): 169–89.

Cobb, John B., Jr., and Charles Birch. *The Liberation of Life: From the Cell to the Community*. Cambridge: Cambridge University Press, 1981.

Cottingham, John. "'A Brute to the Brutes?' Descartes' Treatment of Animals." *Philosophy* 53 (1978): 551–59.

Dalai Lama. *Ethics for the New Millennium*. New York: Riverhead Books, 1999.

Davis, Richard S. "Whitehead's Moral Philosophy." *Process Studies* 3 (1973): 75–90.

Dawkins, Marian Stamp. "Animal Minds and Animal Emotions." In *The Animal Ethics Reader*, edited by Susan J. Armstrong and Richard G. Botzler, 94–99. New York: Routledge, 2003.

Descartes, René. *The Correspondence*. In *The Philosophical Writings of Descartes*, vol. 3, translated by Anthony Kenny et al. Cambridge: Cambridge University Press, 1991.

———. *Description of the Human Body*. In *The Philosophical Writings of Descartes*, vol. 3, translated by Anthony Kenny et al. Cambridge: Cambridge University Press, 1991.

———. *Discourse on Method*. In *The Philosophical Writings of Descartes*, vol. 1, translated by John Cottingham, Robert Stoothoff, and Dugald Murdoch. Cambridge: Cambridge University Press, 1985.

———. *Meditations on First Philosophy*. In *The Philosophical Writings of Descartes*, vol. 2, translated by John Cottingham, Robert Stoothoff, and Dugald Murdoch. Cambridge: Cambridge University Press, 1985.

———. *Principles of Philosophy*. In *The Philosophical Writings of Descartes*, vol. 1, translated by John Cottingham, Robert Stoothoff, and Dugald Murdoch. Cambridge: Cambridge University Press, 1985.

Devall, Bill. "The Deep, Long-Range Ecology Movement: 1960–2001—A Review." *Ethics and the Environment* 6 (2001): 18–41.

Devall, Bill, and George Sessions. *Deep Ecology: Living As If Nature Mattered*. Salt Lake City: Gibbs Smith, 1985.

Dewey, John. *Experience and Nature*. 2d ed. La Salle, Ill.: Open Court, 1929.

———. "Time and Individuality." In *John Dewey, the Later Works*, vol. 14, edited by JoAnn Boydston. Carbondale: Southern Illinois University Press, 1991.

Dombrowski, Daniel A. *Babies and Beasts: The Argument from Marginal Cases*. Urbana: University of Illinois Press, 1997.

———. *Hartshorne and the Metaphysics of Animal Rights*. Albany: State University of New York Press, 1988.

———. "The Replaceability Argument." *Process Studies* 30 (2001): 22–35.

Everett, Jennifer. "Vegetarianism, Predation, and Respect for Nature." In *Food for Thought: The Debate over Eating Meat*, edited by Steve F. Sapontzis, 302–14. New York: Prometheus, 2004.

Felt, James W. "Proposal for a Thomistic-Whiteheadian Metaphysics of Becoming." *International Philosophical Quarterly* 158 (2000): 253–64.

———. "Whitehead's Misconception of 'Substance' in Aristotle." *Process Studies* 14 (1985): 224–36.

Ferré, Frederick. *Being and Value: Toward a Constructive Postmodern Metaphysics*. Albany: State University of New York Press, 1996.

———. *Knowing and Value: Toward a Constructive Postmodern Epistemology*. Albany: State University of New York Press, 1998.

———. *Living and Value: Toward a Constructive Postmodern Ethics*. Albany: State University of New York Press, 2001.

Fesmire, Steven. "Morality as Art: Dewey, Metaphor, and Moral Imagination." *Transactions of the Charles S. Peirce Society* 35 (1999): 527–50.

Field, Richard W. "William James and the Epochal Theory of Time." *Process Studies* 13 (1983): 260–74.

"Fighting to Eradicate World Hunger." United Nations World Food Program. http://www.wfp.org/newsroom/downloads/2002/action2002-E-web.pdf (accessed October 14, 2004).

Ford, Lewis S. "An Appraisal of Whiteheadian Nontheism." *Southern Journal of Philosophy* 15 (1977): 27–35.

———. "Boethius and Whitehead on Time and Eternity." *International Philosophical Quarterly* 8 (1968): 28–67.

———. "Can Whitehead Provide for Real Subjective Agency? A Reply to Edward Pol's Critique." *Modern Schoolman* 47 (1970): 209–25.

———. "Can Whitehead Rescue Perishing?" *Personalist* 54 (1973): 92–93.

———. "The Divine Activity of the Future." *Process Studies* 11 (1981): 169–79.

———. "The Duration of the Present." *Philosophy and Phenomenological Research* 35 (1974): 100–106.

———. "Efficient Causation within Concrescence." *Process Studies* 19 (1990): 167–80.

———. *The Emergence of Whitehead's Metaphysics 1925–1929*. Albany: State University of New York Press, 1984.

———. "Genetic and Coordinate Division Correlated." *Process Studies* 1 (1971): 199–209.

———. "The Modes of Actuality." *Modern Schoolman* 67 (1990): 275–83.

———. "Nancy Frankenberry's Conception of the Power of the Past." *American Journal of Theology and Philosophy* 14 (1993): 287–300.

———. "The Non-Temporality of Whitehead's God." *International Philosophical Quarterly* 13 (1973): 347–76.

————. "On Genetic Successiveness: A Third Alternative." *Southern Journal of Philosophy* 7 (1969): 421–25.

————. "The Past as Given by Mannoia." *Modern Schoolman* 64 (1986): 45–51.

————. "Recent Interpretations of Whitehead's Writings." *Modern Schoolman* 65 (1987): 47–59.

————. "The Reformed Subjectivist Principle Revisited." *Process Studies* 19 (1990): 28–48.

————. "Subjectivity in the Making." *Process Studies* 21 (1992): 1–24.

————. *Transforming Process Theism*. Albany: State University of New York Press, 2000.

————. "Whitehead on Subjective Agency: A Response to Edward Pols." *Modern Schoolman* 49 (1972): 151–52.

Ford, Lewis S., and Marjorie Suchocki. "A Whiteheadian Reflection on Subjective Immortality." *Process Studies* 7 (1977): 1–13.

Fouts, Roger, and Stephen Tukel Mills. *Next of Kin: My Conversations with Chimpanzees*. New York: Living Planet Books, 1997.

Francione, Gary L. "Animals—Property or Persons?" In *Animal Rights: Current Debates and New Directions*, edited by Cass R. Sunstein and Martha C. Nussbaum, 108–42. Oxford: Oxford University Press, 2004.

Frankenberry, Nancy. "The Logic of Whitehead's Intuition of Everlastingness." *Southern Journal of Philosophy* 21 (1983): 31–45.

————. "The Power of the Past." *Process Studies* 13 (1983): 132–42.

Frey, R. G. "Pain, Amelioration, and the Choice of Tactics." In *Earth Ethics: Environmental Ethics, Animal Rights, and Practical Applications*, edited by James P. Sterba, 52–63. Englewood Cliffs, N.J.: Prentice Hall, 1995.

Garland, William J. "The Ultimacy of Creativity." In *Explorations in Whitehead's Philosophy*, edited by Lewis S. Ford and George L. Kline, 212–38. New York: Fordham University Press, 1983.

Gendin, Sidney. "The Use of Animals in Science." In *Earth Ethics: Environmental Ethics, Animal Rights, and Practical Applications*, edited by James P. Sterba, 29–37. Englewood Cliffs, N.J.: Prentice Hall, 1995.

Gier, Nicholas F. "Whitehead, Confucius, and the Aesthetics of Virtue." *Asian Philosophy* 14 (2004): 171–90.

Goheen, John. "Whitehead's Theory of Value." In *The Philosophy of Alfred North Whitehead*, 2d ed., edited by Paul Arthur Schilpp, 435–60. La Salle, Ill.: Open Court, 1951.

Gómez, Juan Carlos. "Are Apes Persons? The Case for Primate Intersubjectivity." In *The Animal Ethics Reader*, edited by Susan J. Armstrong and Richard G. Botzler. New York: Routledge, 2003.

Gray, James R. *Process Ethics*. Lanham, Md.: University Press of America, 1983.

Greek, C. Ray, and Jean Single Greek. *Sacred Cows and Golden Geese: The Human Cost of Experiments on Animals*. New York: Continuum, 2000.

Griffin, David Ray. *Reenchantment Without Supernaturalism*. Ithaca: Cornell University Press, 2000.

Hargrove, Eugene. "The Aesthetics of Wildlife Preservation." In *Earth Ethics: Environmental Ethics, Animal Rights, and Practical Applications*, edited by James P. Sterba, 138–44. Englewood Cliffs, N.J.: Prentice Hall, 1995.

———. "Ecological Sabotage: Pranks or Terrorism?" In *Earth Ethics: Environmental Ethics, Animal Rights, and Practical Applications*, edited by James P. Sterba, 353–54. Englewood Cliffs, N.J.: Prentice Hall, 1995.

———. "The Historical Foundations of American Environmental Attitudes." *Environmental Ethics* 1 (1979): 209–40.

Harrison, Peter. "Descartes on Animals." *Philosophical Quarterly* 42 (1992): 219–27.

Harrison, R. K. "A. N. Whitehead on Good and Evil." *Philosophy* 28 (1953): 239–45.

Hartshorne, Charles. "The Aesthetic Matrix of Value." In *Creative Synthesis and Philosophic Method*, 303–22. La Salle, Ill.: Open Court, 1970.

———. "The Aesthetics of Birdsong." *Journal of Aesthetics and Art Criticism* 26 (1968): 311–15.

———. "Bell's Theorem and Stapp's Revised View of Space-Time." *Process Studies* 7 (1977): 183–91.

———. "Beyond Enlightened Self-Interest: A Metaphysics of Ethics." *Ethics* 84 (1974): 210–16.

———. "Can Man Transcend His Animality?" *Monist* 55 (1971): 209–17.

———. "Cobb's Theology of Ecology." In *John Cobb's Theology in Process*, edited by David Ray Griffin and Thomas J. J. Altizer, 112–15. Philadelphia: Westminster Press, 1977.

———. "The Environmental Results of Technology." In *Philosophy and Environmental Crisis*, edited by William. T. Blackstone, 69–78. Athens: University of Georgia Press, 1974.

———. "Ethics and the Assumption of Purely Private Pleasures." *International Journal of Ethics* 40 (1930): 496–515.

———. "Foundations for a Humane Ethics: What Human Beings Have in Common with Other Higher Animals." In *On the Fifth Day*, edited by Richard Knowles Morris, 154–72. Washington, D.C.: Acropolis Press, 1978.

———. "The Kinds and Levels of Aesthetic Value." In *The Zero Fallacy and Other Essays in Neoclassical Philosophy*, edited by Mohammad Valady, 203–14. La Salle, Ill.: Open Court, 1997.

———. "Process as Inclusive Category: A Reply." *Journal of Philosophy* 52 (1955): 94–102.

———. "The Rights of the Subhuman World." *Environmental Ethics* 1 (1979): 49–60.

———. "Why Study Birds?" *Virginia Quarterly Review* 46 (1970): 133–40.

———. "The Zero Fallacy in Philosophy: Accentuate the Positive." In *The Zero Fallacy and Other Essays in Neoclassical Philosophy*, edited by Mohammad Valady, 161–72. La Salle, Ill.: Open Court, 1997.

Haught, John F. "The Emergent Environment and the Problem of Cosmic Purpose." *Environmental Ethics* 8 (1986): 139–50.

Hausman, Carl R. *Charles S. Peirce's Evolutionary Philosophy*. New York: Cambridge University Press, 1993.

Henning, Brian G. "Getting Substance to Go All the Way: Norris Clarke's Neo-Thomism and the Process Turn." *Modern Schoolman* 81 (2004): 215–25.

———. "On the Possibility of a Whiteheadian Aesthetics of Morals." *Process Studies* 31 (2002): 97–114.

———. "On the Way to an Ethics of Creativity." *International Journal for Field-Being* 2, no. 3 (2002). http://www.iifb.org/ijfb/BGHenning-3.htm.

Hobbes, Thomas. *Leviathan*. Edited by C. B. Macpherson. New York: Penguin, 1968.

Hocking, Ernest William. "Whitehead as I Knew Him." In *Alfred North Whitehead: Essays on His Philosophy*, edited by George L. Kline, 7–17. Englewood Cliffs, N.J.: Prentice Hall, 1963.

Hoff, Christina. "Kant's Invidious Humanism." *Environmental Ethics* 5 (1983): 63–70.

Hooper, Sydney E. "A Reasonable Theory of Morality: (Alexander and Whitehead)." *Philosophy* 25 (1950): 54–67.

"How Many Vegetarians Are There? A 2003 National Harris Interactive Survey Question Sponsored by the Vegetarian Resource Group." *Vegetarian Journal*, May–June 2003.

Hume, David. *A Treatise of Human Nature*. Edited by Ernest C. Mossner. New York: Penguin, 1969.

James, William. "The Moral Philosopher and the Moral Life." In *The Will to Believe and Other Essays in Popular Philosophy*, 184–215. New York: Dover, 1956.

———. *A Pluralistic Universe*. In *William James' Writings 1902–1910*. New York: Library of America, 1987.

———. *Principles of Psychology*. 2 vols. New York: Dover, 1890.

Janik, Del Ivan. "Environmental Consciousness in Modern Literature: Four Representative Examples." In *Deep Ecology for the 21st Century: Readings on the Philosophy and Practice of the New Environmentalism*, edited by George Sessions, 104–12. Boston: Shambhala, 1995.

Johnson, A. H. "Whitehead as Teacher and Philosopher." *Philosophy and Phenomenological Research* 29 (1968–69): 351–76.

Jones, Judith A. *Intensity: An Essay in Whiteheadian Ontology*. Nashville: Vanderbilt University Press, 1998.

Kant, Immanuel. "Duties towards Animals and Spirits." In *Lectures on Ethics*, translated by Louis Infield. New York: Harper and Row, 1963.

———. *Groundwork of the Metaphysics of Morals*. Translated by H. J. Paton. New York: Harper Torchbooks, 1964.

Kerr, Andrew J. "Ethical Status of the Ecosystem in Whitehead's Philosophy." *Process Studies* 24 (1995): 76–89.

———. "The Possibility of Metaphysics: Environmental Ethics and the Naturalistic Fallacy." *Environmental Ethics* 22 (2000): 85–100.

Kinast, Robert L. "Non-violence in a Process Worldview." *Philosophy Today* 25 (1981): 279–85.

Kline, George L. "Form, Concrescence, and Concretum." In *Explorations in Whitehead's Philosophy*, edited by Lewis S. Ford and George L. Kline, 104–48. New York: Fordham University Press, 1983.

Kraus, Elizabeth M. "Existence as Transaction: A Whiteheadian Study of Causality." *International Philosophical Quarterly* 25 (1985): 349–66.

———. *The Metaphysics of Experience: A Companion to Whitehead's Process and Reality*. New York: Fordham University Press, 1998.

Lango, John W. "Does Whitehead's Metaphysics Contain an Ethics?" *Transactions of the Charles S. Peirce Society* 37 (2001): 515–36.

Lappé, Frances Moore. *Diet for a Small Planet*. New York: Ballantine Books, 1991.

Lappé, Frances Moore, and Anna Lappé. *Hope's Edge: The Next Diet for a Small Planet*. New York: Putnam, 2002.

Lawrence, Nathaniel. "The Vision of Beauty and the Temporality of Deity in Whitehead's Philosophy." In *Alfred North Whitehead: Essays on His Philosophy*, edited by George L. Kline, 168–78. Englewood Cliffs, N.J.: Prentice Hall, 1963.

Leclerc, Ivor. "Being and Becoming in Whitehead's Philosophy." In *Explorations in Whitehead's Philosophy*, edited by Lewis S. Ford and George L. Kline, 53–68. New York: Fordham University Press, 1983.

———. *Whitehead's Metaphysics*. Highlands, N.J.: Humanities Press, 1958.

Leftow, Brian. "Eternity and Simultaneity." *Faith and Philosophy* 8 (1991): 148–92.

Leopold, Aldo. *A Sand County Almanac*. New York: Ballantine Books, 1966.

Llewellyn, Robert R. "Whitehead and Newton on Space and Time Structure." *Process Studies* 3 (1973): 239–58.

Lockwood, Michael. "Singer on Killing and the Preference for Life." *Inquiry* 22 (1979): 157–70.

Lombardi, Louis G. "Inherent Worth, Respect, and Rights." *Environmental Ethics* 5 (1983): 257–70.

Lonergan, Bernard. *Insight: A Study of Human Understanding*. Toronto: Toronto University Press, 1992.

Lucas, George R., Jr. "Agency after Virtue." *International Philosophical Quarterly* 28 (1988): 293–311.

———. "Hegel, Whitehead, and the Status of Systematic Philosophy." In *Hegel and Whitehead: Contemporary Perspectives on Systematic Philosophy*, edited by George R. Lucas Jr., 3–16. Albany: State University of New York Press, 1986.

———. "Moral Order and the Constraints of Agency: Toward a New Metaphysics of Morals." In *New Essays in Metaphysics*, edited by Robert C. Neville, 117–39. Albany: State University of New York Press, 1987.

Mason, David R. "Whitehead's Analysis of Perception as a Basis for Conceiving Time and Value." *Zygon* 10 (1975): 398–418.

McDaniel, Jay. "Land Ethics, Animal Rights, and Process Theology." *Process Studies* 17 (1988): 88–102.

———. "Physical Matter as Creative and Sentient." *Environmental Ethics* 5 (1983): 291–317.

Menta, Timothy. "Clare Palmer's *Environmental Ethics and Process Thinking*: A Hartshornean Response." *Process Studies* 33 (2004): 24–45.

Midgley, Mary. *Animals and Why They Matter*. Athens: University of Georgia Press, 1983.

———. "Is a Dolphin a Person?" In *The Animal Ethics Reader*, edited by Susan J. Armstrong and Richard G. Botzler, 166–74. New York: Routledge, 2003.

Mill, John Stuart. *Utilitarianism*. In *Utilitarianism, On Liberty, Essay on Bentham Together with Selected Writings of Jeremy Bentham and John Austin*, edited by Mary Warnock. New York: Meridian Books, 1962.

Millard, Richard M. "The Ghost of Eternalism in Whitehead's Theory of Value." *Philosophical Forum* 9 (1951): 16–22.

Miller, Michael. "The Meaning of Descartes' Animal Agnosticism." Forthcoming.

Morris, Bertram. "The Art-process and the Aesthetic Fact in Whitehead's Philosophy." In *The Philosophy of Alfred North Whitehead*, edited by Paul Arthur Schilpp, 461–86. La Salle, Ill.: Open Court, 1951.

Moses, Gregory James. "Process Ecological Ethics." *Center for Process Studies* 23, no. 2. http://www.ctr4process.org/MembersOnly/MemberPapers/vol23no2.htm (accessed February 2, 2001).

Moskop, John C. "Mill and Hartshorne." *Process Studies* 10 (1980): 18–33.

Naess, Arne. "A Defence of the Deep Ecology Movement." *Environmental Ethics* 6 (1984): 265–70.

———. "The Principle of Intensity." *Journal of Value Inquiry* 33 (1999): 5–9.

———. "The Shallow and the Deep, Long-Range Ecology Movements: A Summary." In *Deep Ecology for the 21st Century: Readings on the Philosophy and Practice of the New Environmentalism*, edited by George Sessions, 151–55. Boston: Shambhala, 1995.

Nairn, Thomas A. "Hartshorne and Utilitarianism: A Response to Moskop." *Process Studies* 17 (1988): 170–80.

Nicols, Terence L. "Aquinas' Concept of Substantial Form and Modern Science." *International Philosophical Quarterly* 36 (1996): 303–18.

Nobo, Jorge Luis. *Whitehead's Metaphysics of Extension and Solidarity*. Albany: State University of New York Press, 1986.

———. "Whitehead's Principle of Process." *Process Studies* 4 (1974): 275–83.

———. "Whitehead's Principle of Relativity." *Process Studies* 8 (1978): 1–20.

O'Connell, Robert J. "'The Will to Believe' and James's 'Deontological Streak.'" *Transactions of the Charles S. Peirce Society* 28 (1992): 809–31.

O'Neill, John. "The Varieties of Intrinsic Value." *Monist* 75 (1992): 119–37.

Palmer, Clare. *Environmental Ethics and Process Thinking*. Oxford: Clarendon Press, 1998.

———. "Response to Cobb and Menta." *Process Studies* 33 (2004): 46–70.

Peirce, Charles Sanders. *The Essential Peirce: Selected Philosophical Writings*. 2 vols. Edited by Nathan Houser and Christopher Kloesel. Indianapolis: Indiana University Press, 1992.

Pepperberg, Irene Maxine. *The Alex Studies: Cognitive and Communicative Abilities of Grey Parrots*. Cambridge: Harvard University Press, 1999.

Pluhar, Evelyn B. "The Right Not to Be Eaten." In *Food for Thought: The Debate Over Eating Meat*, edited by Steve F. Sapontzis, 92–107. New York: Prometheus, 2004.

Press, Howard. "Whitehead's Ethic of Feeling." *Ethics* 81 (1971): 161–68.

Putnam, Ruth Anna. "The Moral Impulse." In *The Revival of Pragmatism: New Essays on Social Thought, Law, and Culture*, edited by Morris Dickstein, 62–71. Durham: Duke University Press, 1998.

———. "Perceiving Facts and Values." *Philosophy* 73 (1998): 5–19.

Pybus, Elizabeth M., and Alexander Broadie. "Kant and the Maltreatment of Animals." *Philosophy* 53 (1978): 560–61.

Rachels, James. "The Basic Argument for Vegetarianism." In *Food for Thought: The Debate Over Eating Meat*, edited by Steve F. Sapontzis, 70–79. New York: Prometheus Books, 2004.

———. "The Challenge of Cultural Relativism." In *The Elements of Moral Philosophy*. 4th ed. New York: McGraw-Hill, 2003.

Reese, W. L. *The Dictionary of Philosophy and Religion*. Highlands, N.J.: Humanities Press, 1980.

Regan, Tom. *The Case for Animal Rights*. Berkeley: University of California Press, 1983.

———. "The Case for Animal Rights." In *Ethics: History, Theory, and Contemporary Issues*, edited by Steven M. Cahn and Peter Markie, 821–29. Oxford: Oxford University Press, 1998.

———. "The Nature and Possibility of an Environmental Ethic." *Environmental Ethics* 3 (1981): 19–34.

Reynolds, Charles H. "Somatic Ethics: Joy and Adventure in the Embodied Moral Life." In *John Cobb's Theology in Process*, edited by David Ray Griffin and Thomas J. J. Altizer, 116–32. Philadelphia: Westminster Press, 1977.

Rodman, John. "Four Forms of Ecological Consciousness Reconsidered." In *Deep Ecology for the 21st Century: Readings on the Philosophy and Practice of the New Environmentalism*, edited by George Sessions, 121–30. Boston: Shambhala, 1995.

Rolston, Holmes, III. "Are Values in Nature Subjective or Objective?" *Environmental Ethics* 4 (1982): 125–51.

———. "Duties to Endangered Species." In *Earth Ethics: Environmental Ethics, Animal Rights, and Practical Applications*, edited by James P. Sterba, 317–28. Englewood Cliffs, N.J.: Prentice Hall, 1995.

———. *Environmental Ethics: Duties to and Values in the Natural World*. Philadelphia: Temple University Press, 1988.

———. "Nature, the Genesis of Value, and Human Understanding." *Environmental Values* 6 (1997): 361–64.

Rosenfield, Leonora Cohen. *From Beast-Machine to Man-Machine: Animal Soul in French Letters from Descartes to La Mettrie*. New York: Octagon Books, 1968.

Rotenstreich, Nathan. "The Superject and Moral Responsibility." *Review of Metaphysics* 10 (1956): 201–6.

Russell, Paul. "Strawson's Way of Naturalizing Responsibility." *Ethics* 102 (1992): 287–302.

Sagoff, Mark. "Animal Liberation and Environmental Ethics: Bad Marriage, Quick Divorce." In *Earth Ethics: Environmental Ethics, Animal Rights, and Practical Applications*, edited by James P. Sterba, 166–72. Englewood Cliffs, N.J.: Prentice Hall, 1995.

Sapontzis, Steve F., ed. *Food for Thought: The Debate over Eating Meat*. New York: Prometheus Books, 2004.

———. "The Moral Significance of Interests." *Environmental Ethics* 4 (1982): 345–58.

Savage-Rumbaugh, Sue, and Roger Lewin. *Kanzi: The Ape at the Brink of the Human Mind*. London: Doubleday, 1994.

Schilpp, Paul A. "Whitehead's Moral Philosophy." In *The Philosophy of Alfred North Whitehead*, edited by Paul Arthur Schilpp, 561–618. 2d ed. La Salle, Ill.: Open Court, 1951.

Schindler, David L. "Whitehead's Inability to Affirm a Universe of Value." *Process Studies* 13 (1983): 117–31.

Schrader, David E. "Simonizing James: Taking Demand Seriously." *Transactions of the Charles S. Peirce Society* 34 (1998): 1005–28.

Schweitzer, Albert. "The Ethics of Reverence for Life." In *Animal Rights and Human Obligations*, edited by Tom Regan and Peter Singer, 32–38. 2d ed. Englewood Cliffs, N.J.: Prentice Hall, 1989.

Sessions, George. "Western Process Metaphysics (Heraclitus, Whitehead, and Spinoza)." In *Deep Ecology: Living As If Nature Mattered*, edited by Bill Devall and George Sessions, 236–42. Salt Lake City: Gibbs Smith, 1985.

Sherburne, Donald W. *A Key to Whitehead's Process and Reality*. Chicago: University of Chicago Press, 1966.

———. "Responsibility, Punishment, and Whitehead's Theory of the Self." In *Alfred North Whitehead: Essays on His Philosophy*, edited by George L. Kline, 179–88. Englewood Cliffs, N.J.: Prentice Hall, 1963.

———. *A Whiteheadian Aesthetic*. New Haven: Yale University Press, 1961.

Singer, Peter. *Animal Liberation*. 3d ed. New York: Avon Books, 2002.

Sprigge, T. L. S. "Metaphysics, Physicalism, and Animal Rights." *Inquiry* 22 (1979): 101–43.

Stapp, Henry Pierce. "Quantum Mechanics, Local Causality, and Process Philosophy." *Process Studies* 7 (1977): 173–82.

Sterba, James P. "Introduction." In *Earth Ethics: Environmental Ethics, Animal Rights, and Practical Applications*, edited by James P. Sterba, 1–17. 2d ed. Englewood Cliffs, N.J.: Prentice Hall, 2000.

Stump, Eleonore, and Norman Kretzmann. "Eternity." *Journal of Philosophy* 78 (1981): 429–58.

Sunstein, Cass R., and Martha C. Nussbaum, eds. *Animal Rights: Current Debates and New Directions*. Oxford: Oxford University Press, 2004.

Taylor, Paul W. *Respect for Nature: A Theory of Environmental Ethics*. Princeton: Princeton University Press, 1986.

Thomson, Judith Jarvis. "A Defense of Abortion." *Philosophy and Public Affairs* 1 (1971): 47–66.

Wallace, R. Jay. *Responsibility and the Moral Sentiments*. Cambridge: Harvard University Press, 1996.

Warren, Mary Anne. "The Rights of the Nonhuman World." In *Earth Ethics: Environmental Ethics, Animal Rights, and Practical Applications*, edited by James P. Sterba, 175–89. Englewood Cliffs, N.J.: Prentice Hall, 1995.

Wee, Cecilia. "Cartesian Environmental Ethics." *Environmental Ethics* 23 (2001): 275–86.

Weston, Anthony. "Beyond Intrinsic Value: Pragmatism in Environmental Ethics." *Environmental Ethics* 7 (1985): 321–39.

White, Villard Alan. "Whitehead, Special Relativity, and Simultaneity." *Process Studies* 13 (1983): 275–85.

Whitehead, Alfred North. *Adventures of Ideas*. New York: Free Press, 1933.

———. *The Aims of Education and Other Essays*. New York: Free Press, 1929.

———. *The Concept of Nature*. Cambridge: Cambridge University Press, 1920.

———. "Explanatory Note." In *The Philosophy of Alfred North Whitehead*, edited by Paul Arthur Schilpp, 664–65. 2d ed. La Salle, Ill.: Open Court, 1951.

———. *The Function of Reason*. Princeton: Princeton University Press, 1920.

———. "Immortality." In *The Philosophy of Alfred North Whitehead*, edited by Paul Arthur Schilpp, 682–700. 2d ed. La Salle, Ill.: Open Court, 1951.

———. *An Introduction to Mathematics*. London: Oxford University Press, 1948.

———. "Mathematics and the Good." In *The Philosophy of Alfred North Whitehead*, edited by Paul Arthur Schilpp, 666–81. 2d ed. La Salle, Ill.: Open Court, 1951.

———. *Modes of Thought*. New York: Free Press, 1938.

———. *Process and Reality*. Corrected edition. Edited by David Ray Griffin and Donald W. Sherburne. New York: Free Press, 1978.

———. *Religion in the Making*. Edited by Judith A. Jones. New York: Fordham University Press, 1996.

———. *Science and the Modern World*. New York: Free Press, 1925.

———. *Symbolism: Its Meaning and Effect*. New York: Fordham University Press, 1927.

Whiten, A., et al. "Culture in Chimpanzees." In *The Animal Ethics Reader*, edited by Susan J. Armstrong and Richard G. Botzler, 125–33. New York: Routledge, 2003.

Wiehl, Reiner. "Time and Timelessness in the Philosophy of A. N. Whitehead." Translated by James W. Felt. *Process Studies* 5 (1975): 3–30.

Wilcox, John R. "Whitehead on Values and Creativity." *Philosophy and Theology* 6 (1991): 39–53.

Williams, Bernard. "A Critique of Utilitarianism." In *Ethics: History, Theory, and Contemporary Issues*, edited by Steven M. Cahn and Peter Markie, 566–83. Oxford: Oxford University Press, 1998.

Williams, Daniel D. "Moral Obligation in Process Philosophy." *Journal of Philosophy* 56 (1959): 263–70.

Index

abortion, 20, 193n17
actual entity. *See* actual occasions
actual occasions, 66, 78, 101, 114, 146; as
 active, 34, 44, 97; and agency, 95–96;
 aim of, 6, 99; coordination of, 68,
 72–74, 90–91, 94–95, 97, 105,
 118–119, 161, 163–64; definition of,
 31–32; as discrete and distinct, 60,
 82–83, 85–87, 94; interdependence
 of, 33, 57, 59, 69, 85; as living, 71, 96;
 and perishing, 37, 44–45, 52, 56, 69,
 92, 93, 156, 160, 205n1; as present in
 others, 32–34, 86; as self-caused
 (*causa sui*), 36–37, 39, 52–53, 198n62,
 202n37; as unique, 139; unity of, as
 subject-superject, 51–53, 54–57, 58,
 131–32, 134; value of, 58, 59, 60,
 132–34, 144, 177. *See also* concrescence; entities; individuals; societies
actual world, 62, 125, 129; and concrescence, 35–36, 39, 101, 139; definition
 of, 31–33; status of, 47, 52–54, 133.
 See also past
actuality, 22, 29, 55; aim of, 99, 118–19,
 129–31, 133, 134, 146, 155, 178, 187;
 as experience, 4, 23–24, 32, 34, 38–39,
 41, 62, 68, 85, 102, 143; as extending
 to subject and object (superject), 5,
 51–57, 58, 131–32; as inherently
 beautiful, 103, 109, 134, 146, 185; as
 intensity of contrast, 54–57; as limited to subjectivity, 4, 42–46, 48,
 130–31; single genus of, 68, 72–73,
 81, 183; as temporal modes, 46–50;
 triadic structure of, 41, 62–64, 178.
 See also experience; intrinsic value,
 of actuality; process; subject, as actuality in attainment; superject, as attained actuality; vacuous actuality
Aesthetic Circle, 102–3; and dimension,
 comparative, 107–12; and dimension of harmony, 103–5, 153–54; and

dimension of intensity, 106–7,
 153–55. *See also* beauty
aesthetic education. *See* education, obligation of
aestheticism, 6, 126–27, 129–35
aesthetics, 55, 99, 109, 110, 146, 153;
 definition of, 100–2. *See also* aestheticism; beauty; education, obligation of metaphysics; morality,
 relation to aesthetics
agency. *See* moral agents; societies, collective agency of
agriculture, 170
American Dietetic Association, 168
American philosophy. *See* pragmatism
anesthesia, 105, 117, 148, 149, 151,
 167–70; definition of, 113–15. *See
 also* beauty; evil; tameness; violence
animals, nonhuman, 161, 175, 181, 182;
 definition of, 163–65; as lacking civilization, 112; mechanistic view of,
 13–15, 21–22; as monarchy, 162–63;
 moral comportment toward, 166–72,
 179, 189; as persons, 209n63; and
 rights, 180. *See also* bodies, animal;
 consciousness
animal experimentation. *See* experimentation, animal
animal rights. *See* animals, nonhuman;
 experimentation, animal; predation;
 rights; vegetarianism; vivisection
animism, 38–39
anthropocentrism, 15–16, 175, 181, 187,
 190, 212n19. *See also* biocentrism;
 kalocentrism
Aquinas, Thomas, 44, 83, 85, 90, 193n12
Aristotle, 16, 18, 44, 48, 66, 79, 94; view
 of morality, 103–4, 107, 109,137, 151,
 153; view of nature, 12–13; view of
 substance, 29, 32, 34, 83, 85–86, 90.
 See also substance; teleology
art, 99, 100, 115, 128

moral significance of, 188–89; as
succession of selves, 82–83, 93–94.
See also consciousness; moral agents;
nature, human beings as part of;
person, definition of; societies, personally ordered
Hume, David, 18–19, 139, 203n63;
Whitehead's acceptance of, 38–39
hunger. *See* starvation

idealism, 22, 38, 194
importance, 7, 63, 71; definition of,
126–28, 134; as extending to subjects
and objects, 132; as limited to subject, 46, 130–31. *See also* beauty, as
equivalent to importance (value);
morality, as maximization of importance; process, importance as aim of;
value, importance as equivalent to
inclusivity. *See* morality, as requiring inclusivity
independent existence. *See* individuals,
as independent
individualism, 43. *See also* individuality,
classical liberal view of
individuality, 91, 148; classical liberal
view of, 33, 60, 63; dualistic view of,
12–17; mechanistic view of, 12–15,
21–22; need for systematic account
of, 2; organic model of, 5, 31–33, 37,
59, 62, 66–98; substance view of, 23,
29–33, 38–40, 59, 67, 83. *See also* actual occasions; entities; individuals;
societies; substance
individuals: as a career, 24–25, 93; as determined by human interests and
scale, 80–81, 157, 217n39; as differing by degree not kind, 5, 23–25,
67–68, 73–76, 97–98, 156, 161, 165,
185–186, 186; as enduring, 66–69,
83, 88, 92–93, 98, 110; identity and
unity of macroscopic, 5, 27, 66–98;
as independent 12, 15, 19, 23, 28–31,
60, 63, 71, 83, 87; as interdependent
and interrelated, 26, 30–31, 37, 62,
85–87, 97, 101, 120, 147, 152, 160,
182–83; as internally related, 23,
26–27, 31, 32–34, 55–56, 60, 77–79,
85–87, 90, 145, 156, 159–60, 162, 163,
179; microscopic, 5, 27, 64, 66, 75,
83, 85; as unique, 143, 156, 174,

178–79; and whole, relation to, 100.
See also actual occasions; entities; individuality; societies; substance
inherent value. *See* intrinsic value
instrumental value. *See* value, instrumental
intensity, 62, 75, 97, 131, 140, 148, 186; as
aim of process, 55, 130; of experience,
106, 163, 178; and past, 33; value, 40,
41, 60, 61, 98. *See also* actuality, as
intensity of contrast; Aesthetic Circle, and dimension of intensity;
beauty, and harmony and intensity;
category of subjective intensity
interests, 11, 131, 161, 162, 187; and importance, 126, 128; of the one vs.
many, 3, 112, 119–21, 154, 182,
188–90; self, 133, 145, 148, 152–53;
species lack of, 78, 159; and value,
19, 140. *See also* goodness; individuals, as determined by human interests and scale; moral interest theory;
value
intrinsic value, 4, 7, 17, 212n19; of actuality, 4, 39–40, 41, 64, 71, 143, 145,
174, 176, 178, 179, 181, 185; defined
as including self, other, and whole,
57–65, 133, 143, 156, 174–75, 178,
180; defined as noninstrumental
value, 57, 59–60; defined as objective
value, 58–59; defined by individual's
nonrelational properties, 57–58, 59;
human being as sole locus of, 15–16,
20; matter's lack of, 13–20; and the
problem of subjectivism, 41–43. *See
also* value
intuitionism, 139
invasive species, 161, 225n38
inviolability. *See* human being, inviolability of; value, absolute; autonomy

James, William, 2, 6, 29, 30, 32, 145, 148,
153–55, 171, 195n41, 217n44; and
moral ideal, 141–43; and moral philosophy, limits of, 135–41; rejection
of dualism, 23–26; and role of God,
119–20
Jones, Judith A., 199n68, 200n16, 205n2,
206n13, 217n41, 220n31; and ecstatic
interpretation, 50, 54–57, 61, 75, 105,
130

September 11, 2001, 114, 135, 154
Sessions, George, 183–85, 187
Sherburne, Donald W., 210–11n4
Singer, Peter, 20–21, 165, 175–76, 180
skepticism, 121, 135
Smith, Adam, 64
societies, 156, 162, 186; as aggregate or
collection, 82–83; collective agency
of, 95–96, 213n23; confusion with
actual occasions, 89; definition of,
69–70, 87; as enduring individual,
69, 92–93; as more than aggregate or
collection, 70, 86–88; as nested
within larger environments, 70–71;
personally ordered, 72–74, 91,
94–96, 117, 162–64; regnant, 72,
95–96, 163–64; and self-identity,
92–98; structured, 70–74, 86, 91,
94–96, 162–64. *See also* actual occasions; animals; entities; individuals;
nexus; plants; substance; systems
sociology, 17
Socratic, 136
soil erosion, 170
solipsism, 34, 50, 61–64, 100, 133, 134,
218n47; moral, 200n20, 130–31. *See
also* subjectivism
soul, 12, 39, 95–96, 118, 119, 163, 206n6.
See also societies, regnant
species, 66, 76, 114, 161, 165, 182–83,
225n38. *See also* entities, temporal
formal (species); invasive species;
species extinction
species extinction, 2, 76, 158, 159–60, 167,
172. *See also* invasive species; species
speciesism, 165, 175
Spinoza, 44
Spitzer, Robert, 27
spontaneity. *See* novelty
starvation, 109, 158, 167, 168–69
strenuous mood, 119–21, 135. *See also*
God
subjects, 4, 29, 31, 88; as actuality in attainment, 37, 47, 53; classical interpretation of, 44–46; definition of,
34–37; ecstatic interpretation of,
52–57; as efficient product of past
occasions, 53–54. *See also* actual occasion; ecstatic interpretation; experience; individuals; subjectivism;
superject

subject-superject. *See* actual occasions,
unity of, as subject-superject; ecstatic interpretation
subjective aim, 47, 49, 55; and beauty,
108, 111; definition of, 35–37; as determining degree of novelty, 71,
211–12n11; and value, 120. *See also*
concrescence; teleology
subjective immediacy, 37–40, 44. *See
also* experience; subject
subjectivism, 4–5, 34, 41–43, 129–31,
134, 177–78, 200n12; and classical
interpretation, 46–48; solution to,
51, 54, 57. *See also* moral interest
theory, Whiteheadian ethics as
substance: as abstraction, 30, 73, 118;
as basis of unity and identity, 84–86,
95; as dynamic, 82–85, 87, 89, 95;
etymology of, 196n47; rejection
of, 23, 38–40, 71, 79, 83, 86–89,
97–98, 145; and systems, 90–92.
See also Aristotle, view of substance;
Descartes, view of substance; dualism; entities; facts; individuality,
substance view of; individuals,
identity and unity of macroscopic;
societies
suffering, unnecessary, 21, 175–76, 185.
See also pain; vegetarianism
superject, 4, 34, 41; as active, 36–37;
51–57, 131–35; as attained actuality,
37, 44, 47, 53; classical interpretation
of, 44–46; as ontologically distinct
from subject, 44–48, 130. *See also* actual occasions, unity of, as subject-
superject; ecstatic interpretation;
past; subjects
subjective form, 55
systems, 87, 182, 208n56; definition of,
90–92, 208–9n59. *See also* ecosystems; societies

tameness, 105, 110, 114. *See also* anesthesia
teleology, 6; and Aristotle, 12, 16; and
self-determination, 35–36, 52, 55,
198n63. *See also* actuality, aim of; actual occasion, aim of; beauty, as aim
of universe (process); finality; process,
importance as aim of; purpose; subjective aim

DATE DUE
